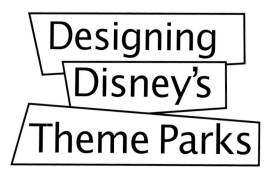

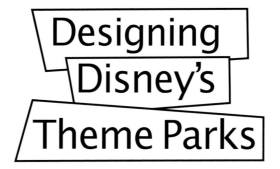

The Architecture of Reassurance

Edited by Karal Ann Marling

Centre Canadien d'Architecture/Canadian Centre for Architecture
Montréal

Flammarion
Paris - New York

This book accompanies the exhibition *The Architecture of Reassurance: Designing the Disney Theme Parks* organized by the Canadian Centre for Architecture (CCA) with Karal Ann Marling, guest curator.

The CCA gratefully acknowledges the extraordinary co-operation of Walt Disney Imagineering, Walt Disney Attractions, and The Walt Disney Company in the preparation of this exhibition.

The exhibition has been made possible by the generous support of the Dayton Hudson Foundation on behalf of Target Stores, Mervyn's, Dayton's, Hudson's, and Marshall Field's.

This publication is supported by a grant from the Graham Foundation for Advanced Studies in the Fine Arts.

The CCA also thanks the J.W. McConnell Family Foundation for its generous support of the public programs accompanying the exhibition as well as Bell Canada, Royal Bank of Canada, and Teleglobe Canada Inc. for their contributions in support of the exhibition and publication.

The CCA benefits from the operating support of the Ministère de la Culture et des Communications du Québec and the Conseil des arts de la Communauté urbaine de Montréal.

Library of Congress Cataloging-in-Publication Data

Designing Disney's theme parks : the architecture of reassurance / edited by Karal Ann Marling : Canadian Centre for Architecture.
  p.   cm.
  "Published in conjunction with the exhibition 'The Architecture of Reassurance: Designing the Disney Theme Parks,' at the Canadian Centre for Architecture in Montreal, 17 June–28 September 1997"– –T.p. verso.
  Includes bibliographical references and index.
  ISBN 2-08-013639-9 (hardback). — ISBN 2-08-013638-0 (pbk.)
  1. Disneyland (Calif.)—History. 2. Walt Disney Company– –Buildings—Catalogs. 3. Architecture, Modern—20th century– –Catalogs. 4. Amusement parks—Design—Catalogs. 5. Centre canadien d'architecture—Catalogs. I. Marling, Karal Ann.
  II. Centre canadien d'architecture.
  GV1853.3.C22D47 1997
  791'.06'879496—dc21   97-19033

Flammarion:
Editorial Direction: Suzanne Tise
Editorial Management:
Philippa Hurd
Designed and typeset by
Agence Comme Ça
Copy-editing by Christa Weil

Canadian Centre for Architecture:
Manager, Publications Services:
Christine Dufresne
Copy-editing by Marcia Rodriguez

Copyright ©1997 Canadian Centre for Architecture, for texts.
Copyright © 1997 Disney for illustrations, unless otherwise noted.

Fig. 24: © Henry Ford Museum and Greenfield Village; Fig. 32 © Capitol Records Archives; Figs. xiv, xv: photograph: © Peter Aaron/Esto; Photographs pp. 6, 8, 12, 18, 28, 53, 106, 133, 153, 167, 178, 190, 200, 208, 214, 223: © Catherine Wagner, CCA, Disney.

Published by Flammarion in 1997.
Reprinted in April 1998.
All rights reserved. No part of this publication may be reproduced in any form or by any means, electronic, photocopy, information retrieval system, or otherwise without written permission from the copyright holders.

Flammarion
26 rue Racine
75006 Paris

200 Park Avenue South, Suite 1406
New York
NY 10003

Website: www.flammarion.com

ISBN: 2-08013-639-9 (hardback)
ISBN: 2-08013-638-0 (paperback)
Numéros d'édition:
FA 363907 (hardback)
FA 363806 (paperback)
Dépôt légal: June 1997
Printed in France

Note on the captions:
All dimensions are in inches; height precedes width.

The exhibition *The Architecture of Reassurance: Designing the Disney Theme Parks*
has been made possible by the generous support
of the Dayton Hudson Foundation on behalf of Target Stores,
Mervyn's, Dayton's, Hudson's, and Marshall Field's.

Itinerary of the Exhibition

Canadian Centre for Architecture/Centre Canadien d'Architecture, Montreal
June 17, 1997 to September 28, 1997

Walker Art Center, Minneapolis
October 26, 1997 to January 18, 1998

UCLA at the Armand Hammer Museum of Art and Cultural Center, Los Angeles
May 9, 1998 to August 2, 1998

Cooper-Hewitt National Design Museum, New York
October 6, 1998 to January 10, 1999

Modern Art Museum of Fort Worth, Fort Worth
February 14, 1999 to April 11, 1999

CONTENTS

Foreword 9
Nicholas Olsberg, *Chief Curator, Canadian Centre for Architecture*

The Artist as Imagineer 13
Marty Sklar, *Vice-Chairman and Principal Creative Executive, Walt Disney Imagineering*

Expository Expositions: Preparing for the Theme Parks 19
Neil Harris

Imagineering the Disney Theme Parks 29
Karal Ann Marling

Making Imagination Safe in the 1950s: Disneyland's Fantasy Art and Architecture 179
Erika Doss

Disneyland: Its Place in World Culture 191
Yi-Fu Tuan with Steven D. Hoelscher

Forty Years of Overstatement: Criticism and the Disney Theme Parks 201
Greil Marcus

Interview with Frank Gehry by Karal Ann Marling and Phyllis Lambert 209

Catherine Wagner.
Beanstalk outside Sir Mickey's Store;
Fantasyland, Disneyland Paris,
Marne-la-Vallée, France.
Collection CCA.

Sources 214
Chronology 219 compiled by *Andrew Landsbury*
Photographs 223 *Catherine Wagner*

Catherine Wagner. *Autopia; Tomorrowland, Disneyland, Anaheim, California*. Collection CCA.

FOREWORD

From the moment it opened in July of 1955, Disneyland has been a key symbol of contemporary American culture, celebrated and attacked as the ultimate embodiment of the consumer society, of simulation and pastiche, of the blurring of distinctions between reality and imagery. As Disney's architectures of illusion have expanded—to Florida, to Japan, to Paris—"Disneyfication" has entered the language as a synonym for sham. At the same time, Disney's approaches to designing recreational space, to the representation of historic architecture, and to the shaping of an urban narrative have had a massive impact on the "real-world" architecture of the shopping center and the resort, and on public expectations of the townscape.

For all the inflammatory power of Disneyland as cultural metaphor, and for all of its acknowledged effect on the built landscape of our time, little has been done to reconstruct how the first park was conceived and realized or to identify its ancestry and intent. Even less has appeared to suggest how profoundly the parks and their purpose have changed since Disney first assembled his team of studio artists into the design unit that became known as "Imagineers." Originally envisioned simply as a means of amusing visitors to the Disney Studios in Burbank, the parks' agenda gradually became more ambitious. As plans for the first Disneyland evolved, Disney began to see it both as fun fair and civic center. With a Grandmother's Farm and a faithful reproduction of Main Street appearing in the first design, the park was to be a soothing reminiscence of the all-American small town, home to parent-teacher associations, Boy Scout troups, Rotary clubs, and science fairs. With the acquisition of land in Florida, Disney began planning, alongside a sort of permanent World's Fair, a fully fledged prototype for the city of the future. Once built, the Florida parks did indeed dramatically alter the scale and scope of Disney's architecture, setting up the solemnly didactic world of EPCOT and self-consciously experimenting with new techniques for transportation and infrastructure. Latterly, Imagineering has begun to reflect the growing sophistication, self-reference, and irony of its Hollywood home: the increasingly familiar, dull, and studied optimism of its "Tomorrowlands" gives way to playfully sinister views of the near future and often satirical takes on contemporary "reality." At the same time, as Imagineers carry their designs outside the parks into such ventures as the wittily themed Disney Stores, they complete a process of becoming in which fantasy architectures finally merge into the city street and suburban mall.

The idea of an exhibition and publication that would look behind the multiple myths of Disneyland, in order to trace the impulses and mechanisms that made and changed it, emerged from discussions at Imagineering with Marty Sklar, its creative director. We shared a sense that there was a remarkable tale to be told about the methods of Disney design among the thousands of sketches and drawings preserved in the Disney Art Library. Marty had himself nursed most of them into life, and all of them demonstrate the unorthodox sequence through which the artist's rendering initiates rather than closes the imaginative process. It was also apparent that the story of Disneyland's origins and intentions commented eloquently on the transformation of the postwar United States into a suburban, automobile-centered, televisual society, and that Disney's architectural fabrication of this "essence of America as we know it—the nostalgia of the past, the exciting glimpses of the future" had done much to define both its own cultural memory and its popular image overseas. The project thus assumed a central place in the CCA's American Century exhibition series, much of it concerned with the changing image, at home and abroad, of an ideal America.

From the start, Marty and the CCA agreed to recognize the theme parks as a cultural phenomenon in the public domain and to insist together that only an exhibition and publication curated and edited with complete independence could effectively account for it. While aiding curator, researchers, photographer, and authors with astonishing generosity—not a file has been closed to us, and not a needed service denied—the Disney team has assiduously distanced itself from the content and argument of the exhibition and of the book. We are immensely grateful to Walt Disney Imagineering, Walt Disney Attractions, and The Walt Disney Company for their confidence, restraint, and cooperation. We are deeply indebted to Karal Ann Marling—curator of the exhibition and the project's director of research—for the balance between sympathy and rigor with which she has approached this first opportunity to move the discussion on Disney's lands from speculative critique to informed analysis.

We warmly thank the Dayton Hudson Foundation for its generous support. We also gratefully acknowledge the support of the Graham Foundation for Advanced Studies in the Fine Arts, the J. W. McConnell Family Foundation, and of Bell Canada, Royal Bank of Canada, and Teleglobe Canada Inc.

Nicholas Olsberg
Chief Curator, Canadian Centre for Architecture

Catherine Wagner. *Mickey Mouse's House; Mickey's Toontown, Disneyland, Anaheim, California.* Collection CCA.

THE ARTIST AS IMAGINEER

At the moment I'm feeling a lot like Aladdin must have: I let the genie out of the bottle and, with my first "wish," I helped create this phenomenal, one-of-a-kind exhibition.

For a long time, many years in fact, *The Architecture of Reassurance: Designing the Disney Theme Parks* could never have happened. In the first place, traditional museums have not often regarded the world of theme parks, or the artworks and artists behind them, as "legitimate" subjects for their sacred halls. Personally, I never quite understood this attitude, because World's Fairs and International Expositions have "traditionally" showcased great art and artists. See Alexander Calder and Salvador Dalí at the 1939 New York World's Fair; Michelangelo's *Pietà* and the works of Lichtenstein, Warhol, Rauschenberg, Pollock, Rosenquist, et al. at the 1964 New York World's Fair; and retrospectives of Picasso and Chagall at Seville's Expo '92. One of my fond memories of the 1964 New York World's Fair was the Vatican Pavilion, where the *Pietà* was featured. The pavilion also presented the contrast of exquisite, tiny "peek-a-boo" religious scenes created by Sister Corita, and the huge, colorful banners designed by Norman LaLiberté, a Canadian whose wonderful, often whimsical creations now grace not only many public spaces, but my home as well.

A second reason for exclusion was Imagineering's own paranoia about the fifty thousand pieces of original artwork it created for the Disney theme parks over the past forty-five years. Except for occasions when they were used for reference in creating new concepts for future projects, these artworks have remained safely locked in our own vaults for almost half a century. Only an occasional "treasure," such as John Hench's twenty-fifth-birthday portrait of Mickey Mouse or Herbert Ryman's *New Orleans Square* concept painting for Disneyland, both loaned to American embassies around the world, has found its way into limited public view.

A third reason was Disney management's viewpoint that WED Enterprises (as Walt Disney's theme park design group was originally known), and now Walt Disney Imagineering, should remain as invisible to the public as possible. After all, they reasoned, the public is not really interested in the beginning of a Space Mountain or the symbolic Tree of Life in Disney's Animal Kingdom, but in the ultimate *experience* these great attractions offer: the plunge in a racing vehicle through the darkness of outer space, or the secrets of nature's tiny but most abundant creatures, insects, unlocked in the 3-D "inner space" adventure *It's Tough to Be a Bug*. (The show is presented in a theater *inside* the Tree of Life at Disney's Animal Kingdom, opening in 1998 at Walt Disney World.)

Some have likened the way we work to the Renaissance, when the inspirational work of artists in two dimensions fueled designers of three-dimensional spaces and creations. The architecture of the Renaissance was indeed inspired by the sketches, paintings, and concepts of Leonardo da Vinci, Michelangelo, and their peers, much as the artistry of Ryman, Hench, McKim, Goff, Hennesy, Anderson, Davis, Martin, Bushman, Redmond, and others instructed the early designs for Disneyland, and its Disney successors around the world.

Ryman, Hench, Goff. Do I dare mention the names of these "unknowns" in the very same breath (and paragraph) as Michelangelo and Leonardo? What's going on here?

The fact is that from the early 1950s through the mid-1960s, Walter Elias Disney brought together, in a quintessential organization bearing his initials, a group of artisans who were to make history—entertainment history, at least—in the most anonymous way: hardly a single one of them was, or is, known to the 1.2 billion guests who have visited a Disney theme park around the world since the opening of Disneyland in Anaheim, California, on July 17, 1955.

This was not *deception* but rather a studied and relevant *conception*, in the true mode of the master-apprentice-artisan world of the Renaissance. As Walt Disney once explained to me, "I'm not 'Walt Disney' anymore. Disney is a thing, an attitude, an image in the eyes of the public. I've spent my whole career creating that image, and I'm a great believer in what Disney is. But it's not me, the person, anymore."

In retrospect I realize that this was my first "out-of-body" experience. For Walt Disney, at least, seeing through and beyond the obvious, as well as into the past and the future, was an everyday storyteller's experience.

Using the words "storytellers" and "experience" together brings me full circle back to the Disney theme parks. For if nothing else, we believe that this unique traveling exhibition will suggest to you that the people, the process, and the projects represented in these spaces constitute a body of work perhaps unequaled in its impact on people around the globe.

Even Walt Disney would be rather surprised to find that today, the little seed he planted with a handful of Imagineers in 1952, when WED Enterprises was formed, has grown into what we believe is the largest creative design and development organization in the world, with nearly two thousand employees and more than one hundred separate and distinct talent disciplines. But all of us—artists and engineers, model makers and architects, writers and designers of ride systems, costumes, restaurants, shows, landscaping, graphics, Audio-Animatronics®, interiors, lighting, special effects, vehicles, transportation systems—all of us owe our present and future roles to a handful of those original Renaissance Imagineers.

Among them were the motion-picture set designers Dick Irvine and Marvin Davis. Dick was the leader of the band, Walt's right hand in the three-dimensional world of design from the beginnings of Disneyland through the opening of Walt Disney World in 1971, while Marvin was proud of the fact that his Master Plan #7 (for nearly 28,000 acres) became reality in Florida, when it took 69 master plans for less than 200 acres in Anaheim. Two "partners" from animation background-painting days at the Disney Studio, Claude Coats and John Hench, became the world's foremost designers of three-dimensional show spaces. Who will ever forget Claude's layout for the quintessential Pirates of the Caribbean, and John's classic Space Mountain?

One of Walt Disney's earliest collaborators on Disneyland design was another motion-picture designer, Harper Goff (of *20,000 Leagues under the Sea* and *Willie Wonka and the Chocolate Factory*). Harper's concepts for Main Street and his black-and-white illustrations, as well as those of Sam McKim, established the fact that a story would be told by architectural facades and interior designs (see the rich color sketches for Main Street and New Orleans Square by Dorothea Redmond) as well as in the attractions, shows, and adventures. And Harper Goff's original rendition of Adventureland's Jungle River Cruise, the boats inspired by the Bogart-Hepburn *African Queen*, was easily the greatest of all the new Disney "ride" genres at the park's opening in 1955.

Walt Disney's own genius lay not just in the ideas he himself generated, but in the casting of talents—many of whom were Disney Studio veterans embarked on "new careers" in the second half of their creative lifetimes. None surpassed those former animators whose signatures remain to this day indelibly inscribed on Disney ride adventures and experiences: Marc Davis, creator of pirates, hitchhiking ghosts, singing bears, and the frolicking children and animals of It's a Small World; Blaine Gibson, without peer as a sculptor in three dimensions of all Marc Davis's two-dimensional characters; and Yale Gracey, who set a standard for special effects that even the newest technologies have not eclipsed.

Arguably, the greatest of all the amazing talents was Herbert Dickens Ryman. A graduate of the Chicago Institute of Art, Herbie came to the Disney Studio after years of watercolor painting; illustrating set designs, concepts in live-action movies, and books; and traveling (and behind-the-scenes sketching) with the Ringling Brothers Circus in the days of outdoor tenting. Herbie's palette was broad, ranging from the smallest sketch (see his twelve-by-sixteen-inch pencil-sketch concept for Cinderella's Castle at Walt Disney World) to the largest canvas (everything from the first overall illustration of Disneyland to his inspirational paintings of concepts for Tokyo Disneyland). Because of their detail and his complete understanding of space and scale, Herb Ryman's paintings from the very beginning gave audiences around the world a chance to "walk into" these fantasy environments long before construction even began. He was truly "one of a kind."

The continuity of Disney theme-park design is clearly one of its greatest strengths. A personal story will illustrate this fact. I first met this remarkable cast of characters as a twenty-one-year-old starting his Disney career a month before Disneyland's opening. Twenty-five years later, as Vice President of Concepts and Planning, and working side by side with my principal mentor John Hench, I directed many of these same talents in the creation of EPCOT. Harper Goff led the design effort for the World Showcase pavilions. His sense of scale and the relationship of iconography, the use of symbols (for example, a Moroccan tower contrasted to the Eiffel Tower), and all the movie "tricks" like forced perspective—made for a tour-de-force trip around the world.

(Of course, he also had the hand and eye of Bob Jolley, who could make new wood and recently cut stone look as if it had been around for centuries, "aging" in the Florida sunshine.)

Bill Martin, earlier a designer of Fantasylands and Frontierlands, headed the Italy and Mexico pavilions architecturally. The story and character sketches by Herb Ryman and Sam McKim were the products of great storytellers who taught us all the importance of research for EPCOT shows. Herbie's painting of EPCOT's entrance said it all: this was not Magic Kingdom stuff, but instead a cosmopolitan center where cultures and technologies merged and flourished.

EPCOT (originally EPCOT Center at its opening in October 1982) was in many ways the last hurrah of the Walt Disney-originated concepts. It was Imagineering's attempt to take a complex idea for an entire "living community" (EPCOT = Experimental Prototype Community of Tomorrow) and synthesize it into the theme-park genre.

We must have been successful, without closing the door on the building of a true living community at Walt Disney World. EPCOT celebrates its fifteenth birthday on October 1, 1997. At the same time, Celebration will be well into its second year as a "new town" being developed on 4,900 acres surrounded by a 4,700-acre protected greenbelt. The master plan, created by Robert A.M. Stern Architects and Cooper, Robertson, and Partners, includes "downtown" buildings designed by internationally renowned architects in addition to education, health, commercial, retail, and recreational facilities for a resident population that one day may number twenty thousand. (Not by chance, perhaps, this was the number envisioned by Walt Disney for his living community.) The Disney Institute (opened in 1996 as a "vacation of discovery" for mind and body) together with the more than twenty thousand resort hotel rooms, campgrounds, championship golf courses, water parks, and other recreation amenities—and, of course, the theme parks—convince many of us that Walt Disney's original vision for this Florida land has indeed been realized at Walt Disney World.

My "partner" in the challenging game of developing EPCOT as a theme park was John Hench, without question the most influential person after Walt Disney in creating the Disney theme-park vernacular. John originally joined the Disney Studio to work on *Fantasia* in 1939. Now, at age eighty-eight in 1997, he is still going strong in his fifty-eighth year at Disney. His groundbreaking, original body of design has established the visual language of the Disney parks: everything from how the "close-ups" must reinforce what the "long shots" introduce visually, to theories of color played out in the flat gray skies of Anaheim, the bright sun of Florida, and the dark winter afternoons of Tokyo and Paris. But his work on EPCOT, especially his design and engineering solutions to Spaceship Earth, are truly remarkable.

It would be difficult to imagine an undertaking more demanding than EPCOT. As Disney's first "non-Disneyland" theme park it often broke from traditional thinking, while at the same time holding fast to major principles. Second, it had to *complement* (not compete with) the Magic Kingdom at Walt Disney World. And third, it had to keep its foundations rooted in Walt Disney's goal of marrying the technological know-how of American free enterprise (that is, corporate sponsors) with Disney storytelling.

Nevertheless, the process Imagineering used in developing EPCOT was basically the same one we followed in designing those parks that came before—Disneyland and the Magic Kingdom—and those that followed—Tokyo Disneyland, the Disney-MGM Studios at Walt Disney World, and Disneyland Paris. Recognizing that the six parks bearing the Disney name rank one through six in theme-park attendance around the globe as of 1997, that same process is currently at work in the three Disney parks now under development: Disney's Animal Kingdom, opening in spring 1998 at Walt Disney World; Disney's California Adventure, opening in 2001 adjacent to Disneyland; and Tokyo DisneySea, the next-door neighbor to Tokyo Disneyland beginning in 2001.

That process begins with what we call our "Blue Sky" phase, so called because "the sky's the limit" when Imagineers are brainstorming new ideas. Disney's California Adventure, the last theme-park concept we have developed to date, may suggest that the process has reached a new standard. It began with a "concept charrette," when Imagineers joined CEO Michael Eisner, Disneyland leaders, and a sprinkling of other experts from inside and outside the company for two days of "no idea is a bad idea" discussions in the very blue-sky summer atmosphere of Aspen, Colorado. Out of this came at least three ideas that evoked passionate support, and one—the idea of a park based on the dreams, the myths, the iconography, and the reality of the Golden State of California—leapt to the head of the class. Within a year, having survived a gauntlet of conceptual and financial feasibility analyses, it was being capitalized as the eighth major park to carry the Disney name. (Tokyo DisneySea will be the ninth.)

In process terms, that means that "Blue Sky" has given way to Design Development, which will segue into Schematics and Feasibility. During these phases, the project is scrutinized from A to Z: everything from a detailed storytelling analysis of each attraction to engineering doability, schedule makeability, and budgetary reliability. In everything we do, a project has to stand on more than one leg to be "turned on." And no wonder, because a complete theme park now costs in the neighborhood of $800 million to $1 billion and more in corporate investment, and is five to seven years in the making.

If a live-action movie fails to excite the public at the box office, it can be gone and forgotten within a week or two. But our projects, standing in concrete and steel, must live long beyond their adolescence to justify the scale of investment. In the business of theme parks and resorts, risk taking is not just a philosophy. It's a way of life.

We all grew up imbued with the philosophy of Walter Elias Disney, which since 1984 has also been strongly endorsed and followed by Michael Eisner. Walt Disney summarized it in three words: "Take a Chance." As Walt said, "Now I'm a grandfather and have a good many gray hairs and what a lot of people would call common sense. But if I'm no longer young in age, I hope I stay young enough in spirit never to fear failure—young enough still to take a chance and march in the parade."

Me too.

Marty Sklar
Vice-Chairman and Principal Creative Executive, Walt Disney Imagineering
October 1, 1996 (on the occasion of Walt Disney World's 25th Anniversary.)

Catherine Wagner. *World Bazaar; Tokyo Disneyland, Tokyo*. Collection CCA.

EXPOSITORY EXPOSITIONS

PREPARING FOR THE THEME PARKS

Neil Harris

Many believe it all began with a fair. It might have been a World's Fair, perhaps an industrial or commercial fair, or maybe even a local or county fair. But some kind of exposition inspired the founder to do his work.

There is, to be sure, no universal agreement. Other authorities posit a more mundane experience occurring in 1930s Los Angeles, perhaps a frustrated day-long quest for wholesome entertainment by Walt and his family. The search for a single moment, the germ of the impulse that sired the magic kingdoms, has, understandably, been intense. Historical logic seems to require that, like James Watt with his tea kettle and Isaac Newton with his apple, Walt Disney received his vision at some definite point in time, propelled by a transforming experience.

But it might also be argued that in creating his theme-park empire, Walt Disney was a child of broader circumstances, building upon generic conditions and aspirations. Rather than the inspiration of any particular fair, it was the fair experience itself, with its amusement strips, disciplined crowds, and park-like settings, that supplied the necessary nurture. American expositions provided visions of a higher life set amid heavenly landscapes. Enveloping in their scale, their novelty, their string of surprises, they punctuated their decades like giant exclamation marks. Fairs and expositions molded the fantasies and sharpened the expectations of several generations of Americans. They shaped national assumptions about the social functions of public spaces. They helped spawn a series of cultural institutions, from museums of art and science to amusement parks and convention centers. They spread a notion of structure: aesthetic, social, and racial. Pilgrimage sites in an emerging tourist culture, they provoked an astonishing volume of souvenirs and memorabilia. Above all, they performed as sites for self-discovery, camp meetings for a dominating middle class.

Contemporaries accepted the significance of fairs. Looking back at Philadelphia's Centennial Exposition of 1876, *Harper's Weekly* solemnly boasted in 1890 that "no one act of the American people, except their successful wars, has ever done so much to give the United States a standing among the nations." "The finest architectural view that has ever been beheld on our planet," cried Denton Snider of Chicago's Columbian Exposition. That 1893 fair, exclaimed another enthusiast, marked "a point in civilization never before reached by any people," "the dawn of a new era." Such views, so long disparaged by hard-headed anti-sentimentalists, have recently gained ground, however modified by different outlooks. The great fairs are now worshipped as revelatory texts, keys to open the lock box of national values and prejudices. The exposition plans turn out to be maps of the American sensibility.

Similarly venerated by millions of Americans today, the Disney theme parks have produced their own legions of interpreters (and imitators). Play has always been serious. Now it has become self-conscious as well. Such a journey deserves some equally serious and self-conscious commentary. Excursions into illusion, excitement, myth-making, and role-playing, the fairs—and their sibling pleasure gardens, amusement parks, and theme parks—have evolved into the laboratories, churches, and amphitheaters of a new culture.

The great urban expositions of the modern era were not products of immaculate conception. Fairs were ancient marketplaces and the notion of devoting pieces of land to active, popular, fee-paying public pleasures also goes back far into time. Students of urban history often begin this story with the pleasure gardens that were established in European cities like London and Paris during the seventeenth and eighteenth centuries. Patrons eager to escape city congestion met entrepreneurs prepared to manage their diversions, resulting in creation of some immensely popular pleasure grounds.

One of the earliest such enterprises, London's Vauxhall Gardens, opened in the 1660s as New Spring Garden. Renovated and renamed in the following century, it was sustained, in various forms, for almost two hundred years, lending its name and celebrity to imitators on two continents. Visited (and written about) by John Evelyn, Samuel Pepys, Horace Walpole, Oliver Goldsmith, James Boswell, Tobias Smollett, Charles Dickens, and W. M. Thackeray, among others, and sketched by George Cruikshank and Thomas Rowlandson, by the late eighteenth century Vauxhall commingled garden walks and arbors, mazes, statuary, shops, replicas of ruins, illusionistic paintings, dining pavilions, and obelisks, to give a partial list of its features. And it hosted balls, parties, concerts, fireworks, balloon ascensions, and all manner of festivities.

Throughout their history, critics claimed that Vauxhall, and counterparts like Ranelagh Gardens, were becoming centers of vice and social infection, but one aspect of their appeal lay precisely in the atmosphere of (controlled) risk they contained, the casual and unpredictable encounters they offered. Later amusement parks would build on this tradition, never losing their association with a darker, more dangerous side.

Vauxhall Gardens, some historians have suggested, had another, political dimension, one which would also set precedents. A cockpit of antigovernment feelings for part of the eighteenth century, it was a place where those out of sympathy with the Crown and its ministries gathered to exchange their grievances. More significantly, Vauxhall and some Parisian imitators allowed broad segments of the public to discover one another, and to enjoy themselves without dependence upon royal condescension or hierarchical organization. Such sites, writes John Goodman, were perceived as places "where established social taxonomies broke down," planting images "of social self-sufficiency in the minds of their largely middle-class clientele." Indeed these highly theatrical settings projected their own utopian vision: a new, harmonious sense of community built around the consumption of pleasure. Connections between amusement parks and political values were made well into the twentieth century, sometimes with surprising conclusions. It is significant that "America's two principal funfairs are situated cheek by jowl in the heart of Goldwater-Reagan territory," conservative pundit Russell Kirk wrote in the 1960s. Disneyland was more than a commercial enterprise; its "terrestrial paradise" was a paean to traditional values, insisted Kirk, and others besides himself found the affinity unsurprising.

The United States had its own profit-seeking Vauxhalls in its young seaboard cities, as well as some Ranelaghs, Tivolis, and a Bathsheba's Bath and Bower (in Philadelphia), but far greater energy would soon pour into creation of public recreational grounds, open without charge to everyone. American parks were presented to local taxpayers as safety valves, public health measures, real estate subsidies, and wholesome antidotes to urban congestion. In the second half of the nineteenth century, brilliant landscape architects like Frederick Law Olmsted, Horace Cleveland, and George Kessler developed programs for cities across North America, providing spacious correctives to the increasing noise and bustle.

While park makers often promoted their landscapes as alternatives to busy, self-absorbed urban lifestyles, naturalist settings that encouraged communion with nature and screened out intrusive distractions, a range of social functions was also served. Parks were becoming miniature cities themselves. Human delight in seeing others and being seen, as well as in active amusements, was served by the public park and boulevard systems of the late nineteenth-century city. "People insist upon playing in groups," acknowledged the City Club of Milwaukee, in a pre-World War I survey of that city's amusements and recreations. In time, zoos, carousels, skating rinks, mazes, band shells, tennis courts, golf courses, baseball fields, refreshment stands, and other amenities would entice visitors on holidays and weekends. A mere twenty years after he had begun to work on his greensward plan, Frederick Law Olmsted assured a journalist that Central Park was "going to the devil," and confessed that his dream of producing an urban arcadia had been doomed from the start. Gotham had despoiled his sylvan retreat.

The changes Olmsted bemoaned did not arrive without resistance. Like so much else in the urban world, municipal parks were contested settings, and defenders of open space fought bitterly against more active uses. "The intrusion into natural scenery of buildings, no matter how beautiful in themselves, and of formal gardens, no matter how charming and instructive . . . is wrong," *Harper's Weekly* insisted in 1897, fighting the creation of a botanical garden in a Bronx park.

In any event, the construction and maintenance of city parks were expensive, and taxpayers frequently abandoned their early, costly commitments; many cities never put ambitious plans into effect. It often took the presence of a great event, like an exposition, to galvanize energies and stimulate political leadership to action. In their wake the expositions in Chicago, Buffalo, St. Louis, Atlanta, Nashville, and elsewhere left a string of considerably altered urban parks, newly landscaped or much enlarged, either for purposes of receiving the fairs in the first place or to return the grounds to public use after the expositions had closed.

From one angle, the expositions were giant parks themselves, supervised settings that projected utopian visions of space and history. Short-lived, with admission fees, fairs could afford high maintenance and policing charges. The high polish that resulted frequently energized dormant plans for municipal park systems, and dramatized their civic appeal. The disciplined crowd behavior at expositions reassured those who worried about public drunkenness and violent behavior, and demonstrated, once more, the advantages of careful planning. "Courtiers in the garden alleys of Versailles or Fontainebleau could not have been more deferential and observant of the decorum of place," wrote John J. Ingalls of the multitudes attending Chicago Day at the Columbian Exposition of 1893. "It was like a veteran army on the march or in the bivouac, without captains or commanders." The fairs' zoning features—grouping structures by function—their controls on commercial distraction, as well as their exemplary systems of movement and communication, provoked widespread admiration, an admiration that translated into a distinctive tradition of urban planning.

The fairs had still another impact, however. Close by their cultivated urban parks, sometimes even within them, lay concentrated groupings of exotic restaurants, thrilling rides, illusionistic concessions, and alluring performers. Variously termed Midway, Pike, Zone, Pan, Warpath, Pay Streak, or Gay Way, these clusters of concessions contributed mightily to the success of their larger hosts; indeed exposition managers quickly realized that their financial success hinged largely on the selection of concessionaires. There were many "dignified reasons" why an international exhibition should host an amusement district, Frank Morton Todd declared in his history of San Francisco's 1915 Panama-Pacific Exposition: precedent, a need for relaxation, the exhibition of exotica. "But we may as well admit the main reason, which is that people want to have some fun, and there is no reason why they shouldn't have it to the profit of the undertaking."

Tested by market demand and precisely measured by gate receipts, these attractions could then be transferred from an exposition to a permanent amusement park setting. One of Coney Island's first major novelties was directly imported, in 1877, from the Philadelphia Centennial of the year before: the Sawyer Observatory, a three-hundred-foot iron tower which provided visitors with spectacular views of the surrounding landscape.

Such innovations were a two-way street. Amusement park developers like LaMarcus Adan Thompson, the roller coaster pioneer, and George Tilyou, builder of Steeplechase Park, developed their own, highly original attractions, many of which were quickly imported by exposition managers. By the 1880s, one historian argues, Coney Island was filled with midwestern entrepreneurs, lured to the East by the Philadelphia Exposition. Tilyou was one of them, sufficiently fascinated by World's Fairs to spend his honeymoon at Chicago's Columbian Exposition in 1893. There he gaped at the first Ferris wheel (Fig. i), as important an influence on his professional goals as "A Trip to the Moon," an illusionistic voyage featured by Buffalo's Pan-American Exposition of 1901. Midwestern migrants, now gone West, would help shape the twentieth-century amusement world as well.

By the turn of the century, after half a dozen important fairs had come and gone, commercially operated amusement parks flourished all across the country. They were linked, physically and spiritually, to the industrial and technological changes transforming the lives of millions of people, and were physically connected by electric transit lines to the homes and neighborhoods of their visitors. Fed by the expositions before them, they varied considerably in size and sophistication. New York's Coney Island, with three different parks in full operation by 1910, had become the fabled industry leader, but there were dozens of such complexes in large cities like Boston, Chicago, Philadelphia, and Cincinnati, with counterparts in smaller towns. The formulaic blending of electrically powered thrill rides, gambling and games of chance, athletics, vaudeville acts, spectacular reenactments of great disasters, fun houses, daredevil stunts, and girlie shows, almost guaranteed success, particularly when housed within elaborately appointed and extravagantly lit fairground settings. Fantasy, danger, exoticism (and, sometimes, sexuality) mixed together in what contemporaries agreed were high-powered environments, mirroring rather than relieving the daily life of the modern city. The parks' owners and operators, acclaimed as shrewd businessmen, went so far as to share their management philosophy with the readers of popular magazines.

The notion that amusement was a business, and that catering to the taste of millions could be refined to a science, vaguely reassured some Americans who otherwise might have dismissed the function of entertainment as frivolous or trivial. The planners of fairs, like the owners of amusement parks, invited respect for their hard-headedness, as well as admiration for their creative energy. "Things move so smoothly in the White City that one hardly appreciates how much is owing to those who help to make them move smoothly," Richard Harding Davis wrote of Chicago's 1893 fair. The "executive part of it" he thought the most impressive. Fair managers and amusement managers alike linked their success to knowledge of human psychology, insight into the American character, as well as a commitment to a wholesome atmosphere. Showmen learned, wrote the scientist and journalist Edwin Slosson in 1909, that "decent people have in the aggregate more money to spend than the dissipated, even tho they spend it more sparingly." Americans, wrote Frederic Thompson a year earlier, could take public morality for granted, and their showmen concentrate on awakening the carnival spirit.

But while gaiety was not immoral, neither was it spontaneous, Thompson continued; it had to be manufactured. There was nothing wrong in the creation of frolic; this was the showman's business. In fact, the reason so many large expositions failed financially was that they were rarely run by showmen. Too many were led by educators or aestheticians. "It is foolish to make people serious or to point a moral." It was wiser to keep the rides short and fast. After all, people resting on benches were not paying customers, and the carnival spirit was expensive to manufacture.

Were didactic aims inherently at odds with the pleasure principle? Could instruction and gratification be combined? Exposition managers believed in their merger, and remained insistent promoters of high culture and refinement. A self-righteous tone ran through their apologias. Up through the early twentieth century, the strongest permanent links expositions had with their surrounding communities lay in the museums of art, history, and natural science that they generated. Fair buildings, designed to display, on a palatial scale, art and artifacts from around the world, formed obvious sites for the municipal institutions that were the hallmarks of cosmopolitanism. Expositions offered many Americans their first serious art exhibition, symphony orchestra, or presentations of national history, natural science, and the logic of the new technology. Charmed by the displays, impressed by the crowds, and eager to retain temporary collections for permanent use, local philanthropists often joined with public authorities in salvaging parts of these exhibits for the community. Some cities even tried to retain the entire exposition as a permanent institution. The dream landscapes produced instant nostalgia, anxiety that what had been so painfully put together suffered so short a life. Indeed the intensity of the fair experiences rested partly on the knowledge that they would not be around for very long.

Despite the powerful institutions that flowed out of expositions, fairs were basically events rather than places, memory pieces, performances, once-in-a-lifetime experiences. They were simply too expensive to keep. A "white elephant would be a mere trifle" compared with the cost of maintaining something as gargantuan as St. Louis's Louisiana Purchase Exposition, the *New York Times* commented in 1904. The sooner the ground was cleared "the better for the peace of mind of the people of St. Louis and for the solvency of its Treasury." Local citizens often seemed far more interested in preserving the rides than the larger landscapes. The closing of the Ferris wheel in Chicago, in the fall of 1893, actually occasioned a riot. While moralists and educators lamented the loss of the larger educational setting, the disappearance of the amusement midways occasioned more intense regret, at least until the amusement parks had sufficiently recreated their range of exotic entertainments.

By World War I, they had managed to do so. The America of Disney's youth possessed, in its larger cities, hundreds of these parks, wonderlands devoted to thrills and Sunday sports, legacies of the taste left by the larger expositions. In Whalom in Massachusetts, Willow Grove near Philadelphia, Olympic Park in New Jersey, Riverview in Chicago, illusion as well as excitement played its role. Day Allen Willey, describing the trolley parks for readers of *Cosmopolitan*, juxtaposed the miniature railroads with their pygmy locomotives, and the "aquaramas," "where you pay your dime to drift with the current along the mysterious river, passing an ancient castle with its frowning battlements, plunging into darkness as your craft goes through what seems to be a tunnel." Along with the rides there were vaudeville shows, dance halls, and swimming pools.

Smaller towns, lacking such complexes, compensated through the attentions of visiting carnivals. Estimates had more than 150 of these troupes touring the country in the mid-1920s. While the amusement parks and Coney Islands of the world had apparently cleaned themselves up and abandoned the more salacious and dishonest attractions, the traveling carnivals constituted a clear menace to public morals, their girlie shows as dangerous to health as the germ-laden pink lemonade they peddled. Tawdry, violent, dishonest, the carnivals represented the dark side of the recreational dream, excursions into forbidden territory that had to be cleansed or at least monitored. State legislation now mandated periodic inspections, while an association of carnival owners declared itself ready to police the ranks. The quest for sanitized decency that Walt Disney adopted had a lengthy American pedigree.

By the 1920s, rural Americans were feeding their dreams in movie palaces rather than carnival midways. In fact, even the great expositions, for decades symbols of the coexistence of education and entertainment, didacticism and escape, seemed threatened by the rise of radio and cinema. The big fair of the period, Philadelphia's Sesqui-Centennial Exposition of 1926, the largest such enterprise since the San Francisco and San Diego extravaganzas of the teens, was a bust, an almost unqualified disaster (everywhere but in the pages of Philadelphia's most loyal booster, the *Saturday Evening Post*). Indeed the *Nation* asked whether such extravaganzas were not

i. View of the Ferris wheel, World's Columbian Exposition, Chicago. Charles Dudley Arnold, photographer. Gelatin silver print, 6 x 8. 1893. CCA PH1978: 078:002.

anachronisms, killed by film, radio, and cheap illustration. "Today every child has seen Javanese and Ceylonese villages on the screen," it contended. Taking solace in the successful centennial pageant put on by Baltimore's great railroad, the *Nation* concluded that exhibitions were not dead after all. But merely raising the question indicated that some kind of turning point had been reached. The Philadelphia Sesqui-Centennial, unlike the fairs in St. Louis, Chicago, Buffalo, and San Francisco, left no parks or museums in its wake. It was tied, firmly if stolidly, to an expanding popular and commercial culture. Its links were closer to a new stadium and convention hall, vessels serving the city's appetite for sports and for business. The trolley and amusement parks were still flourishing in the 1920s, but more and more they were serving youthful audiences, teenagers, adolescents, who found roller coasters, tunnels of love, Ferris wheels, and cotton candy a recipe for romance, summer escape, and playing hooky. The competitors from Hollywood and radio were much stronger than anything the showmen could manage.

Overtaken, first by technology, then by the Depression, the exposition-amusement park axis received an unexpected boost in the 1930s. World's Fair enthusiasm revived. *Newsweek* described the masses who closed Chicago's Century of Progress Exposition in 1934 (Fig. ii) as combining "the exuberance of an Army-Navy football crowd with the hysteria of a Day of Judgment throng." In its two-year season it enjoyed almost fifty million visitors. New York's World's Fair of 1939–40, not as profitable as Chicago's, attracted nearly as many people. There were elements of continuity with the older expositions. High and low continued to have a presence. While local art museums were already well stocked, and the managers of the New York World's Fair, themed "The World of Tomorrow," tried briefly to get away without any art exhibition, special loans and masterpiece displays ultimately acknowledged the role of high culture and a continuing commitment to uplift.

Girlie shows and thrilling rides, moreover, remained staples of these fairs, indeed penetrated them as never before. "We take our amusements more integrally with our culture than our fathers did," the *Christian Century* observed, commenting upon the fact that high art lay outside the walls of the Century of Progress Exposition, in the Art Institute, while the Midway sat securely inside. Chicago's sky ride offered visitors an exciting overhead view of the fair, a tribute perhaps to the growing role of air travel, and New York's parachute jump was reconstructed at Coney Island after the World's Fair had closed. There were many gestures to sentimentalism and nostalgia: a replica of Fort Dearborn and relics of Lincoln's youth entertained Chicago patrons, while New York's fair contained reconstructions of Shakespeare's England and the city itself half a century earlier.

But the Depression-era fairs also contained some fundamental changes, as the *Christian Century* suggested, among them the emergence of the business corporation as a public personality and a heavy emphasis on futurism. The fairgrounds were clotted with elaborate and expressive corporate pavilions, planned by some of the most prominent industrial designers in the country. Their exhibits, along with a number of official displays, projected a vision of tomorrow that retained its capacity to startle and excite, rivaling the novelties of film and radio. Where once huge models had reconstructed the past—Saint Louis in 1904 featured a miniature city of Jerusalem—now they projected the coming age, as in General Motors' enormously popular Futurama at New York's World of Tomorrow in 1939. New products—nylon, Lucite, plexiglass, fluorescent lighting, television—and vast models of futuristic cities, robots, and innovative entertainments sated the crowds. Ford, Firestone, and Chrysler participated prominently (Fig. iii). In Chicago an industry-sponsored "Wings of a Century," a pageant of transportation, featured hundreds of people and dozens of trains and locomotives. Lincoln Kirstein was particularly caught by the transportation show: "Here men and machines, with music, live horses, and solid wheels, steel and wood, flashing in the paling light of day, are a splendid show of relevant activity." Open-air spectacle had combined with radio amplifiers. In a lyrical mood, Kirstein imagined future pageants built around the words of Walt Whitman.

Sharp criticism was also plentiful. The only big new idea the *New Republic* found in Chicago's Century of Progress Exposition was Sally Rand's fan dance. All else seemed rather derivative. The future, the publication argued, too closely resembled the past, and visitors seemed almost oblivious to the present, either ignorant of or indifferent to the misery that lay around them. The exposition, moreover, adjacent to Chicago's black neighborhoods, was almost entirely white in its personnel and its clients, having rebuffed efforts made by African-Americans to gain more employment or present exhibitions. This increased the indignation of those who found the fair conservative in its ideology as well as authoritarian in its management. Even the "modern" architecture the fair boasted was derided by no less an authority than Frank Lloyd Wright as a travesty—superficial, gussied up, and trivialized. The commercialism and salaciousness of the amusement zone brought condemnation from a whole range of moralists, secular and religious, who felt the Streets of Paris did not belong on the shores of Lake Michigan.

But the Century of Progress, like the World of Tomorrow, showed that American appetites for expositions had not disappeared, indeed they had barely diminished. Fairs had a special gift for looking backward and forward simultaneously, for making the pleasure principle acceptable by cloaking it with useful information. They also fed, as nothing before them had, the passion for searching out the next generation of consumables. The fairs of the 1930s, acknowledging the potent appeal of the

Expository Expositions 25

ii. Looking east from Skywide Tower, International Exhibition, Chicago. Unnumbered plate from the album *A Century of Progress, International Exhibition, Chicago, 1933–1934*. Unknown photographer. Gelatin silver print. 8 x 11. 1934. CCA PH 1990: 0323:013.

new mass media, indeed deploying radio and film within their enormous systems of publicity and public relations, linked up with the new celebrity culture by exploiting public familiarity with the products of Hollywood and the airwaves. Far more broadly than their predecessors, these fairs accepted the commercially shaped, nationalized, media-driven middle-class culture that was coming to dominate America. No longer did visitors require the reassuring presence of state buildings and hospitality houses to welcome them to the exposition. Provincialism had been shaken by the power of the media. Nor did the sentimentalized cultures of the old country need quite so many costumed peasants in their ethnic restaurants.

Film had endowed many Americans with a somewhat more elaborate and infinitely more effective sense of time and space, and, in any event, many of the European exhibitors in New York (the only fair of the decade to enjoy extensive foreign participation) presented themselves as entirely modern and up-to-date, flaunting the latest in architecture, industrial design, and political authoritarianism. The fairs no longer had to serve as bridges between high and low; they could, instead, acknowledge the broad middle without apology, accepting commercialism and mass culture without any need to gild their exhibitions with the trappings of venerated art. As it turns out, science and technology, in the form of new products and materials, were far more inspirational. In acknowledging the broad middle and embracing brand-name merchandise, they were simply anticipating the style of amusement management that would follow upon World War II.

That this would be pioneered in California was not wholly surprising. There the landscape had naturally absorbed the kinds of exotic fantasy that had once been the monopoly of fairs and amusement parks. For decades, a steady drumbeat of incredulous commentary, mainly from Eastern or foreign visitors, had captured the astonishing spectacle of Los Angeles's streetscapes. The "highest form of popular art is found in the decoration of filling stations," Bruce Bliven reported to readers of the *New Republic* in 1927; "one tours them as one does the *château* country of France." It was, he stated admiringly, a "middle-class heaven"; in no other place in America did "all classes do so nearly the same thing at the same time." "Here you see," Edmund Wilson remarked four years later, "mixturesque beauty," a "Pekinese pagoda made of fresh and crackly peanut brittle—there a snow-white marshmallow igloo—or a toothsome pink nougat in the Florentine manner, rich and delicious with embedded nuts." On either side of the coastal highway "fabricated features amaze us . . . a trapper's cabin made of plaster pine logs that sells lime and lemon dope-flavored pop and unbuttered barbecue sandwiches, a monster papier-mâché ice-cream freezer." It was a land where "every prospect appeases and the goofs hang like ripe fruit." Many others expounded during the interwar years on the exaggerated character of Southern California, contrasting the scale, color, and astonishing shapes to be found with the hordes of midwesterners who had, with surprising abruptness, thronged its capital, Los Angeles. "Suddenly Southern California woke to find these people descending like an invasion," wrote Sarah Comstock in 1928; lured by the climate, Iowans and Kansans had discovered the "paradise of the Corn Belt." "They fill the streets, gaping at the sights; they 'eat out,' an unspeakable luxury to the women after years of making pies and 'baking hens' for the harvest crew." This was not so far from descriptions of exposition crowds in the days when America was rural, agricultural, and largely innocent of metropolitan ways.

Comstock made the exposition connection even closer, admiring the local Dutch bakeries, built to resemble windmills, their blades whirling in the air to attract customers: "In short, one buys one's daily bread under the illusion of visiting a Midway Plaisance." California seemed on the verge of becoming an enormous carnival, a "Christmas play where the plum cake has grown into a house and Jack is waving his cap from a beanstalk as high as a steeple." Los Angeles, wrote another at about the same time, "is the child of Hollywood out of Kansas," the "Middle-Westerner's Nirvana, his reward for years of toil, economy, or shrewdness," a permanent real estate boom with the sustained excitement of a camp meeting, a "prairie city transplanted to a luxuriant subtropical setting." This "new Greece," an amalgam of the Middle West and the movies, was the land of the happy ending, bereft, critics charged, of critical intelligence, a traditional class structure, good taste, and a willingness to face unpleasant facts.

Decades later this rhetoric would be easily if casually applied to another California phenomenon: its pacesetting theme parks. Far from being inhospitable between the wars to middle-class recreational needs, the charge brought to explain Disney's search for alternatives, Southern California abounded with options: amusement piers at Long Beach and Santa Monica, miniature golf courses, and above all, those fantasy buildings created by restaurateurs, haberdashers, piano distributors, and ice-cream chains, making the drive down a highway an *Alice in Wonderland* journey. Two fairs of the 1930s, the California Pacific International Exposition in San Diego and the Golden Gate International Exposition in San Francisco added to this feast for middle-class consumption, somewhat more romantic in their physical appearance than their Eastern counterparts, and building on the vacationland symbolism of their surrounding cities.

California, as so often, provided a forecast. Recreation became a national obsession, especially during the dark years of the Depression, with heavy emphasis on extending its varieties to an enlarged class of white-collar and blue-collar workers. In half a dozen years the Works Progress Administration (WPA) actually spent more than one billion dollars to create forty thousand new sports and recreation facilities, from skating rinks and ski runs to municipal golf courses and school gymnasiums. The Little League was founded in 1939. And, after the war, the rise of the automobile was demonstrated by the presence of thousands of drive-in movie houses, constituting, at their peak in the 1960s, one-third of all American theaters. The collapse of mass transit, the demographic shifts transforming metropolitan landscapes, the suburbanizing trends, threatened the popularity of the established amusement parks. And, despite their popular success in the 1930s, international fairs went into eclipse in the United States, experiencing a twenty-year hiatus until revived in Seattle in 1962.

The first Disney park appeared during this pause, amid rumors that the taste for expositions was as dead as the expiring amusement parks. But the appetite for fantasy had not disappeared, nor the special ability of a three-dimensional landscape to feed it. Experienced showmen had long argued that the best rides were participant-directed; feelings of self-directed movement, control, and choice stimulated public patronage. "The keynote of the idea is the active cooperation of the spectator in his own entertainment," Julian Hawthorne observed on Buffalo's Pike in 1901. So ingeniously were the elaborate illusions of the midways carried out that "instead of viewing a performance on a stage, we are ourselves participants in the scene." The Disney parks accepted this notion. The challenge was to design a product that matched form and content, and no longer took refuge in elevating popular taste by honoring high culture.

Disney was able to retain the exposition's moralism without harnessing himself to its heavy didacticism. He did so, in large part, by harnessing childhood nostalgia for his own creations to the historical myths and futurist conceits that fairs had employed. His landscapes, moreover, were far more specialized and efficient than the sprawling, comprehensive settings that were fairgrounds. Fairs certainly were more coherent than most American cities, but Disney outdid even their polish and proverbially intensive maintenance. By concentrating on popular science, mass amusements, patriotic nostalgia, and industrialized mythology, by frankly abandoning high-minded ambitions in favor of the existing taste of his customers, the Disney parks promoted a form of self-discovery, as revolutionary, perhaps, as the Vauxhall experience once had been. The Disney parks celebrated not Columbus, the Panama Canal, the Louisiana Purchase, or the building of bridges, as had some earlier expositions. They celebrated themselves and their audiences. These joint ventures in spectacle management, like the Vauxhalls and Ranelagh Gardens of another day, endowed their visitors with a new vision of themselves, lending dignity to the commercial culture that had been feeding their hearts and minds for so many decades. Champions of high and low alike might bemoan this vision of America, vulgarized, standardized, and sanitized as it seemed, but visitors voted with their feet, as they had at World's Fairs. Radicals, reformers, purists, and populists from Louis Sullivan and Lewis Mumford to Frank Lloyd Wright and Edmund Wilson, had found the great expositions reactionary, racist, repressive, or superficial. That did not dim their exultant receptions.

The expositions, however, did help establish the most fundamental feature of all, and one Disney eagerly built upon: a periodically recurring rhythm of mass movement, a faith in destination as social restorative, a system of travel designed to reaffirm belief—in the future, in the past, or, especially for twentieth-century Americans, in one another. With Disney the Pilgrim's Progress had become a family tour and Vanity Fair the Heavenly City. But the transforming dream, so long nurtured by the expositions, that search for social happiness, remained in place.

iii. View of Chrysler Building, New York World's Fair. Frank Navara, photographer. Gelatin silver print. 9 5/8 x 7 5/8. 1939. CCA PH 1981: 0276.

IMAGINEERING THE DISNEY THEME PARKS

Karal Ann Marling

Disneyland is so much a part of the American landscape that it's hard to imagine a time when the park wasn't there (Fig. 1). A time, back before the freeway was invented, when the site along Harbor Boulevard in Anaheim was just another orange grove, dozing in the warm California sunshine. Like the Grand Canyon or Chicago or the Golden Gate Bridge, Disneyland is a key American place-marker, an icon, a picture vignette on the national road map, striking and memorable and singular. A place. A place as real as any mountain range or metropolis.

Except that it isn't. Not quite. It didn't just happen, over eons of geological time, for one thing, nor did it develop through generations of pioneering toil. Movie mogul Walt Disney deliberately created Disneyland in that orange grove in 1955 with money borrowed against his life insurance policy (Fig. 2). And it isn't entirely real, either. It's a film set, an illusion. The buildings at Disneyland often fool you into thinking that they are turn-of-the-century business blocks or Third World trading posts, but actually they are 1950s-style malls (Fig. 3). Malls and sprawling megastructures slip-covered in a period decor that makes the bleakest functional architecture look cozily quaint—or hauntingly odd, all parabolic curves and weightless cantilevers, like some gleaming spaceport on Mars in the year 2000-something. Thanks to forced perspective and fiberglass, nothing here is as it seems to be. In Disneyland, even the natural features of the terrain are unnatural. The 1/100-scale Matterhorn mountain added to the park in 1959 was made out of 2,175 steel girders and enough lumber to build a new subdivision.

Nor is Disneyland unique any more, a one-of-a-kind place. For after Disneyland (Fig. 5) came the Magic Kingdom at Walt Disney World in Florida (1971), Tokyo Disneyland (1983; Fig. 4), and Disneyland Paris (formerly Euro-Disney, 1992). They differ in size, and in detail. But they all have a live steam railroad line, a pedestrian Main Street modeled after the turn-of-the-century streetscape of a little American city, a tall castle to orient the visitor in space, and a variety of fictive "lands" based on scenes in Disney movies and Walt's personal vision of history (Fig. 6). They all have a peripheral berm, a barrier separating the enclosed precincts of the park from the outside world. And they all have similar footprints: a heart-shaped plan, with a single entry at the point, centered on a

1. Aerial view of the Disneyland site in the orange groves of Anaheim, California. Construction began in July 1954. The Santa Ana freeway bisects the photograph from left to right, just above the park.

2. Laying out the trolley tracks on Main Street, Disneyland, 1955.

Left: Catherine Wagner. *Storybook Land; Fantasyland, Disneyland, Anaheim, California.* Collection CCA.

hub affording both visual and physical access to every segment of the park.

Today, too, there are little bits of Disneyland everywhere: actual, working structures situated outside the parks proper but based on their internal logic of make-believe. Walt Disney Imagineering—Walt's own term: imagination + engineering = "Imagineering"—has conceived a whole range of retail stores, galleries, and hotels, expressly calculated to create and sustain a mood. In the Contemporary Hotel on the grounds of Walt Disney World, that mood was futuristic optimism, c. 1969 (Fig. 7). A giant concrete and steel A-frame into which prefabricated room modules were slotted, the Contemporary was planned as a showplace of tomorrow's building techniques, a technology dramatized by the interior decor. In the guest rooms, plastic chairs and tables borrowed from some outer-space fantasy of modern living once perched expectantly on single, sci-fi legs (Fig. 8). Down below, and visible from the open corridors outside each door, a streamlined monorail still glides silently through the towering lobby, an emissary from a time that never came.

And there are new Disney parks that are not Disneylands at all. EPCOT (1982), at Walt Disney World, began life as Walt's utopian dream of a real city for upwards of twenty thousand people, a perfect city with dependable public transportation, a soaring civic center covered by an all-weather dome, and model factories concealed in greenbelts that were readily accessible to workers housed in idyllic suburban subdivisions nearby (Fig. 9). As EPCOT Center was built by his corporate heirs

3. Disneyland under construction in 1954. Seen from above, it is obvious that the Main Street buildings consist of large blocks decorated with Gay Nineties facades. The prefabricated industrial sheds used in Fantasyland for reasons of speed and economy are also visible in the background.

4. "Fun Map" of Tokyo Disneyland, sold as a souvenir. Printed version: Terry Smith. 28 11/16 x 43 9/16. 1989.

after Walt's death, it became a kind of permanent World's Fair instead, with one section devoted to corporate pavilions and another to national product shows housed in replicas of the Eiffel Tower, the Piazza San Marco, and similar must-see stops along the tourist itinerary. Initial plans, however, were for that real city that Disneyland was not, or not quite. Code-named "Project X," the original EPCOT was a bold New Town scheme intended to show that the problems of present-day American cities were not beyond solution. That it was possible, for example, to eliminate the automobile from the urban equation, or at least minimize its depredations by running service roads under and around city centers and providing cheap, efficient forms of mass transit.

But Disneyland had already presented a powerful critique of the manifest ills of Los Angeles in 1955. Like Project X, Disneyland included pedestrian spaces free from vehicular traffic. In the form of rides (or "attractions," in park lingo), it spotlighted every imaginable kind of people-moving device that did not entail a driver piloting himself through increasingly congested streets—and chewing up the landscape in the process: trains, monorails, passenger pods, canal boats, riverboats, and double-decker buses (Fig. 10). If Disneyland was a place of amusement and escape, it was also, in its own way, a kind of pre-EPCOT utopia, a better, cleaner, more pleasant and resonant American place than 1955 afforded the average urbanite who drove to Anaheim on the interstate and the Santa Ana freeway. There was, after all, something blessedly real about Disneyland.

Disney-MGM Studios (1989), another addition to the Florida property, mimics L.A. in the 1940s when, at least in memory, every building was a gleaming Art Deco masterpiece, every woman was a glamour-girl under contract to one of the studios, and everybody rode the Pacific Electric red car to premieres at Grauman's Chinese Theater (Fig. 11). The faux-Oriental movie palace is the MGM equivalent of the familiar Disneyland castle (Fig. 12). And like Disneyland, this park casts a baleful eye on Los Angeles as it is, preferring a city that never was—and yet contrives to flourish anyway in fiberglass and false fronts, like a mirage, in the dazzling, shimmering heat of a central Florida afternoon.

The Ideal City: Walt Disney's Burbank Studio

The Reluctant Dragon, released in June 1941, showed actual glimpses of that beautiful Los Angeles neverland flashing past the window of a speeding car. The first Disney feature to incorporate extensive live-action footage, *The Reluctant Dragon* sends humorist Robert Benchley motoring off to the new Disney studios in Burbank with a children's book of the same name: Mrs. Benchley thinks it would make a great cartoon. In the finale, Mr. Benchley at last meets Walt in a screening room where the staff is about to preview his latest animated film. It is, predictably enough, *The Reluctant Dragon*. But the movie captures Disney at an unhappy moment of tension and change, when the notion of building a theme park—of translating animation from a flat

5. Popular souvenir maps show how important the "place-ness" of Disney parks is to their meaning. Printed "Fun Map" of Disneyland: Sam McKim. 30 x 44. 1957. Collection of David Wurtz.

6. Main Street, U.S.A., Magic Kingdom, Walt Disney World, Orlando, Florida. As in all the Disney parks, this street leads from the point of entry to the Castle.

7. Contemporary Hotel, Walt Disney World, under construction, c. 1970. The supporting beams for the monorail are visible on either side of the atrium lobby, which doubles as a monorail station. The architect is said to have threatened to withdraw from the project because he objected to the idea of his building being invaded by an amusement park "ride."

32 Designing Disney's Theme Parks

8. Design for a table in a typical guest room of the Contemporary Hotel. Richard Hebner. Watercolor on paper. 12 x 16. 1969.

screen to the three-dimensional world—first presented itself as an appealing alternative to the movie business. The painstaking art of animation was, after all, the art of perfecting the world. In his cartoons, Walt always made good triumph over evil. The sun was shining. The birds sang. The magic of ink and paint made bunnies giggle, dragons recite verse, and elephants fly through the air. It was a world over which Walt Disney exercised total, beneficent control. What if he could do the same thing in real life? At his own studio, for instance?

The fifty-one-acre Burbank lot on the edge of Griffith Park was Walt's initial foray into building the ideal city and he went about it in an ad hoc manner that would characterize his later approach to Disneyland. Moving from outmoded quarters on Hyperion Avenue to the Park Avenue of the studio district was a major accomplishment for Disney. Furthermore, the move came during the making of *Fantasia*, the animated interpretation of classical music that announced Walt's claim for legitimacy in the realm of the fine arts. Because the studio was a visible manifestation of his own hard-won status—his sense of self—he did not employ a conventional architect who might have been tempted to stamp the buildings at the corner of Buena Vista and Riverside with marks of a competing artistic personality. Although California industrial stylist Kem Weber (a sometime set designer for Paramount) was the "supervising designer" of record, Walt began the project in 1939 by setting up his own in-house design unit to work out a master plan based on the efficient movement of materials along a sort of conceptual assembly line. The relationship between each brick or concrete-block building and the next depended on the steps in the animation process, from drawing to cel to motion picture film.

The same team also determined the placement of underground utilities and solutions to a number of special problems dictated by the animation business: structures were aligned to internal streets (named Dopey Drive and Mickey Avenue) on a true north-south axis, for example, to provide optimal lighting conditions for artists, and windows were equipped with special metal awnings adjustable by the occupants of each office (Fig. 13). An air-conditioning system built to order by General Electric kept dust from ruining the painted celluloid sheets and added to the creature comforts of the new studio. Weber's low desks and sofas, his blond wood animation tables and bent plywood "Airline" chairs, also contributed to a feeling of friendly informality and concern for the welfare of the employee at odds with the industrial efficiency the company sometimes stressed in its own publicity about its model factory.

In *The Reluctant Dragon*, the new studio is the real star, a well-manicured, campus-like utopia, luxuriously furnished and, above all, special—notably different from the world outside the gate, where Benchley is forced to abandon his car (Fig. 14). Inside this magical kingdom, drawings talk and move; railroad trains snort to life on paper; musicians, artists, and paint chemists stroll along tree-shaded streets named for Mickey Mouse and his friends; and everyone seems happy and

9. Walt Disney explained his plans for a utopian EPCOT—an Experimental Prototype Community of Tomorrow—to the camera in October 1966, only months before his death.

10. The ceremonial opening of the Disneyland monorail line, June 14, 1959. The Nixon family and other dignitaries who visited the park helped to make it a national institution.

11. The Disney-MGM Studios Theme Park in Orlando presents Main Street, U.S.A. again, this time in the guise of Los Angeles in the 1940s. Note the billboard for the Red Car (the monorail of the 1940s) and the facade of Grauman's Chinese Theater in the place of the usual Disney castle.

34 Designing Disney's Theme Parks

12. Grauman's Chinese Theater serves as the castle for the Disney MGM-Studios Theme Park. Study for paint and finish colors, Grauman's Chinese Theater at the Disney-MGM Studios Theme Park. Katie Olson. Colored pencil, acrylic, and ink on blackline. 23 x 30. 1987.

productive. Except, perhaps, for the saturnine boss, painfully twisted into his viewing-room chair, his legs drawn up under him, as if recoiling in horror from his own creation. Somehow, despite his best efforts, the lovely vision of order and harmony presented in the film was a just another Hollywood illusion. When *The Reluctant Dragon* opened in L.A., it was greeted by a line of angry pickets demanding higher wages and union representation for the artists, and enraged by the on-screen suggestion that the Disney studio was some kind of workers' paradise.

Early in the 1950s, *New York Times* critic Bosley Crowther came to see the Disney complex and found his old friend utterly disinterested in making movies. Disney was, he wrote, "almost weirdly concerned with the building of a miniature railroad engine and a string of cars." (Fig. 15). Although most critics and moviegoers never noticed, the change had begun a decade earlier, with the bitter strike, the ultimate failure of *Fantasia*, and Walt's growing determination to build something tangible and true, something perfect, a place where nothing could ever go wrong. Children love dollhouses and toy train sets because they give little fingers mastery over the dangerous, forbidden, frustrating world of grown-up things.

So, when Walt's doctors advised him to forget the studio for a while and get a hobby, he turned to miniatures, tiny replicas that differed from the beautifully appointed rooms of his own new studio in only two respects: they were much smaller, of course—and they were wholly subject to his control.

Fairs and Miniatures

It all began with the 1939 New York World's Fair. Like other fairs, this was an instant city, a city (or cities) in miniature, thrown up overnight to celebrate progress and forward thinking. The fair was American urbanism as it ought to be. Committees laid out broad axial boulevards, each one pointed toward some giant statue or oddly shaped tower. Artists mandated a palette of distinctive exterior colors that brought an illusion of harmony to competing architectural schemes and established functional zones or districts—for industry, transportation, foreign nations, government—by tonal means alone. Unlike its predecessors, this was a bicoastal fair, with outposts in New York and San Francisco. And in both locations, the rational decision-making, the neat subdivisions of the plan, and the sheer spit-and-polish newness stood in studied contrast to the down-at-the-heels vernacular of the host cities after ten years of economic depression. The New York fair, at which Disney was represented by a specially commissioned Mickey Mouse cartoon in the Nabisco pavilion, is best remembered for its series of dramatic displays about the shining city of tomorrow, which repetition made seem all but inevitable. It was a tangible fact, this Democracity, this Futurama, as real as the clever dioramas in which autos of the future winked past shrunken skyscrapers on tiny freeways, bound for suburbs laid out in tidy, geometric patterns. And each little house in each little cul-de-sac was painted in the same cheery, scientifically chosen color as the one next door.

13. The 1941 film *The Reluctant Dragon* showed off the new Disney studio in Burbank. The public was clamoring for studio tours and the movie tried to address that demand. But the ongoing interest suggested to Walt Disney that he might someday build a little park across the street especially for tourists in search of Mickey Mouse.

14. The layout of the Disney plant, correlating to the way in which animated films were made, is apparent in this still from *The Reluctant Dragon*.

Although his own blueprint for EPCOT would owe something to the hypothetical worlds of tomorrow conjured up at Flushing Meadow, there is no convincing evidence that Walt Disney ever set foot on the New York fairgrounds (Fig. 16). But he did attend the Golden Gate International Exposition in San Francisco in 1939. This fair was less determinedly futuristic in style than its East Coast counterpart. A strange mixture of Latin American and vaguely Pacific motifs, with overtones of Art Deco streamlining, the architecture is best described as festive or fantastic. Turrets, castles, palaces, and towers sprouted everywhere (Figs. 17, 18). The centerpiece—the Tower of the Sun—resembled a rocket ship carved in ersatz stone by a Mayan seer. But every big thing had its own Lilliputian version: bold structures like the four-hundred-foot Tower gained added stature, somehow, by contrast with a plethora of much-too-little things. So the Vacationland Palace, sponsored mainly by the railroads, featured a model train that chugged its way through a layout composed of well-known landmarks in the American West, all reproduced at toy-town scale.

And while many of the exhibits called upon fairgoers to imagine a wondrous world to come, San Francisco's tomorrow was, by and large, a rocketless near future, premised on the homely verities of today. It was a domestic tomorrow of suburbs and ranch-style homes. Crowds nonetheless flocked to see furnished rooms from the kinds of practical new houses in which Californians of taste and moderate means might actually find themselves dwelling next year or the year after that. Kem Weber was one of the designers chosen to show how linoleum, plastics, laminates, and an abstract sculpture by Isamu Noguchi could add up to an ideal living room, as relaxed and practical as Walt Disney's Burbank office. But despite the feasibility of the model rooms—and the voyeuristic pleasure always attached to tiptoeing through somebody else's house in the absence of the inhabitants— it was the miniature rooms that won the hearts of San Franciscans.

The Thorne Room Miniatures consisted of thirty-two little shadowboxes, each one about three feet wide, eighteen inches deep, and two feet high. Peering in through the missing front wall, the viewer saw fully furnished English and early American period rooms—or the prelude to the full-size modern rooms nearby. The difference was in the microscopic size of the chandeliers, the wallpaper patterns, the cabinetry, carpets, and bibelots that added up to a vivid impression of life as it was lived by a race of tiny beings with exquisite taste. Socialite Mrs. James Ward Thorne, of Chicago and Santa Barbara, got the idea of building her rooms in the 1920s, when dollhouses and period rooms both became fashionable. In 1924, Queen Mary of England was presented with a dollhouse; the work of thousands of British artists and handicrafters, it was endlessly photographed and exhibited as an exemplar of English design, past and present. The American movie actress Colleen Moore had her famous Fairy Castle, too, a mansion with tiny portraits of Mickey and Minnie Mouse hanging over the mantelpiece. Begun in the late twenties, Moore's dollhouse had been furnished with the help of several Hollywood art

---

15. Walt Disney's backyard railroad on Carolwood Drive in Holmby Hills, 1951. Testing and construction are still in progress. Disney built an earthen berm around the house to protect the neighbors from the noise and to preserve the illusion of scale on his layout.

16. The layout of EPCOT Center, as it was ultimately built, reflects design features of World's Fairs: oddly shaped "theme" buildings, axial boulevards, large plazas, artificial lagoons.

17. The castle became the trademark of the Disney parks and the Walt Disney Company. Color reference chart for Cinderella's Castle, Tokyo Disneyland. Miyuki Iga. Gouache, pen, and colored pencil on blueline. 32 x 21. 1980.

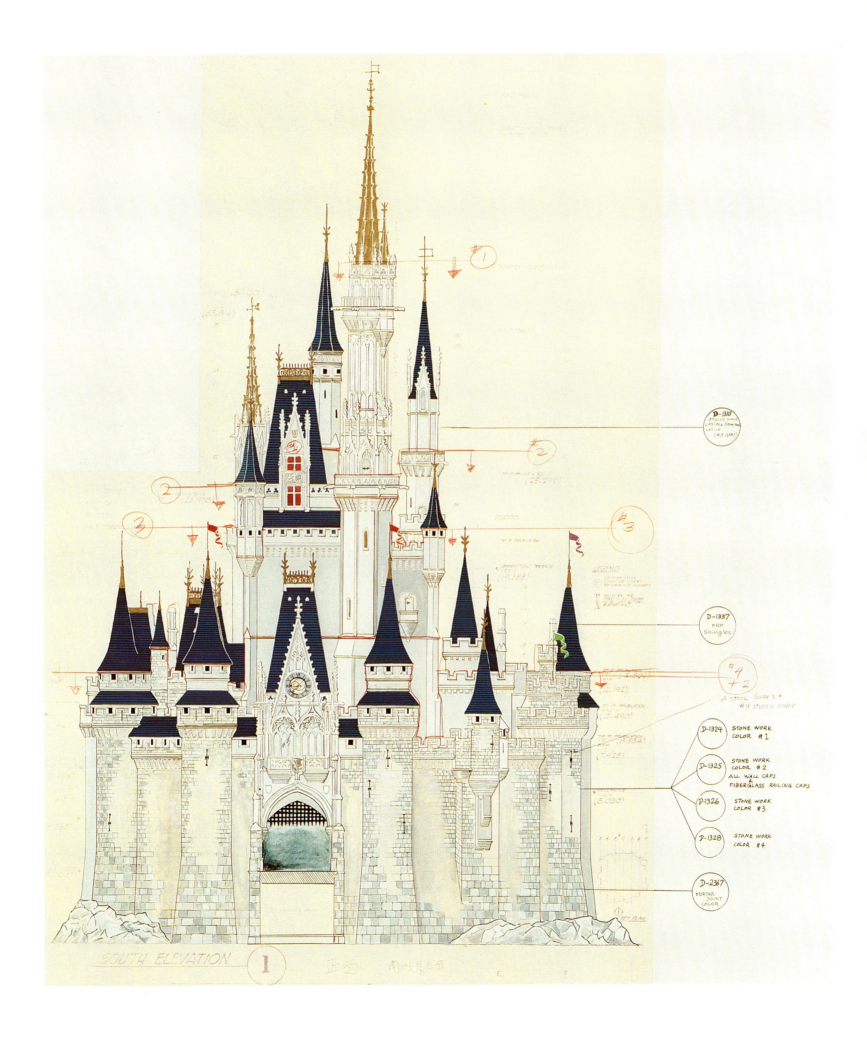

directors, including, according to legend, the young Walt Disney. In the 1930s, eleven rooms of the Fairy Castle toured the country. A 1935 display in the window of Macy's New York City department store stalled sidewalk traffic for blocks.

The passion for tiny things—and miniatures were as popular among ordinary dads and secretaries as they were with royalty—is explained by the customary reaction to these dollhouses for grownups. How intricate the workmanship! How miraculous the detail! And all made by hand! Imagine that! Mrs. Thorne's little rooms in San Francisco, and a second set on simultaneous view in New York in 1939, were handwrought rebukes to the machine age idolized by World's Fairs. They were a human protest against modernity, against an impersonal, dehumanized world of factories that cranked out the linoleum and the plastics found in model rooms of tomorrow. The period rooms Mrs. Thorne copied were also a key feature of American museums in the 1920s, intended to offer tacit instruction in the rules of proper living, as they harked back to times and places presumably more virtuous than a modern era of naughty movies, short skirts, fast cars, and bootleg gin. O tempera! O mores! Rampant nostalgia at the scale of one inch to the foot. Walt Disney came home from San Francisco and began to collect miniatures.

It wasn't just the craftsmanship, although Walt began to find real relaxation in making his own small-scale models. It wasn't simply nostalgia, either, although, as life at the studio grew more complicated, he invoked childhood memories of the family farm outside Marceline, Missouri, more and more readily. No. There was a powerful drama about Mrs. Thorne's little rooms, despite their smallness. The format resembled a stage, a proscenium arch through which an interior could be viewed but never entered. That feeling of exclusion existed in the theater but was stronger here, somehow, since the minute size of the furnishings precluded any possibility of actual participation. Like Lewis Carroll's Alice on the other side of her looking glass (and Disney commissioned Aldous Huxley to write the script for such a film in 1945), the onlooker could only peer inside and yearn to be a part of that perfectly ordered domain.

In all of Mrs. Thorne's rooms, objects pertinent to the absent owners were scattered about like clues in a country-house mystery: a discarded book, the open door of a cabinet, a chair turned toward a window, a tiny cup and saucer abandoned on the very edge of a table. And the things they left behind conjured up stories in the heart of the observer. Love letters unanswered. A sudden quarrel. A three-dimensional world that could charm and delight and tell a story: in an odd way, this was animation without the quarrelsome animators who would throw up a picket line around the new studio on May 29, 1941.

Parks and Railroads

By all published accounts, Walt Disney had

18. King of his domain, Walt Disney walks through the Disneyland Castle, 1957.

thrown himself into the planning of the twenty-five-building Burbank complex with characteristic enthusiasm. But there are signs that he was hedging his bets from the beginning, searching for ways to change the nature of his business—looking for a product more like Mrs. Thorne's rooms and less like conventional cartoons. Even as the swank new plant was rising on Riverside Drive, he sent supervising animator David Hand out to the construction site one afternoon to find a suitable spot for a kiddie park nicer than the grubby ones he patronized on Sundays so his own little girls could ride the merry-go-round (Fig. 19). Children from every corner of the country wrote to Walt now, wanting to come to Hollywood and see the place where Mickey Mouse lived. Public demand had forced some of the other studios to sell paper-bag lunches and maps of their backlots, for fans bent on a behind-the-scenes glimpse of the movie business. The segment of *The Reluctant Dragon* in which Alan Ladd pretends to make an animated film was Walt's answer to the studio tour. Tourists would be bored stiff by the painstaking technicalities of animation, he thought. There really wasn't much to see.

But a little park, with statues of Mickey and the other characters, with picnic tables, grass, and trees. A place for all the kids who wanted to meet Mickey. A place where happy, non-unionized employees could bring their families on the weekends. Now that was another story. What kinds of things belonged in such a park? Some little houses, perhaps, like the Snow White cottage in the Disney family's own backyard, a seven-dwarfs-size playhouse with a white picket fence built by the studio model shop in 1937 in tribute to the release of the first feature-length animated film. Word was that the Disney daughters, Diane and Sharon, were soon bored by the cottage. Walt was the one who cherished each tiny gingerbread gable. What about *more* little houses? And a little train. His park would be altogether different from those "dirty, phony places, run by tough-looking people," he said. Something new. "Some kind of family park." With a train.

19. The earliest site plans for a hypothetical Disney park on Riverside Drive in Burbank all revolve around a miniature railroad. First concept sketch for a Disney park adjacent to the studio. Harper Goff. Watercolor, opaque watercolor, and colored pencil on paper. 8 1/4 x 33 1/2. 1951.

A steam train with a whistle and a bell and a little caboose.

After the fact, the art directors and animators who suddenly, in the winter of 1952, found themselves working at a company called Walt Disney Inc. (later WED Enterprises, for Walter Elias Disney; today, Walt Disney Imagineering) building something called Disneyland agreed that the trains had been the first clue to the boss's intentions. In 1938, Ward Kimball, one of the few actual studio artists to appear in *The Reluctant Dragon*, bought himself an honest-to-gosh railroad train, after years of drawing cute ones for Walt. He had an 1881 narrow-gauge Baldwin locomotive hauled to his home in rural San Gabriel, laid nine hundred feet of track, and thus became the first private citizen in the United States to own a railroad—the Grizzly Flats line—for his own personal use. Fellow animator Ollie Johnston started building a miniature ride-on live-steamer in 1946 in his Santa Monica backyard. Neither man was surprised to find a little Lionel layout in Walt's office just before Christmas of 1947. Ostensibly a gift for a nephew, the train was Disney's latest hobby and the two railroad buffs found him busily adding trees and buildings to the tabletop landscape through which it chugged. It was clear from the gleam in his eye that the toy train was only the beginning. "This is [just] an electric train," Walt told Roger Broggie, the head of the studio machine shop. "Now what's for real?"

Soon he and Broggie were scouring California for ideas and authentic details, taking photographs of working trains, talking to hobbyists like Johnston who built their own steam engines, and planning Walt's Carolwood Pacific line, named after the street in Holmby Hills where his $1/8$-scale model of a Central Pacific locomotive of the 1870s circled the garden of his brand new home via a forty-foot timber trestle, two tunnels, eleven switches, and twenty-six hundred feet of rail. Although he represented the train to his wife and children as a happy inspiration of the moment, the landscaping done as the house was being built was arranged with a future right-of-way in mind. Like Disneyland, the Carolwood Avenue house was screened from the pricey real estate around it by a steep earthen berm. "That's where I started it," Walt admitted to daughter Diane years later. "I built that bank up in the canyon so when I was down there playing with my trains, my neighbors wouldn't be annoyed."

The berm was his idea—and the train was his handiwork, built in the machine shop at Burbank with expert help. The first trial run of Walt's "Lilly Belle" engine took place on Christmas Eve 1949, on a loop of track in Studio One (Fig. 20). But the yellow caboose that was his pride and joy was built on stolen weekends in a little red barn out behind the Carolwood house. The barn was a miniature rendition of the one he remembered as a boy on Crane Farm, the forty-eight-acre Disney spread in Linn County, near Marceline, Missouri, c. 1906. And the caboose was a miniaturist's dream. Every detail was correct, down to the acanthus leaves on the legs of the pot-bellied stove and the text of the little newspaper tossed aside by a sleepy switchman whose unseen presence could be deduced from the rumpled little bunk alongside the stove (Fig. 21).

20. Walt Disney testing his train at the Burbank studio, 1951.
21. Disney originally crafted this miniature stove for his own caboose and later sold copies commercially.

22. Surrealist artist Salvador Dalì takes a ride on the Carolwood Pacific line.

23. It seems likely that the first, tentative sketches for the townscape of a new Disney park were made at Walter Knott's Berry Farm in Buena Park, California. Later studies continue to echo the flavor of Knott's Ghost Town. Harper Goff. Pencil on animation paper. 12 x 22. 1952–53.

Never at ease in social settings, the railroad finally gave Walt something to do at his own parties. Red Skelton, Edgar Bergen, and Salvador Dalì were among the celebrity guests who perched precariously atop a boxcar or a gondola for a circuit of the yard in 1951, 1952, and 1953 (Fig. 22). His train friends from the studio came, too, to help with the technicalities of keeping up a head of steam and to admire his craftsmanship. But in the late 1940s and early 1950s, just about everybody was a railroad buff. The craze for old trains was an aspect of the broader popular interest in "Americana"; antiques gave mobile Americans a sense of rootedness. Beyond that, however, the railroad whistle in the midnight air, the hiss of steam, were part of the collective memory of a whole generation of boys who became men with money and time for leisure in the postwar era. Like Walt Disney, they remembered the Missouri Pacific roaring past a little house in Kansas City, the Santa Fe bound for California. Those wonderful old trains were no more. Diesels whooshed silently past now, in dwindling numbers. Goods moved by truck, along the new interstate highways. Travelers were apt to catch a plane. Kimball's first steam train, once the pride of the Nevada Central, was one of many being sold off for scrap. And collected by those for whom the vanishing past was precious.

In the same spirit, Walter Knott, the owner of a thriving berry farm near Anaheim, started buying up whole towns as if they were clusters of little buildings on a model train layout. The first such structure was the Old Trails Hotel, found in an abandoned settlement outside Prescott, Arizona, and shipped back to Buena Park, California, in 1940. Soon, Knott had a complete Western "ghost town" to entertain folks waiting in line for one of his wife's famous chicken dinners, and a monthly magazine, *Ghost Town News*, devoted to the virtues of American life as the gritty old-timers had lived it in the nineteenth-century West (Fig. 23). Knott rescued an old mine train, too: in 1952, the Ghost Town and Calico Railway began operations in among his growing collection of false-front saloons, schoolhouses, and mercantiles.

The Chicago Railroad Fair

The railroad industry acknowledged the interest in models, memorabilia, and the old steamers in the summer of 1948. Against the backdrop of Lake Michigan, on the site of the 1933 Century of Progress Exposition, thirty-eight major American carriers, including the Santa Fe, organized a gala Railroad Fair. The stated reason for the celebration was the hundredth anniversary of the first steam locomotive to enter Chicago, the nation's greatest railroad center. The real reason was to revive an industry hard hit by competition and burdened with an inventory of rolling stock all but worn out by hard use during World War II. In keeping with the futurism endemic to fairs, this one trotted out its sleek new engines, its glass-domed observation cars, and a mysterious "X" train, said to be capable of speeds in excess of 150 mph. But by design, the overall tenor of the Railroad Fair was retrospective. Experts had put the number of railroad hobbyists and model makers at one hundred thousand; their total annual investment ran to some $10 million. Organizers of the Chicago fair of 1948 were eager to tap this reservoir of interest and goodwill. And so, with a perfunctory nod to tomorrow, they set out to indulge the growing American appetite for cowcatchers, pistons, smokestacks, old cabooses—and the fabled historical romance of the rails.

Ordered by his doctors to get away from the studio again, Walt went out to Chicago for the big show in August. He took Ward Kimball along for company and the latter's home movies show Disney in a state of unrestrained bliss from the moment the Santa Fe Super Chief left the Pasadena station. The railroad knew he was coming: the engineer let him ride in the cab and toot the whistle at level crossings. The fair had acres of famous engines and working replicas thereof and Kimball's film suggests that the pair inspected every last one of them. Disney caught Kimball at the throttle of an ancient engine; Kimball, in turn, took pictures of Disney, in a top hat and vest, acting the part of a hungry passenger stopping to dine at a trackside Harvey House during the twice-a-day pageant of railroad history performed by a cast of historic trains and a troupe of costumed attendants. Among the earliest sketches for the Disneyland railroad is a train based on the distinctive double-decker coaches of the *Atlantic*, lent to the pageant by the Baltimore and Ohio and highlighted in Kimball's footage (see Fig. 19).

But the Chicago Railroad Fair had a deeper impact on Walt's vague notions of doing something new involving working trains, models, and a park. At the fair, as would be the case in Disneyland, a railroad defined the boundaries

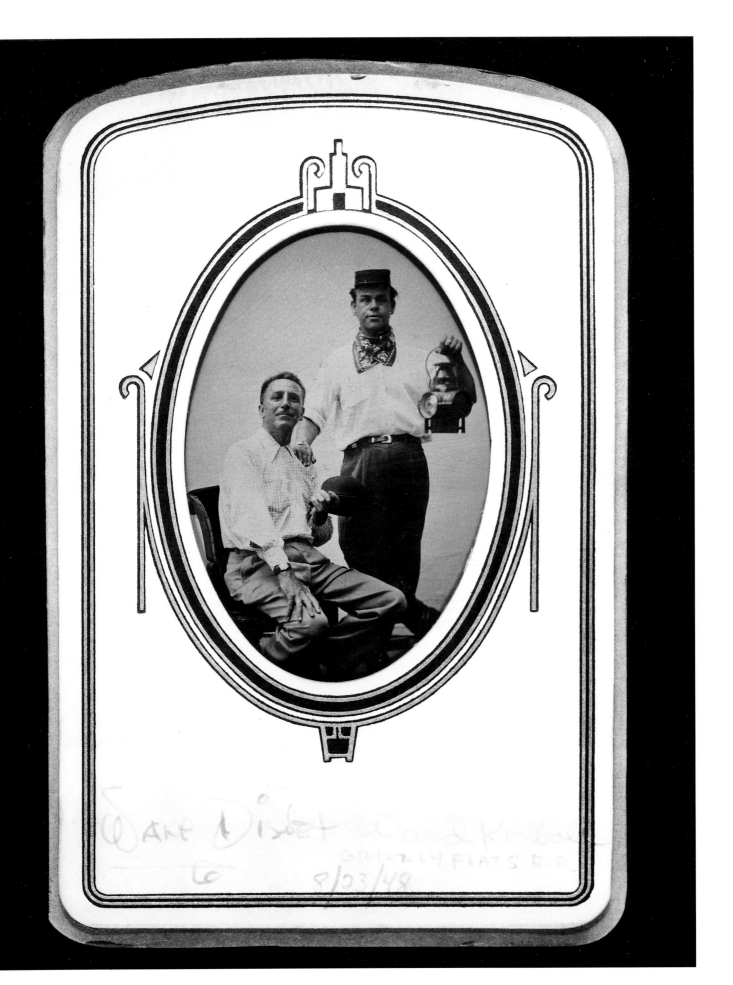

of the grounds, served as the major artery of internal transportation, and ultimately determined the scale of the buildings adjacent to the tracks. Anxious to promote the railroad as a kind of magic carpet to vacationland, participating lines presented a series of prototypical "lands" or villages, recreating well-known tourist meccas along their respective routes. The Illinois Central set up a replica of the French Quarter in New Orleans. A consortium of western lines built a dude ranch and slice of a generic national park with a mechanical geyser guaranteed to erupt every fifteen minutes. And the Santa Fe, of course, had Indian villages: pueblos, trading posts, tepees, and all. In each venue, the illusion of being there was sustained by workers in appropriate garb and by restaurants with matching cuisine. As Walt made mental notes about the menus and the outfits, the future Frontierland, Fantasyland, Adventureland, and Tomorrowland of Disneyland were only a daydream away.

World's Fairs had long exhibited artifacts from foreign cultures in picturesque "villages." In fact, the Railroad Fair occupied the portion of the old Century of Progress site once devoted to the Alpine, Hawaiian, and Spanish Villages. What was different about the 1948 railroad extravaganza was the coherence and concentration of the experience, the sensation of having taken the train on a whirlwind journey through most of the nation's beauty spots in a single day. What was different, too, was the dramatic unity enforced by the pageant, which gave every exhibit a place in a powerful narrative whole. All the way home, Walt talked to his fellow train lover about building a park something like the Railroad Fair. "Disneyland was already forming in his mind," Kimball remembers. "Of course, he thought [it] should have a full size steam train . . . that he could have fun operating himself on days when the park was closed."

On the way, they stopped off in Michigan, at Henry Ford's Greenfield Village. Ford was a tinkerer, like Disney, and a utopian whose town contained an idiosyncratic mixture of historic buildings of particular interest to the founder and period replicas that housed pet Ford projects, such as schools in which hand-picked pupils were educated on a spartan intellectual diet of McGuffey readers and manual training. Alongside structures of some historic value—Stephen Foster's house, Thomas Edison's laboratory, the schoolhouse to which the little lamb of the famous children's verse once followed Mary—were the farmhouse where Ford grew up and the woodstoves and gas lamps he associated with his youth, in the horse and buggy days, before the advent of factories, assembly lines, and Ford cars.

Walt had been there before, when Ford was still alive. Like his father, Elias Disney, Walt admired Ford for his attempt to build an ideal industrial system, with the worker paid enough to spend the money needed to strike a balance between production and consumption—and the leisure time in which to do so. And Walt's trackside barn, raised early in 1950, clearly echoed Ford's will to live in the utopia of his own prettified memories. But mostly, Disney played the role of a famous tourist on holiday at Greenfield Village. An issue of the student newspaper for April 1940, pictures Walt drawing Mickey Mouse on the blackboard to the delight of the assembled scholars; according to the accompanying article, the afternoon's entertainment consisted of Disney and a well-known automotive designer, who drew streamlined trains and a portrait of Walt for the kids. This time, Walt and Kimball posed for old-

fashioned tintype portraits. Walt sports a derby. Kimball wears a bandanna and a stiff conductor's hat and carries a signal lantern. Red for stop. Green for go (Fig. 24).

Back in California, three synergistic projects —the railroad, the miniatures, and the park—suddenly kicked into high gear and converged on a single track. Within days of his return, Walt had circulated an internal memo proposing the lot across the street from the studio as a suitable site; since it was just across the flood plain from Griffith Park, where kiddie trains already ran on a desultory schedule, he wondered if he could loop his own railroad through the park and enhance both operations. He sent away for working drawings of the *Atlantic* and catalogues of locomotive parts.

24. Walt Disney and Ward Kimball tintyped at Greenfield Village, 1948. Courtesy Henry Ford Museum and Greenfield Village Research Center.
25. Walt Disney working on one of his engines, c.1950.

26. This set for the 1949 Disney live-action film, *So Dear to My Heart*, was precious to Walt Disney because it reminded him of the sights of his Missouri boyhood.

He looked at other people's steam trains and at trains for sale, including five small-scale engines from the Venice Pier and another, stranded in a backyard in Los Gatos, once used at the 1915 San Francisco World's Fair. Walt began machining parts for the Lilly Belle in September (Fig. 25). And, in the meantime, he put animator and art director Ken Anderson on his personal payroll to paint a series of detailed interior scenes from the American past, in the manner of a Norman Rockwell illustration or a historic house in Henry Ford's village. Using the paintings as guides, Walt intended to build a set of twenty-four miniature rooms, like Mrs. Thorne's, but less chilly, less pedantic. His rooms would be full of atmosphere, color, and sentiment and the first of them—the test model—was the farmhouse that haunted his dreams.

Disneylandia

The farmhouse was, in fact, Granny Kincaid's cabin, a scene from one of his own films, *So Dear to My Heart* (Fig. 26). The time was 1903. The place, Fulton's Corners, a small town somewhere in the Midwest. The plot concerned a boy and his pet sheep and the county fair. There were a few short animated scenes, in which picture books seemed to come to life. But *So Dear to My Heart* was mainly a live-action film, like *The Reluctant Dragon*, and for the same reasons. It was expensive to make an animated feature every year or so, and Disney was strapped for cash. The movie never attained the popularity of a *Snow White* or a *Dumbo* (the latter introduced the wonderful Walt Kimball-drawn engine known as "Casey, Jr."). It remained Walt's personal favorite, however, from the time of its release in 1949 through its revival for his new Wednesday-night television show in 1954. He loved the look of its Main Street and its old farmstead: *So Dear to My Heart* could have come straight out of one his own sweet reveries about the good old days, back in Marceline, Missouri.

Despite efforts to contain costs in the postwar period, the studio took enormous pains with the sets for *So Dear to My Heart*. In 1947, Walt sent his art director to Ward Kimball for advice on a proper railroad station. Kimball consulted a rare reference book in his collection—*Buildings and Structures of American Railroads*—and came up with a picture of a gingerbread depot on the Pottsville Branch of the Lehigh Valley railroad in eastern Pennsylvania. And sparing no expense, that was the station built in the form of a three-sided shell, propped up with two-by-fours, on the town set erected in Porterville, California. In the spring of 1948, Walt went out to Kimball's house to ride his train and, noting the absence of a station, offered him the Fulton's Corners depot, proudly observing that it had real working windows. And so the Grizzly Flats line got its best-known icon. Best known because Walt returned in the autumn of the year to see the results and was so pleased that eventually, in 1953, he tried to get the building back from Kimball for use at Disneyland. Failing that, the Frontierland Station in the park was finally built from the original working drawings prepared for *So Dear to My Heart*.

Granny's cabin appears as a full-size building on some early plans for the Disneyland park, too. But in a miniature version, it was the mainstay of an alternative project, the very first conception of Disneyland, sometimes known as Disneylandia. Disneylandia consisted of models of the buildings in an ideal, imaginary, long-ago town that would teach the viewer

about the development of American ideas of work, comfort, domesticity, and urbanism. Walt's own handmade model of Granny Kincaid's cabin came first, an L-shaped room with a hearth, a rag rug, a spinning wheel, and tantalizing views out the doors and windows toward as-yet-unbuilt companion structures. Similar to the New England kitchens popular at World's Fairs of the late nineteenth century, the spinning wheel scene was meant to evoke how the function of the American home had changed in the modern era, away from home-spun production to consumption and pleasure. Walt exhibited his handiwork publicly in 1952 at the Festival of California Living held in the Pan-Pacific Auditorium in Los Angeles. The interior was shown as a shadowbox, recessed in the wall and framed like a painting, at eye

27. Walt Disney shows off his own handmade model of Granny's Cabin at the Pan-Pacific Auditorium, 1952.

level (Fig. 27). Actress Beulah Bondi, the original Granny of the film, recorded a narration that played when the lights went on. But nothing much happened—and that was the problem with the meticulously wrought little cabin. It was kind of boring.

Walt returned to Ken Anderson's secret workroom in 1949 to remedy the defect. This time, the scene to be depicted was the stage of the town Opera House, all gilded plaster and swags of velvet (Fig. 28). And this time, the miniatures would move. In 1946, on one of his therapeutic absences from Burbank, Disney visited New Orleans and brought back an antique mechanical bird that sang and fluttered when its clockwork mechanism was wound. Why not apply the same technology to little figures in miniature environments? Why not bring the old Thorne Room idea to life? Dancer Buddy Ebsen (a future star of Disney's *Davy Crockett* television series) was filmed for study against a measured grid, doing a vaudeville routine. The sculptor Christadoro was hired in September 1950, to carve the jointed, nine-inch figure of the dancing man with the straw hat. And "Project Little Man" commenced in earnest.

The machinery that powered the dancing man occupied a cabinet that was larger than the scene itself—and infinitely more complex to build. But the team pressed on with a third scene, an old-fashioned barbershop, about

28. Disney planned to build the sets and furniture for Disneylandia with his own two hands. The first such set was a music hall; a tiny robotic figure—a Dancing Man—was to perform before the curtains. Preliminary design for the Dancing Man set, Disneylandia. Ken Anderson. Tempera on cardboard. 13 x 19. 1949.

eighteen inches square, with a group of four habitués forming a classical quartet that was to warble "Down By the Old Mill Stream" (Fig. 29). A live group was filmed doing just that. Artists studied a 1936 Rockwell cover for the *Saturday Evening Post* and another, more recent rendition of the same setting, published on April 29, 1950: the former showed the singers, lathered and pomaded, while the latter was an evocative view of Shuffleton's Barbershop from a darkened street, through a plate glass window, the interior aglow with warmth and camaraderie.

The level of detail in the Disney tonsorial parlor was obsessive: a fancy barber chair that pivoted and reclined, a brass cuspidor, mirrors inscribed with the establishment's prices in curlicue lettering, tiny bristle shaving brushes, and rows of little mugs. Walt's relish for making things, for being the working artist instead of the remote executive, never flagged. But he had discovered that there was a whole world of incredible miniatures to be purchased ready-made, if the price was right. Tiny books that could actually be read. Glass and china from the finest manufacturers of full-scale dinnerware. On a trip to Paris in 1949, he was rumored to have spent hundreds of dollars on miniature furniture in a shop whose location he would never disclose. In 1951, scouring London for more miniatures, he met Harper Goff one afternoon in Bassett-Lowke Ltd., a train shop that catered to hobbyists in search of scaled-down railroad accessories. Goff, who had painted the kinds of scenes for magazines and other Hollywood studios that Walt was proposing to make in three dimensions, soon

29. Another Disneylandia scene consisted of an old-fashioned barbershop with a quartet of mechanical singers. Concept sketch for the Barbershop Ensemble, Disneylandia. Ken Anderson. Pencil and conté crayon on paper. 19 x 19. 1949.

joined the clandestine group at work on the barbershop.

Goff's fortuitous encounter with Walt in a train store illustrates the close relationship between Disney's two current hobbies. The backyard railroad, the Carolwood Pacific, was a steam-powered miniature in its own right, from which a thriving business had arisen in 1951. The Walt Disney Miniature Railroad Co. sold plans for the Lilly Belle and parts and castings for locomotive builders (Fig. 30). The fledgling firm also sold little pot-bellied stoves, copies of the one Walt had made for his yellow caboose. "I had a pattern made up," he wrote, "and it turned out so cute with the grate, shaker, and door and all the little working parts. I became intrigued with the idea and had a few made up—one was bronze, another black, and I even made a gold one! Then we made more and started painting them in motifs that fitted the period at the turn of the century." The stoves were so cute that Mrs. James Ward Thorne ordered two of them for her collection.

By day, if he felt pressured by the demands of his real business, Walt set up cardboard dollhouses on his desk and fiddled with the furnishings: the inventory of the contents of his office taken at the time of his death in 1966 includes blueprints for twenty-seven such shoebox-style rooms. By night, he worked on his trains. And all the time, it seemed, he fretted about Disneylandia. Three old Southern Pacific Pullman cars mysteriously appeared one morning on a stretch of track behind the studio complex. Walt's idea was to install his miniature rooms—the cabin, the Little Man, the Barbershop Quartet, and all the rest—in railroad cars, and take them on a national tour. People would walk through the cars, pop their quarters into a slot next to each scene, a curtain would open, and voila! Walter Knott had some old coin-operated carnival toys in his Ghost Town that worked on the same principle.

When Roger Broggie did the arithmetic on the number of quarters it would take to pay for the freight and siding fees demanded by the railroads, and factored in the snail-like rate of speed at which the average viewer was apt to

30. The E. P. Ripley locomotive at Disneyland was developed from the working drawings for Walt Disney's own model engine. Anonymous. Opaque watercolor on paper. 17 1/8 x 41. 1955.

Imagineering the Disney Theme Parks 51

31. Site plan for a park to be located on Riverside Drive in Burbank, with red pencil notations possibly by Walt Disney. Harper Goff. Colored pencil and watercolor on paper. 24 x 36. 1951.

move through the train, he saw no likelihood that Disneylandia would ever recover the costs incurred to date. Besides, the machinery that made the dancer dance and the singers sing was touchy, in need of constant supervision and repair. And even Walt was dismayed by the prospect of schoolchildren picking their way

through some dismal freight yard to find the train. Despite the years of work and the high hopes, Disneylandia looked puny and measly to Walt. "We got as far as building the guy in the chair and the barber behind him," said Broggie. "Then the whole job was stopped and they said, 'We're going to do this thing for real!'" Walt was going to build Disneyland.

The Burbank Park

For a time, however, both plans—the "kiddieland" adjacent to the studio and the miniatures display—moved ahead simultaneously, in their separate, locked rooms, with Walt Disney's imagination the only link between them. Some of his associates said that Disney had begun to talk about building an amusement park back in the 1920s. The idea was certainly discussed in some detail as the Burbank studio neared completion and again, in 1948, when an eight-acre sliver of land on the edge of the property was proposed as a site: future Imagineer John Hench, who was toiling over the color styling and design of *Alice in Wonderland* and *So Dear to My Heart* in the 1940s, as well as babysitting painter Salvador Dalí during his abortive preparations for an animated surrealist ballet along the lines of *Fantasia*, used to look out his window and see Walt pacing the farthest parking lot on weekends, building the imaginary park he saw in his mind's eye. A singing waterfall. Characters from his films. A train.

Disney often talked about his own baleful experiences in the 1930s, when his daughters were young and every weekend was a struggle to find something they could all do together. The kiddie rides on La Cienega Boulevard stranded Daddy on a bench watching Diane and Sharon go round and round. There had to be a better way. What finally kicked his thinking into high gear was a visit to Tivoli Gardens in 1950, during a European vacation with radio host Art Linkletter. Unlike the cheap, curbside funlands of Los Angeles, the 1843 park in Copenhagen had a beautiful natural setting, fine restaurants, high standards of cleanliness, and plenty of mild amusements for families to enjoy as a group. By the time Walt met Harper Goff in London, lured him away from the Warner Bros. studio, and assigned him to draw up plans for a park on a sixteen-acre wedge of wasteland on the flood-control channel across the street from the studio, the "magical little park" in the parking lot had become an American Tivoli, with strong overtones of Greenfield Village or Colonial Williamsburg. Kiddieland no longer, it was Walt Disney's America now. "I don't want to just entertain kids with pony rides and swings. I want them to learn something about their heritage," he told Goff.

Four surviving documents describe this prototypical Disneyland: an August 1948 memo reflecting the strong influence of the Railroad Fair; a 1951 Goff color rendering of a park on the sixteen-acre parcel; a site plan of the same period with red pencil annotations and additions that may be in Walt's hand (Fig. 31); and a six-page prospectus, excerpted in the *Burbank Leader* in March of 1952, when Disney presented the plan to the Burbank city council for approval. The written records are most interesting as illustrations of the twin principles of "blue sky" speculation and long memory that continue to govern the practice of Walt Disney Imagineering.

The 1948 memo, for example, sets forth a detailed description of the Main Street and Frontierland districts later built at Anaheim in 1955. The railroad station, the Town Hall, the streetcars, a stagecoach, and a list of potential stores are all enumerated and what carnival rides are mentioned—roller coasters, a merry-go-round, "the typical Midway stuff"—are of no consequence to the author. "This," the memo says, "will be worked out later." The Burbank prospectus is less specific about the

32. Welton Becket, Capitol Records Tower, Hollywood, California, 1954–55.

Catherine Wagner. *World Bazaar; Tokyo Disneyland, Tokyo.* Collection CCA.

character of the Wild West and the "small Midwestern town at the turn of the century" (to which Granny's Farm has been added, at full scale) but introduces vague references to a whole new category of attractions, geared to fantasy and futurism: a canal boat moving past scenes from Disney fairy-tale films, a spaceship, a submarine ride, and a nature preserve on an island circumnavigated by a paddle-wheeler. And there were to be "no roller coasters or other rides in the cheap thrill category."

In a pattern that would mark the evolution of the Disney parks ever afterward, ideas leapt into being fully fledged at an early stage in the planning process, only to be shifted to the back burner as new ones arose. But they never really disappeared. As more art directors and architects joined the team, as story meetings were held with greater frequency, the final product gradually took shape. Something from that memo. Something from this one. Main Street, U.S.A. Frontierland. Fantasyland. Tomorrowland. Adventureland. In the end, however, the words were far less important than the pictures. It is still the custom at Imagineering to start with your best stuff, your boldest, wildest idea, and to paint it in absolutely convincing detail.

"Eyewash," they call it, good for convincing prospective sponsors to sign on the dotted line but the real point of origin of the whole design process. If you can imagine it, it can probably be built.

Form doesn't follow function, or even common sense. The pictures are what matters. Harper Goff's picture of the Burbank park shows a railroad depot in the foreground, a townscape to the left, a farm to the right, an Indian village, trains of several eras, a stagecoach (see Fig. 19). Victorian gingerbread and a crude frontier water tower. Trestles and trees and lakes, tied together by a series of gentle ovals formed by roadways and right-of-ways meandering through this child's garden of history. John Hench likes to say that Mickey Mouse is universally beloved because he's made out of rounded forms, suggestive of breasts and teddy bears and clouds. Cushiony, comforting shapes that soothe and reassure. The architecture of reassurance began with Harper Goff's pictorial rendition of the Burbank park.

So did the habit of endless revision, or "plussing." The luminously tinted site plan for Burbank enlarges the lake and the island, organizes the town around a central hub, inserts a covered bridge and an old mill, and adds an old-fashioned circus at the corner of the lot. But the pictorial rendering of the park also showed what wasn't there, in large areas of grass-green emptiness. And with impatient stabs of red pencil, somebody—Walt? another critic?—wondered what else could fit on sixteen acres of undeveloped land. A "dwarf's house?" A castle? Even when inscribed in a bold red hand, the words failed to register the urgency of the writer's impatient inventiveness. How would a castle *look* alongside a Midwestern town? Where would it go, exactly? (see Fig 31).

It would not, in the end, go on Riverside Drive in Burbank. Neither words nor images moved the city council to sanction the park. "We don't want the carny atmosphere in Burbank," cried one lawmaker, who must have noticed a carousel annotated in red on the plan. "We don't want people falling in the river, or merry-go-rounds squawking all day long."

Enter the L.A. Architects

The quasi-legend of Disneyland says that the

33. Luckman & Pereira, Disneyland Hotel, Anaheim, California, 1954–55.

real planning began with the 1952 fiscal year when, straight from his setback in Burbank, Walt learned that his brother Roy, who controlled the corporate purse strings, had allocated only $10,000 to research and development expenses on "Kiddieland." And that sum grudgingly, as a sop to the younger Disney's reckless enthusiasms. The budget squeeze was devastating because the project was just starting to be expensive: Walt needed more draftsmen, a new site, pricey architects, and a lot of fresh money. So he sold his vacation home, borrowed against his life insurance policy, set up Walter Elias Disney (WED) Enterprises, and created Disneyland anyway.

In actuality, however, things moved forward by fits and starts, with the automata still being built in the studio shop and Harper Goff assigned to lurk around the Granny's Cabin display at the Pan-Pacific Auditorium and take careful note of public reaction. The press, meanwhile, had been told that the cabin was only a sample of things to come, a sneak preview of something called "Disneyland—a Miniature Historic America" (see Fig. 27). And Walt took himself, his wife, his daughters, and a niece to Europe again, this time to see Maurodam, a new park in Holland consisting of miniature replicas of the famous architectural landmarks of Europe. Little churches.

Windmills. Guild halls, copied in miraculous detail. Maybe what his park needed was some genuine architecture like this. Or, at the very least, some professional architectural advice.

As luck would have it, Walt knew an up-and-coming California architect, his friend and Holmby Hills neighbor, Welton Becket (who lived across the street from the Linkletters). Becket had made a name for himself in the 1930s and 1940s as a specialist in movie-star houses, done in the then-fashionable period styles that seemed to lend new money instant respectability and to reinforce the make-believe of the Hollywood film industry. Actor Robert Montgomery, for instance, found himself at

34. Elevation study for Main Street stores. Marvin Davis. Colored pencil on brownline. 11 x 38. c. 1953.

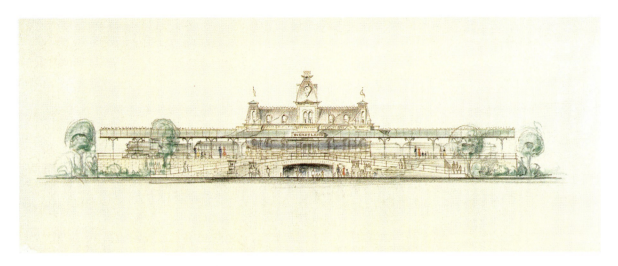

home in a massive, half-timbered Tudor mansion, with a squat, pseudo-thatched turret over the front door, thanks to Welton Becket. The Los Feliz home in which the Disneys lived before their move to Holmby Hills in 1950 was a smaller version of this Hansel and Gretel type, with a similar witch's-hat entryway—and a matching *Snow White* playhouse in the backyard. Becket, like Walt Disney and the rest of the film colony, favored a picturesque, even pictorial architecture, in the spirit of the indigenous fantasy vernacular that had already adorned the major intersections of Los Angeles with restaurants made in the image of Mother Hubbard shoes, hot-dog stands in the shape of giant frankfurters, and camera-shaped photo shops.

Becket came into his own in the postwar years with two major commissions: Bullock's branch department store in Pasadena (1948) and the Capitol Records Tower (1954–55) in Hollywood. Perched on the edge of the freeway like a stack of flying saucers from Mars, the Capitol Tower looked just like Disney's Tomorrowland—or the mooring mast for a spacecraft sightseeing over L.A. (Fig. 32)! It was Los Angeles fantasy architecture carried to a glorious extreme, a perpetual ad for the company, and a practical solution—or so Becket maintained—to any number of problems with conventional office buildings, including a reduction in the total area of exterior wall and thus of heat transfer. But above all, the building looked wonderful. It was one of Frank Lloyd Wright's too-tall dream buildings actually standing there, at 1750 Vine Street, all steel sunshades and twenty-first-century pizzazz.

35. Entry/railroad station on Main Street. Marvin Davis. Colored pencil on brownline. 7 1/4 x 18. 1953.
36. Artist Harper Goff later said that Fort Collins, Colorado, was a major influence on his vision of Main Street; Goff's father had worked for a newspaper in Colorado similar to the one shown in this sketch. Concept sketch for Main Street newspaper office. Harper Goff. Pencil on animation paper. 12 x 23. 1952–53.

The commission for the department store came from an executive who had seen a number of Becket houses and encouraged him to plan the interior as a series of artfully decorated rooms in a private home, themed to the merchandise casually displayed—without price tags or sale signs—in areas devoted to sporting goods, kitchenware, and so forth. Lighting came from floor and table lamps, customers were encouraged to settle into easy chairs, and the usual retail apparatus of stock bins and cash registers was tucked away, backstage. Created especially for the motorized carriage trade, the illusion was one of sumptuous, gracious living. But Bullock's was strictly business when it came to getting shoppers into the store through the series of "motor courts" that surrounded and penetrated the building.

In this and in a string of department store commissions that followed, Becket combined pictorial illusionism with a pragmatic approach to the realities of American life in the automotive age. Bullock's was also the first instance of the "total design" concept that became the philosophic basis of the Becket firm's subsequent practice. Total design meant working on all aspects of the building problem: interiors, traffic flow, mechanical systems. Even the corporate letterhead and the shopping bags were subject to intensive research and planning. It was, Becket maintained, architecture for the client, intended to serve every purpose for which the building was being erected. Frank Lloyd Wright, during Congressional hearings on the design of the projected Air Force Academy campus in 1955, disparaged Becket for neglecting the art of architecture in favor of an exaggerated regard for his clients' wishes. "I see no reason," Walt's friend replied, "why I should express Welton Becket."

Walt Disney had been similarly unfazed by Wright, a bitter critic of *Fantasia* and a guest lecturer at the studio in the late 1930s. When one of the animators in attendance on that occasion gushed over the good fortune of hearing the great Frank Lloyd Wright in person, Walt assured him that Wright was the lucky one: "Why, he can learn as much from you

37. Concept sketch for Main Street, Disneyland, showing interior of the General Store. Harper Goff. Pencil on animation paper. 13 x 31. 1952–53.

guys as you can from him!" During the building of Disneyland, architectural masterpieces of the Wrightian variety interested Walt very little. One early rendering for a Main Street building got the ax because he thought the "fellow was attempting a monument to himself rather than designing something that is for people." He also rejected out of hand preliminary studies for Disneyland drawn up by the firm of William Pereira and Charles Luckman, drawings that corresponded in no particular to his mental image of the park. Would his fellow train buff, Welton Becket, help him now? "Walt, no one can design Disneyland for you," Becket answered. "You'll have to do it yourself."

Yet the mark of L.A. architecture in the 1950s remains on Disneyland despite the fact that Walt took his friend's advice and set a cadre of Hollywood art directors to work on his park instead. For one thing, as Becket's son Bruce points out, Hollywood techniques and values permeated the profession. Art directors—the people who drew the pictures of how a café in Casablanca or a ruined mansion in Georgia was supposed to look and feel and smell, and what the camera ought to see in order to make moviegoers share those sensations—were virtual seasonal workers, who bounced back and forth between the studios and architects' offices when things were slack in one business or the other. Or that was how things worked in Becket's shop. Conversely, many of the art directors, animators, and layout men Disney hired when his studio geared up for feature-length animation in the late 1930s were trained architects, without much hope of finding work at their trade during the Great Depression.

William L. Pereira was, admittedly, an extreme case, but he practiced architecture while making movies as a Paramount art director, a production designer, and a special-effects expert (who won an Oscar in the latter category). For that reason, perhaps, he has not received much serious attention, nor has the whole generation of movie-inspired Los Angeles architects to which he belonged. In the 1940s, Pereira designed the flagship theater of the Pan-Pacific chain in collaboration with the Becket firm and thereafter tended to specialize in show-biz projects, including the CBS Television City (1952–53; his brother Hal was, by then, a major television producer), Marineland of the Pacific (1954–55), and the posh Robinson department store in Beverly Hills (1952) in which shops were arranged around "wide-vision sales theaters" laid out in open competition with Becket's Pasadena plan. In 1950, he joined forces with the flamboyant Charlie Luckman, former president of Lever Brothers, who, it was rumored, had lost his job over that company's trademark skyscraper on Park Avenue, the first to break the street line in an un-urban gesture of blatant, commercial self-aggrandizement. Together, Pereira and Luckman built the Flamingo Hotel in Las Vegas, the Tomorrowland-skyscraper-style Disneyland Hotel on the edge of the park (then owned by Jack Wrather, whose wife, Bonita, was a movie star), and a variety of buildings in which a certain theatrical insouciance was combined with a patent desire to glamorize the activities of the client and the everyday lives of his customer (Fig. 33). They—or Welton Becket—ought to have been the perfect match for Walt Disney.

38. Study for a residential district adjacent to Main Street, including a Haunted Mansion. Harper Goff. Pencil on animation paper. 12 1/2 x 25 5/8. 1952–53.

The Art Directors

After the fiasco with the Pereira and Luckman master plan, Walt finally took Becket's sound advice. He already had Ken Anderson and Harper Goff on his private payroll. Now, in May of 1953, he hired Marvin Davis to translate his ideas into workable site plans and elevations. Davis was typical of the corps of Imagineers Disney recruited to create the park. An art director at 20th Century-Fox, Davis had an architecture degree from the University of Southern California. But he had since learned to build sets by listening to directors and reading scripts. So he was not surprised to find himself in a story conference with Walt and the other members of the Disneyland group.

When Davis arrived, Harper Goff had already worked up a full set of sketches for the site at the studio, employing a predominately Old West theme that dimly echoed the Chicago Railroad Fair of 1948. Disney currently had a much larger piece of property in mind, however, with room for a grander, more expansive series of "lands." At story sessions, Disney would reminisce by the hour about Marceline's Midwestern Main Street: the barbershop, the dry-goods store, and the post office were each laid out in his narrative like scenes in a movie script. "This is scene one, this is scene two and this is scene three and they have this relationship," one of his listeners remembers Walt saying. "Never been done before. Here we [have] a Main Street, that now is kind of passing away. . . . One side [is] related to the other side and to its neighbor." After each meeting, Davis "made a list of everything he mentioned and took it from there."

In July of 1953, with the dimensions and location of the park still up in the air, Davis churned out a remarkable series of elevations that became the basis for Disneyland's Main Street, U.S.A. Brilliantly colored in pencil over brownline reproductions of his sketches, they show long, horizontal bands of buildings arranged in distinct blocks or scenes but unified by a sprightly ruffle of ornament at the cornice line. Railroad buildings, from the station platform to the roundhouse, are the subjects of repeated study (Figs. 34, 35). For scale, there are tiny people standing on the street corners awaiting tiny horse-drawn trolley cars, little passengers disembarking from little steam trains. Davis's distanced, extruded view of the streetscape also reinforces the impression that this is an exquisite miniature city, featuring, perhaps, the facades of Walt's own handmade Barbershop and Opera House.

Davis's buildings are fancy and fussy—two- and three-story, mansard-roofed, false-fronted survivors from the sunlit dawn of the Gilded Age. The formality of the architecture sets them apart from those in Harper Goff's pencil drawings, usually said to be the seminal images of Main Street. The Goff pictures of the business district show low board-and-batten buildings, for the most part: of the clapboard church, the Civil War monument across the street from the humble office of the *Weekly Bugle* (Fig. 36), the bakery, the general store, and the barbershop, only the church rises taller than the second story. These drawings have been assigned a variety of dates. Goff himself often dated them to 1951, while others have ascribed the series to January 1952. In fact,

39. Goff maintained that Disneyland's City Hall was based on the courthouse in Fort Collins. This photo of a c. 1954 model for the civic center district of Main Street shows City Hall and the Fire Station.

1953 seems more likely. Archival records clearly show that Walt sent Goff out to Knott's Berry Farm on a Sunday afternoon just before Christmas 1952 to study the movement of crowds in Ghost Town. But Goff's report concerned the architecture: "The shops and stores were full and people were buying," he observed, "particularly in the old-time General Store," the image of which dominates his so-called Main Street drawings, probably finished in January 1953 (Fig. 37).

Main Street was, in Walt's parlance, "Scene One," the common point of entry, through which every visitor to Disneyland would pass. If Harper Goff did not invent that distinctive gingerbread thoroughfare, he nonetheless made major contributions to it. Several of his undated pencil drawings show an expansive (and never built) residential district, out beyond the church, with the tall structures and mansard details of the Davis elevations (Fig. 38). There was nothing comparable on Knott's grounds but this was the predominant style of Fort Collins, Colorado, where Goff had grown up, the son of the local editor. It was photographs of the local courthouse there (and not some dim memory of Marceline), he maintained, that provided the specific model for Disneyland's City Hall (Fig. 39). Davis's multiple views of the railroad station play with elements of the Fort Collins courthouse, too, recombining, enlarging, and shrinking assorted bits of oculus, molding, and slate to create a pleasing composition that would set the visual tone for the street that began at the tracks of the Santa Fe and Disneyland Railroad. Main Street is not an architectural masterpiece attributable to a single genius (Fig. 40). Like a Hollywood film, it is a collaborative effort between Walt Disney

40. An early overall study of the Disneyland civic center or Town Square shows a different version of City Hall at the right. Dale Hennesy. Colored pencil on brownline. 16 x 50. Late 1953–early 1954.

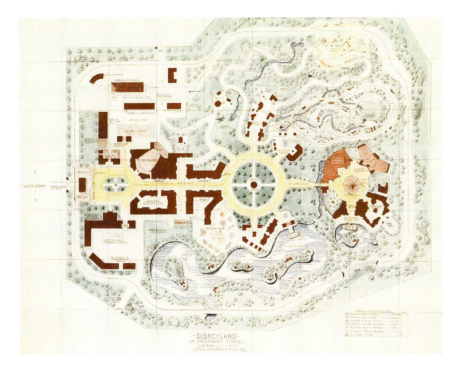

and his art directors. Like a film, it is a mixture of memories, facts, old stories, and fleeting impressions, served up by designers who understood the powerful appeal of old-fashioned curlicues to a culture weaned on plain steel girders and flat glass facades.

Research and Development

Harrison "Buzz" Price, then with the Stanford Research Institute (SRI), tells of being introduced to Disney at a party by Charlie Luckman, early in the summer of 1953. Luckman had buttonholed his one-time client and was giving him a little free advice: namely, that he ought to hire SRI to study the potential sites for Disneyland his own people had already identified. As things stood in July, when the twelve-week study actually began, those parcels of land were all in Southern California, scattered from Chatsworth and Pomona in the north to Tustin and Balboa in the south. Except for a reasonable prejudice against a beachfront location—what can compete with the ocean?—Walt was still not entirely sure that he ought to limit his search to California, although the absence of highly visible tourist attractions in and around the city made the Los Angeles area tempting. The earliest narrative description of the revised and enlarged Disneyland, prepared around this date, stresses the publicity California stood to garner through the television production studios now attached to the park. "It will be a place for California to be at home, to bring its guests, to demonstrate its faith in the future," the white paper concluded.

Along with the other Hollywood moguls

41. Hypothetical plan for a fifty-acre park. Marvin Davis. Colored pencil on brownline. 31 x 46. 1953.
42. Plan for Disneyland on a forty-five-acre site. Marvin Davis. Colored pencil and watercolor on brownline. 30 x 39. May 1953.

of his day, Disney believed in market research. Filmgoers were questioned endlessly on their response to the company product. In a business with a narrow profit margin, where the fickle tide of public opinion meant everything, pollsters were gods and good research was more precious than gold. The SRI site study, submitted in draft form in mid-July and finished on August 28, 1953, recommended an orange grove in Anaheim over seventy-odd abandoned country clubs and failed subdivisions. Good freeway connections to Anaheim were in the works. The climate was temperate, without oceanfront fog or the scorching afternoon heat of the valleys. The one-hundred-eighty-acre tract, adjacent to Harbor Boulevard, twenty-seven miles southeast of downtown Los Angeles, was flat, unencumbered by existing construction, and affordable. Barely affordable. Without much company support, Walt was already deeply in debt, and there was no end in sight. In a companion study on the feasibility of the project, SRI pegged his start-up costs at $11 million.

Meanwhile, back in the so-called Zorro Building, in an obscure corner of the studio lot, Marvin Davis began drawing site plans for a roughly fifty-acre park. The first plan to refer specifically to Anaheim appeared early in August, before the SRI survey was complete. In September, with the location finally settled, designs tumbled from his pencil at two- and three-day intervals (Fig. 41). Plans included a Land of Oz section, based on those L. Frank Baum books to which the studio owned the rights; a castle, or no castle at all; a foreign zone; a town hall in the middle of Main Street, where the courthouse often sat in rural Missouri towns; Lilliputian Land (introduced by a museum of Walt's automata), in which a canal boat would course past miniature versions of the cities of the world as guests nibbled on teensy hot dogs; a residential street, with a white clapboard Harper Goff church, to be used as the backlot for making television shows; a hotel inside the park; a hub, like the Etoile in Paris (Disney and Welton Becket both loved the radiant plan of that city), from which attractions at the end of Main Street pinwheeled off into space; no hub; a dogleg-shaped plan; two hubs; a big castle; circus tents; a little freeway; a single entry under the railroad station (Fig. 42).

No, scratch that idea. What about this instead? A much taller castle, right about here. The original Davis tissues reveal just how improvisational the process of planning Disneyland was. When the Burbank site was abandoned, the Zorro team was told to start over again, from scratch, according to Marvin Davis. To think up new stuff. To think big. They began looking at old Disney movies, he says—*Snow White and the Seven Dwarfs*, *Cinderella*, *Alice in Wonderland*—with the idea of turning them into rides or walk-throughs because the films were one unique and important thing a Disneyland had to offer that nobody else could match.

Say the project was a "dark ride," a vehicle of some kind that transported visitors past a number of illuminated tableaux in an unlit space (Fig. 43). Except for "fun houses"— interior mazes full of mirrored rooms and canted floors—such amusement devices were

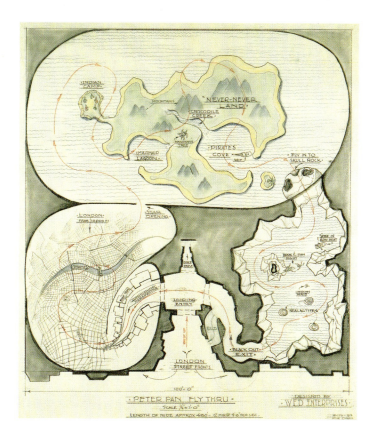

43. Interior layout for a Peter Pan "dark ride" at Disneyland. Bill Martin. Colored pencil and watercolor on photostat. 16 x 19. 1954–55.
44. Plan for a Peter Pan Fly-Thru ride, Disneyland. Marvin Davis. Pencil and colored pencil on tissue. 31 1/4 x 28. August 16, 1953.

not much built in the 1950s. Their heyday had been the turn of the century, when boatloads of World's Fair and Coney Island tourists caught a glimpse of what seemed to be a stark naked Eve in the Garden of Eden on the much-copied "Creation" ride. For laying out their ideas, Davis and his colleagues used cards, like the drawings in a cartoon storyboard, to diagram the experience. First, you see London. Then, Never Land. Then, the flying boat zooms through Skull Rock. Scene one, scene two, scene three. In a new twist on an old idea, the Peter Pan Fly-Thru diagram completed by Davis on August 16, 1953, proposes a cinematic narrative unfolding in three-dimensions through the use of models, dioramas, and statuary figures based on the new Disney Christmas release for that year (Fig. 44). The "guest" who boards the Peter Pan pirate ship for a flight into the J. M. Barrie story becomes one of the Darling children, a character in the movie, swooping over Regent's Park en route to an imaginary place populated by pirates and Indians. Disney would look at the storyboards and then act out the ride, moment by moment, turn by turn, his eyebrows bobbing up and down in delight, like excited caterpillars. When they had eighty-four such ideas crammed into every squared-off inch of Davis's latest plan, Walt sent emissaries forth to America's favorite tourist haunts to test the feasibility.

Other People's Amusement Parks

Walt Disney may have been his own best researcher. For years, he had been hanging around the Pomona Fair, Long Beach, and the Santa Monica Pier, watching the pathways people followed from the Ferris wheel to the hot-dog stand, looking at the expressions on their faces. He had Harper Goff do the same thing at Walter Knott's Berry Farm. And the manager of Tivoli Gardens in Copenhagen was brought to Burbank for face-to-face consultations on crowd flow. But for the big research tour, in June 1954, Walt chose four trusted associates, including Bill Martin, another art director hired on especially for Disneyland, and Bill Cottrell, a longtime Disney story man who had recently married into the family. They went anywhere the tourists went. New York's Fifth Avenue, which they measured, curb to curb, curb to building line. The Mall in Washington, DC. The French Quarter in New Orleans. The Ivanhoe Restaurant in Chicago, a fabulous folly, with underground catacombs complete with bones protruding from cement rockwork, stained glass, suits of armor, and a indoor dance floor that seemed to be outside because it was surrounded by an artificial forest.

Their most intriguing visit was to Chicago's Museum of Science and Industry. In a written report filed at the end of the month, the travelers took note of five features of the museum worthy of further consideration: a series of flashy industrial exhibits sponsored by major corporations; the General Motors "Yesterday's Main Street," c. 1900, with real cobblestones and gaslights; a moving sidewalk;

45. View of Main Street, U.S.A., Disneyland, looking toward the Hub and the park's main "wienie," the Sleeping Beauty Castle. Harry Johnson. Charcoal and colored chalk on paper. 17 x 40. Late 1953–early 1954.

46. Fantasyland poster, showing the canal boats and miniaturized buildings of Storybook Land at Disneyland. Bjorn Aronson. Silkscreen print. 55 x 38. 1956.

Imagineering the Disney Theme Parks 65

47. This model of the Disneyland Castle was photographed up close, as though it were a real building, for use in a presentation book prepared in 1954 to persuade bankers and businessmen to back the project. Anonymous. Tempera on photostat. 19 x 30. 1954.

Colleen Moore's Fairy Castle dollhouse; and a little Santa Fe train. And they linked each of these ideas to the "lands" that seemed to turn up repeatedly in Marvin Davis's plans. Main Street, U.S.A. was already the spiritual heart of Disneyland: the Chicago Main Street was not the source for the idea. But Disney's observers did note its appealing participatory features, including an old-time photo gallery, the interesting displays of historic merchandise in the store windows, and the lavish hand with which detail had been applied to the facades. Disney's Tomorrowland, they thought, should have a moving sidewalk and corporate displays of experimental products, like the Museum of Science and Industry did. Maybe they should think about some miniature rooms in the Disneyland castle, to tell the story of Sleeping Beauty, as well as Walt's handmade set of mechanical miniatures currently slated for their own museum in Frontierland. Perhaps the Disneyland train ought to be a Santa Fe, in tribute to Walt's favorite line (on which Roy Disney, as a boy, had worked as a Fred Harvey "news butcher," hawking cigars and orangeade).

His deputies had brought drawings for Walt's peripheral railroad along on the trip to show to amusement operators, who were holding their annual meeting in Chicago. But the old pros seemed puzzled by Walt's obsession with quality and authenticity. Would the "marks" notice? And the operators failed to grasp the marquee value of the elevated railroad station atop the entrance to Disneyland. Walt wanted strong vertical elements to articulate each section of the park. He used the term "wienie," borrowed from silent-era comedy, to describe tall visual markers that promised to reward the visitor who walked toward them. Wienies were tasty visual treats for pedestrians (Fig. 45). The old pros in the carnival business thought nobody would trudge upstairs to get to the railroad tracks, for example, but Walt's theory was that if the promised goody were good enough, if what was going to be there was clear enough from the environmental cues embedded in the design, then Disneyland's guests would go anywhere and relish the trip.

The pilgrims from Burbank got a more sympathetic hearing at Coney Island of Cincinnati. The owners there kept an architect on retainer and the results were obvious in the pleasant appearance of the buildings, well-maintained and painted in cheerful, festive pastels. The Coney Island folks liked Walt's ideas, too. They looked at the drawings and counseled only that the openings to major attractions be made a little wider, to accommodate the crowds sure to be drawn by the wienies. At the Philadelphia Toboggan Company, where rides were engineered, they advised against trying to run the canal boats on an underwater chain. Long experience had shown that such devices tangled and rusted out (Fig. 46).

The practical tips were much appreciated. On July 21, 1954, three weeks after his search party returned from the wilds of Amusementland, Walt broke ground for Disneyland. There were only 257 working days left until the scheduled opening of the park. Nobody was sure which of Marvin Davis's plans was the final working document. Which of the eighty-four ideas contained therein would stay, and which would go.

48. Bird's-eye view of Disneyland, made for presentation to New York investors. Herbert Ryman. Pencil (with inset park plan designed by Marvin Davis). 43 x 70. September 23, 1953.
49. Frontierland page from corporate presentation book for Disneyland. Herbert Ryman. Photostat of original drawing colored in tempera. 19 x 30. 1954.

Imagineering the Disney Theme Parks 67

50. Tomorrowland as illustrated in a 1954 presentation book. Herbert Ryman. Photostat of original drawing colored in tempera. 19 x 30. 1954.

Castles in the Air

The castle was one idea that did survive the perilous transition from paper plans to fiberglass and lathe. Gilded, turreted, and bespired, the Sleeping Beauty Castle in the middle of Disneyland is the ultimate wienie, so crucial to the meaning of the place and to its spatial comprehension, so distinctively present to the viewer at every turn in the path, that it became, first, the trademark for the park, and finally, the logo for the films from which the park had fitfully evolved (Fig. 47).

The castle dominates the view from Main Street. Early concept drawings, showing how the planned narrative sequence of spaces would unfold from the ticket booths to the farthest reaches of the site, always picture the great towers and battlements rising like a vision of the Emerald City of Oz, or Shangri-La, or the gates of heaven over the mundane commercial bustle of Main Street. Without the castle, this is just another Greenfield Village. With the addition of the castle, it becomes magical. The castle signifies that here is no ordinary history park: its size and presence and sheer peculiarity entice the entering throngs to step along, down the street, past the intersection, to the Hub or central plaza, where all the other equally fantastic and unexpected dimensions of time and place begin. For this is not Marceline, Missouri, or Fort Collins, Colorado, in 1900. Not really. Any more than it's the long-ago frontier, a space colony, a jungle on the banks of an uncharted river, or a land of dreams and legends. It's Disneyland. That's what the castle says, as it plugs the vista that funnels down Main Street into the illustrated pages of a storybook.

On the Goff and Davis plans, castles came and went for several years. A Robin Hood's castle, straight from the 1952 made-in-Britain Disney movie, starring Richard Todd. A

51. This candy mountain proposed for Storybook Land in Fantasyland, c. 1957, was dropped because the model—constructed of real candy—killed all appetite for sweets by virtue of its too-bigness. Claude Coats. Crayon on brownline. 16 1/4 x 36 1/2. c. 1957.

Cinderella palace, from the 1950 animated release. No castle at all. A "Disney Fantasy" building, vaguely castle-like in plan. A castle on axis with the railroad station and prefaced by a hub appeared early in September 1953, only to disappear momentarily toward the end of the month. But it was there again, right in the center, when Herb Ryman spent his fateful weekend closeted with Walt and the plans, and drew the castle that still dominates Disneyland today (see Fig. viii).

By now, the money had all but run out. After years of resistance, however, Roy Disney had agreed to involve the company fully in the project; he was scheduled to leave for the East Coast to scare up backers and fresh capital. So far, no one in a position to help had understood the distinction between Walt's park and the usual, seedy roller coaster-and-sideshow operation. The Disneys needed more than a set of plans and Walt's enthusiasm. They needed pictures of something so enticing, so convincing and new, that the money boys would fall all over themselves to invest. So Walt phoned Herb Ryman on a Saturday morning and asked him to come over to the studio right away. Out by the main gate, eyebrows twitching, he explained his idea for a park. Then he dropped the bombshell.

"Look, Herbie," he said, "Roy is going to New York Monday to line up financing.... I've got to give him plans of what we're going to do. Those businessmen don't listen to talk, you know; you've got to show them what you're going to do."

"Well, where's the drawing?" Ryman asked. "I'd like to see it."

"You're going to make it," Walt replied. And he did.

From that day forward, Herb Ryman became the dominant pictorial force in the genesis of the Disney parks. Unlike Anderson and Davis, Ryman had not been trained as an architect. He was a painter and illustrator, an impressionist with a taste for travel and audacious color. Although he showed his off-duty work in New York and Los Angeles galleries (where Walt had first encountered it), Ryman was a movie artist by trade, a sketch man, all smoke and mirrors. He was a specialist in translating stories and talk into dimly lighted rooms, boulevards thronged with strange and beautiful people, fabulous bazaars—all with the flick of a pencil. His images hung in the air like exotic perfume, pungent but elusive, palpably there but hard to describe afterward with any degree of precision. Walt lured him away from MGM in 1938 for his Latin American trip and for a short time thereafter, in the 1940s, Ryman did occasional work on Disney films—*Fantasia*, *Dumbo*, *The Three Caballeros*—in layout and art direction. He was at Fox when Walt's weekend call sent him to Burbank on September 26, 1953.

Ryman's mother recorded that lost weekend in her diary entry for September 28. "Herbert is helping Walt to do a map of an amusement park," she wrote. "Roy Disney is going to New York soon to talk to the money people about helping to finance Disneyland." But she didn't spell out the terms of the deal. Herbie wouldn't agree to suffer alone, nor would he take responsibility for drawing Disney's park for him. If Walt wanted Ryman,

Walt was going to have to lock himself up for the whole weekend, too, and talk Herb through the plans. Where should he start?

His pencil drawing provides the answer (Fig. 48). Ryman copied the most recent Davis plan on the lower right-hand corner of a big sheet of paper and began to work up the

elevations in perspective as Disney described each of the attractions. Main Street, with the railroad station and the stores, pretty much as Harper Goff and Marvin Davis had begun to see it that summer. The critical Hub. Off to the left, the frontier and a Mississippi riverboat ride (Fig. 49). Off to the right, a secondary wienie, a rocket ship poised for flight above a Tomorrowland housed in the embrace of two matching arcades, like a Martian rendition of Bernini's design for the piazza outside Saint Peter's (Fig. 50). Other things that weren't built, in the end: dead-end side streets off Main Street, and whole neighborhoods approached by thoroughfares running parallel to it. Circus tents. A picnic ground. Brooding over a Lilliputian Land, a mountain made of candy (Fig. 51). Things in the wrong places: Adventure-

52. Fantasyland in 1955.

land set opposite Frontierland, to the east of the Hub, adjacent to the moon-rocket district. But the castle is just where it ought to be, big, majestic, and beautiful.

It is not exactly like the finished Disneyland castle, however. Ryman's first version is much taller, almost cathedral-like with a lofty

westwerk pierced by ranks of arched windows. Detached from the castle proper, which Ryman positions at the back of the keep, the battlements and drawbridge open on a carousel and an assortment of shops set into the walls of the courtyard. At Disneyland, things would be reversed. The castle came first, placed up front, for greater visibility, and Fantasyland, for which funds ran short before the park was completed, hid itself away behind the glamorous facade in a series of prefabricated 60-by-100-foot industrial sheds decorated to resemble tournament pavilions at a medieval joust (Fig. 52, 56).

Marvin Davis cautions against attributing the concept to Ryman. "I guess the one [section of the park] Walt had the most vivid picture of in his mind was Fantasyland with the entrance through a castle," he says. "The castle was his idea—not Herb's." But Ryman did clothe that idea in the make-believe stone walls that still dominate the park. By October of 1954, when Walt unveiled Disneyland on his new Wednesday-night television show of the same name, the Ryman castle had assumed its final, definitive shape (Fig. 53). It was squatter now, blockier, a composition balanced between horizontal fortification walls and vertical turrets, with a greater emphasis on the drawbridge and the portal to Fantasyland that opened at its far end, directly beneath a cluster of towers pointing straight down at the doorway.

This castle demanded entry, and celebrated it in a configuration of parts positioned to make the visitor into a fairy-tale princess bound for the prince's ball, a triumphant knight just back from a fight with a fearsome dragon. The first castle was seen from the air, from a bird's-eye perspective indicated, in Ryman's large drawing, by the presence of a tethered balloon hovering over the park. The castle Walt showed to potential backers and his TV audience in a close-to, color rendering was, however, seen from the front and a little below, as if to put the viewer in the position of a park guest, walking toward the looming castle spires, seeing the doorway, and answering the invitation to plunge into the heart of Fantasyland. No wonder that a glimpse of the unbuilt castle opened every show, teasing a national audience of viewers in Ohio, Florida, Wyoming, and all points between to turn off the set, get in the car, and drive to Anaheim, in time for the gala dedication, on July 17, 1955.

Disneyland: The Place That Was Also a TV Show

The reason Herb Ryman had to draw Walt's park in a single weekend was an upcoming audience with the money men. And most of the money was in television. Ever since he hosted a Christmas Day special in 1950, feeding an insatiable appetite for behind-the-scenes looks at the Disney operation, Walt had been besieged with offers to do a weekly television series. As the head of an independent studio, Walt did not have to contend with the vagaries of the New York-based TV industry, where corporate sponsors seemed to dictate content to the networks. But unlike his fellow Hollywood moguls, Disney was not terrified of the new medium, either. On the contrary, he saw an opportunity to use television to build Disneyland.

The upshot of Roy's trip back east in the autumn of 1953 was an agreement with the ABC television network to supply a show if ABC would provide the line of credit needed to finish the Anaheim project. The television executives were not unduly impressed with the drawings of what they continued to call Walt's "fairground." But, as the third and smallest network, ABC wanted a Disney show, any way they could get it. And Walt began to realize that he needed the show, to explain his dream to potential ticket buyers who weren't going to drive to California to see a mere fairground. He needed a show to sell Disneyland to the people depicted standing in wonder at the castle gate in Ryman's latest drawings. "I saw that if I was ever going to have my park," Walt conceded,

53. Walt Disney introduces Disneyland to his television audience in 1954; here, he points at one of Herbert Ryman's renderings of the trademark Castle.

54. This drawing of the entrance to Frontierland was prepared specifically for use during one of Walt Disney's televised pitches for his park.
Bruce Bushman. Charcoal pencil on paper. 26 x 32. 1954.

72 Designing Disney's Theme Parks

55. Early study for the entrance to Tomorrowland ("Land of Tomorrow") with rocket "wienie" and experimental monorail system. Herbert Ryman. Colored pencil and watercolor on brownline. 14 x 33. 1954.

56. One of the novel new rides in Fantasyland was the Peter Pan Flight, housed in a prefabricated building disguised with turrets and banners. Bill Martin. Colored pencil on brownline. 21 x 36. 1954.

"here, at last was a way to tell millions of people about it—with TV."

"TV," Walt told writer Pete Martin, "was the start of Disneyland." Television also provided the physical structure for the park. The show was organized around a menu of themes, each one corresponding to a part of the park, or to a sprawling roster of "lands" that began to whittle itself down to a manageable four as budgets were fixed and construction began. Each land referred to specific, ongoing Disney projects, as well. Adventureland, for example, was inspired by the True-Life Adventure nature documentaries the studio had begun to make in 1948, and the first of these featurettes, *Seal Island*, was seen during the premiere season of the *Disneyland* show. Frontierland corresponded to live-action westerns for television currently in production, including the wildly popular *Davy Crockett* hours aired on Wednesday nights in 1954 and 1955 (Fig. 54). Tomorrowland was less closely tied to existing Disney films but reflected Walt's ongoing interest in new technologies and in corporate research: television features organized around this subject would include updates from the Bell Laboratories and other contractors working for the space program (Fig. 55). Fantasyland, of course, alluded to the animated features (Fig. 56). And Walt Disney had the best film library in the animation business.

On the *Disneyland* program, the topical "lands" appeared in random sequence: one week (the second, in fact—and the show won an Emmy award), under the Tomorrowland rubric, Walt introduced the stars of *20,000 Leagues under the Sea*, the Jules Verne interpretation of yesterday's tomorrows then being completed in Burbank. The next week, the collection of film clips and new footage shot at the studio could focus on the West or the way in which artists had created a particular segment of a classic animation. Although the series was held together by the overarching Disneyland concept, which was reinforced by frequent field reports from Anaheim, the format emphasized variety and change. As did the layout of the park in which a common entrance to Disneyland ultimately deposited the visitor in the Hub, or *étoile*, in front of Ryman's castle (Fig. 57). From that spot, the four lands pinwheeled outward, each one prefaced by a formal gateway already identified and discussed by Walt on his show.

He spoke about the trademark Hub plan in mostly practical terms. It was reassuring to know that, wherever you wandered, you would always wind up back in that same place. It "gives people a sense of orientation," he said. "They know where they are at all times. And it saves a lot of walking." Not quite true. In the beginning, before routes were plotted out to link one adjacent land to another, the Hub had the opposite effect on the feet: circulation within the park was accomplished only by returning to the Hub and setting forth once more from that same spot, over and over again (Fig. 58).

The Hub was more symbolic and pictorial than practical, despite Walt's protests. Like a Ryman drawing, it established a point of view,

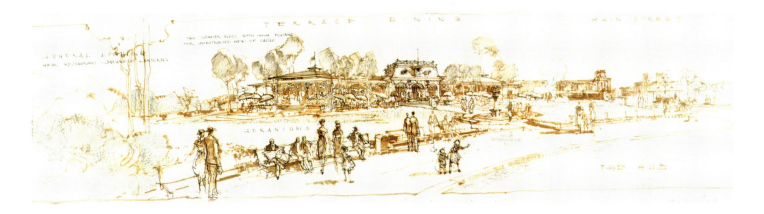

57. Terrace dining area at Main Street Hub, Disneyland. Herbert Ryman. Pen and ink and crayon on tissue. 12 x 42. 1954–55.

the perfect vantage point from which the icons of Disney's world—the Frontierland stockade, the castle drawbridge to Fantasyland, the Tomorrowland rocket, the bamboo portals of Adventureland (Fig. 59)—could all be seen at once. Gates and narrow openings off the Hub framed far-away wienies and thus identified the four quadrants of the park, arranged compass-wise around the Hub. The Hub also diagrammed the concepts of choice and change. Like a Wednesday-night viewer, the tourist standing in the Hub at Disneyland was presented with a whole range of possibilities. Like an impatient viewer in front of the set, the tourist could switch from one channel—oops! land—to another in just a few steps. "I'm tired of museums and fairs where you have to walk your legs off," Walt insisted. "I didn't want anybody at Disneyland to get 'museum foot.'" But this was not a linear, museum-like experience, one era shown after another, ad infinitum. It was a discontinuous narrative, like the weekly TV show called *Disneyland*.

Narrative was what separated Disneyland from all those other parks. The first employees of what would become Walt Disney Imagineering devoted an inordinate amount of time to the brand new, never-before-seen array of story-telling "rides" planned for the precincts of Fantasyland. After old-timers told Walt's research squad to avoid walk-through attractions, because people always bunched up in crowds and impeded the stream of movement, the fledgling Imagineers decided to reinterpret a number of the animated features by means of vehicles moving at a fixed rate of speed past scenes loosely derived from their respective films. The original "dark ride" followed the terrifying adventures of Snow White, as she eluded a murderous huntsman, met the dwarfs, and fell victim to the witch's poisoned apple.

Bill Martin, a member of the touring research group, laid out the track and Ken Anderson, who had been the art director for the original movie back in 1937, picked the scenes to be recreated in three dimensions, with statues of characters that variously swiveled around or popped up as the careening mine car

58. This Disneyland poster describes the position and function of the Castle/Hub complex. Bjorn Anderson. Silkscreen print. 54 x 36. c. 1957.
59. Entrance to Adventureland, c. 1955. The gateway was visible from the Hub.

moved by them (see Fig. 43). Using cardboard mockups, they tried the ride out on Walt in a tabletop version: to duplicate the ultimate effect, he was forced to creep along, knees bent like Groucho Marx, following the route of the moving mine car, with his eyes at the level of the miniature houses and tiny figures. The figure of Snow White was not among them, however. And she was absent in representational form because the spectator was meant to take her place in the story. In other words, it was the family in the mine car that met the dwarfs and fell into a swoon from eating the witch's poisoned apple. The ride was a cinematic narrative, with the rider as star (Fig. 60).

As a movie, *Snow White* succeeds brilliantly for eighty-three minutes. The truncated story line works for the two or three minutes it takes the Disneyland mine car to lurch and twist its way from scene to scene and then back again, into the bright California sunlight. It is much harder to sustain that same narrative drive over the course of a day. So each part of Disneyland became its own narrative—Adventureland, Frontierland, Tomorrowland, Fantasyland, like a line-up of half-hour shows on any given Wednesday evening in Televisionland. The Hub is a giant TV set, showing pictures of what can be found at every side, previews of next week's show, or this afternoon's destination. "Don't touch that dial!" the announcer warns. Please do, says Disneyland. The circle inscribed at the center of the park is the locus of change from Snow White's descent into a kind of cartoon nightmare to a Mark Twain's-eye-view of life on the nineteenth-century Mississippi, from a cruise up the crocodile-infested Amazon to a voyage to a distant star. Go ahead. Touch that dial!

Selling Disneyland

Television was a powerful marketing device. By the time the park opened in the summer of 1955, Disney and ABC were ready to court disaster with unprecedented live, twenty-four-camera coverage of the ceremonies, so great were the potential rewards. Disney had used

60. Fantasyland, 1954. *Snow White and the Seven Dwarfs* was the first feature-length animated film and one of Walt Disney's greatest achievements. But this color study for the facade of the Snow White ride in Fantasyland pays homage to the more abstract graphic design of *Sleeping Beauty* (1959), then in production. Eyvind Earle. Gouache and cel paint on paper. 12 x 30. 1954.

the weekly show to promote his movies; sponsors were quick to capitalize on product tie-ins, offering cardboard castles and other park-related premiums to those who bought their products. However entertaining, Walt's *Disneyland* show was one long, extended ad, a way to sell America on coming to the park of the same name. Week after week, month after month, the symbols of its constituent parts were arrayed across little black-and-white screens in the nation's living rooms, as they would later be displayed on the edge of the Hub in Anaheim, by means of a series of unforgettable icons. Bamboo for Adventureland. The castle for Fantasyland. By the time opening day finally arrived, the mental map of Disneyland was already emblazoned upon the collective consciousness: Train, Main Street, Hub-and-Castle, Lands. Logs and bark for Frontierland. Rocket ship for Tomorrowland (Fig. 61). The pictures made the park. The pictures were the park.

Herb Ryman's original aerial view of Disneyland was attached as an illustration to a six-page booklet describing the park. Booklets were produced by making mechanical reproductions of the drawing—in brownline or photostat, used for such purposes before the advent of the Xerox process—and then coloring the copies by hand. Marvin Davis and Dick Irvine, the 20th Century-Fox art director who had acted as Walt's liaison with Pereira and Luckman on the failed master plan, were both pressed into service as emergency colorists at the end of the famous Ryman weekend. Other booklets and large presentation portfolios, with a number of images mounted on cloth or stiff paper backing for use on a boardroom easel, were created in 1953 and 1954 for meetings with nervous bankers and potential sponsors of concessions or attractions (Fig. 62).

Photos of Walt making his pitch resemble stills from his park-in-progress nights on ABC. Pointer in hand, he stands in front of the stock images that had come to define *Disneyland* (and Disneyland, too, of course). One was painter Peter Ellenshaw's brilliant full-color rendering of the park, a generation beyond Ryman's now, made especially for the introductory television show in October 1954 (Figs. 63). There were also new views of landmarks in Disneyland by Herb Ryman, pictures that seemed to be topographical renderings of places the artist had actually visited and drawn, rather than totally imaginary constructs done while orange trees still dotted an empty site. Ryman drew his views and anybody who was handy painted photostats of them in tempera. Still other pages in the hastily made presentation books contained photographs of little model buildings, the photos painted and retouched to look un-model-like and real.

The models and the booklets were meant to show the people who sold Wurlitzer organs and Swift meats (Fig. 64), Maxwell House coffee (Fig. 65), Kodak cameras and Cole of California swimsuits just how their Main Street

61. Opening day crowds stream into Tomorrowland, July 1955.

shopfronts would look, if they took a chance on Disneyland and signed a lease. They were meant to show bankers and network vice presidents that this was no run-of-the-mill fairground, but a collection of evocative, almost-real environments, complete down to the smallest detail of interior design and costume—miniatures enlarged somewhat for ease of use but still model-like in their fussy, highly wrought perfection. But the models and the bright, larger-than-life paintings were also practical tools in a frantic, complex, ad hoc process of turning ideas into architecture. Disney architecture is picture architecture. Everything starts from an illustration, a concept picture, a slice of an animation storyboard showing characters, or settings, or props, or, best of all, their interaction in space and time.

The picture is a marketing tool but it is also a way for the artist to reach beyond an idea or a conversation about a place toward the making of the place itself. The picture that sold a meat packer on Disneyland was also the picture the model maker measured as a guide in building a miniature meat market (Fig. 66). And the miniature, nicely painted to look like a full-scale building, became a page in a marketing book or a guide for an artist charged with producing a formal elevation drawing that a contractor could follow when the time came to build the actual Main Street. Imagineer David Mumford delights in the tall tales handed down from the pioneer days in Anaheim. He tells one about the heroic artist—George Windrum—stationed in an upstairs office in Disneyland's unfinished City Hall whose task it was to design Main Street as it was being constructed. How the schedule was so tight that he did his design and production drawings almost simultaneously. How he used to have to interrupt himself to sketch a detail of molding, run downstairs, have it milled on the spot, and nail up the pieces, all before lunch time.

When Imagineers go to Disneyland today,

62. The concept and the execution often failed to match, as in the case of this splendid (unbuilt) molecular fountain for the entry to Tomorrowland. When Disneyland opened, Tomorrowland was almost empty. Herbert Ryman. Tempera on photostat. 19 x 30. 1954.

78 Designing Disney's Theme Parks

63. Original bird's-eye view prepared for Walt's ABC-TV introduction of Disneyland, 1954. Peter Ellenshaw. Oil and blacklight paint on storyboard. 50 x 90. October 1954.

to supervise construction of a Mickey's Toontown or an Indiana Jones™ Adventure, they go equipped with models cased for use in the field, highly finished conceptual illustrations of the end product imagined by its designers, films made with tiny cameras dragged though paper mock-ups of interior spaces, conventional elevations, and diagrams indicating the finish desired for each surface. Building Disneyland is still a matter of fluid negotiation between dream, miniature, technical diagram, and the kind of "eyewash" Walt poured in liberal doses over home viewers and investors alike as his park began to rise like a mirage out of the desert soil of Southern California in 1954 (Fig. vii).

The Architecture of Reassurance

Legend has it that Walt Disney never learned to trust blueprints. Like the old-time carpenter who measures rafters by holding every board in place, he believed in things that looked like they really worked, models he could examine from all sides, objects he could touch and turn over in his hands (Fig. 67). There are several important consequences of Walt's unconventional approach to architecture. Because of his devotion to tangible things, for instance, the Disney theme parks are full of compelling, believable detail: they seem more real, somehow, than the world outside the berm, even though the 1800s have vanished, along with the last of the unexplored jungle rivers, and the future still lies up ahead, muffled in hope and the trappings of a thousand bad science-fiction movies. But a creative technique based on models and pictures also favors style over content, clear and simple emotions over a range of more difficult choices.

The gentle fakery of style is entertaining and Disneyland aimed, above all, to entertain. It soothes and reassures the visitor, too, in ways the designers began to understand only after the dust had settled and they could look down from their drafting tables in City Hall and watch the happy crowds streaming down Main Street toward the castle. Some of the feelings generated by Main Street were obvious. The old-fashioned storefronts enhanced the prestige of the businesses inside and gave customers the confidence to shop in an unfamiliar setting. "We've been around a long, long time," whispered the gilded lettering on the windows, the simulated cast-iron pediments above the doorways. Dazzled by the wealth of detail, who would stop to notice that Main Street, while giving the appearance of a place comprising many different buildings, each one novel and delightful, each one about twenty-two feet wide, in fact consisted of only a couple of huge structures decorated with doorways (some false) placed at intervals of eighteen feet (Figs. 68, 69)? Main Street was a strip mall all dressed up in a scintillating Victorian costume that made the products you shopped for at home—film, pianos, bathing suits, even real estate and shoes and lingerie in 1955—seem intriguing all over again (Fig. 70).

The size of things contributed to the aura of well-being, fantasy, and delight. For Main Street was a slightly-larger-than-normal model train layout. "It's not apparent at a casual glance that this street is only a scale model," confessed Walt, who told the press that he had

80 Designing Disney's Theme Parks

64. Exterior elevation of Swift Market House, Main Street, U.S.A., Disneyland. Anonymous. Colored pencil on brownline. 23 x 34. c. 1954.

worked out the dimensions of Main Street by the simple expedient of "blowing up" his backyard engine five times in size for Disneyland and scaling the buildings around it accordingly. So, in theory, every brick and shingle and gas lamp on street level was to be made at five-eighths true size. "This costs more, but made the street a toy," Walt said, "and the imagination can play more freely with a toy. Besides, people like to think their world is somehow more grown up than Papa's was." In practice, the details at sidewalk level are almost life-size. But the second and third stories got smaller and smaller, very quickly; the old art director's trick called "forced perspective" convinced the eye that the upper floors were behaving according to the immutable laws of recession into space whereas the heart knew, secretly, that these were dollhouses, scaled for the private pleasure of the enchanted visitor. So Main Street was reassuring on all counts (Fig. 71).

And there was more. Every part of Main Street—every hitching post and sign and awning, every molding—was of a piece, a complement to all the rest, part of a harmonious picture that admitted no jarring elements (Fig. 72). Main Street was aesthetically unthreatening, different, in that respect, from strip malls and real streets where every store battled with its neighbor in a disquieting cacophony of visual stimuli. "Most urban environments are basically chaotic places, as architectural and graphic information scream at the citizen for attention," John Hench maintains. "This competition results in disharmonies and contradictions that . . . cancel each other [out]. A journey down almost any urban street will

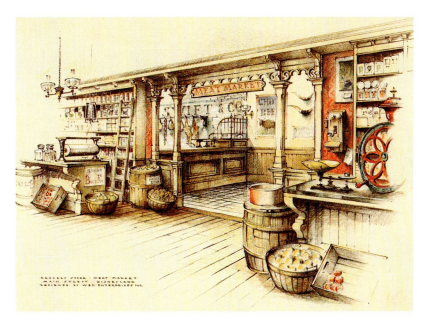

65. Designs were often prepared showing a potential sponsor's signage added to existing or projected buildings for effect.
This elegant coffee house on Main Street was, for a time, sponsored by the Maxwell House brand. Sam McKim. Pencil on tissue. 20 x 23. c. 1954–55.
66. Interior of Swift's Market House on Main Street, showing a meat market. This was part of the decor of a restaurant.
Anonymous. Colored pencil on brownline. 19 x 24. c. 1954.

quickly place the visitor into visual overload as all of the competing messages merge into a kind of information gridlock."

Color was a factor—lots of it, all in the same degree of saturation, the same family of hues. Black is fine when the mood is meant to be mysterious, but on Main Street, the colors were lifted or plussed over the years, made brighter and cheerier and more varied—more colors, new colors—in keeping with an emerging theory of why Americans liked the architecture of the Gay Nineties so much. It was the optimism, Walt's creative successors thought, as they built more Main Streets in Florida (Fig. 73), in Tokyo (Fig. 74), in France (Fig. 75). Anyone could feel the optimism in the variety and sheer exuberant quantity of decorative detail lavished on every surface. It was as comforting as a Victorian parlor stuffed with treasures. As luscious as a birthday cake smothered in pink frosting and silver sugar balls. On Main Street, life suddenly seemed pleasant, manageable and, well—awfully nice.

Things made sense there. In animation, the Disney artists never put anything on the screen that they hadn't intended to be there. "In order to convey ideas, you have to be precise in the way you handle forms. You do not want to introduce any ambiguity, and certainly not contradiction," says John Hench. Like a movie, this place was a fiction, subject to artistic control. And like a movie, it worked over time,

67. Main Street model, 1953–55.

to tell a story that unfolded in three-dimensional space, from train to street to castle. "You don't throw people into the fifth scene, where they cannot make sense of what is happening," Hench cautions. "You begin with the first scene and move through," tugged along from little things close at hand that charm and please by their enhanced familiarity toward big ones, odder in shape, and farther away.

You are emboldened and soothed by clean streets, smiling faces, happy colors, and the implicit promise that here, at least, everything will be OK. It will be fun, you won't get lost, and there are plenty of benches in case your feet get tired. But they won't. Indecision and anxiety make for tiredness. Figuring things out. Not knowing where to go and what to look at. Main Street makes no such demands on the pedestrian. Look at anything. Wander anywhere. It's better than any real street in any turn-of-the-century town had ever been, a vast stage, a film set with the tourist as the actor, comforted on all sides by familiar things that have somehow grown sweeter, gentler, and more appealing than they ever were in Fort Collins or Marceline or her own hometown.

Reassurance and control—the fact that somebody else wrote the script by building outlines of buildings out of two-by-fours and propping them up to test just what you could see from Scene One, when you were standing outside the Main Street Emporium, looking north toward the Hub, or from the start of Scene Two, where Main Street flows gently into the Hub at a corner soda fountain—are not qualities readily associated with the Modernist canon. At least not when control is placed in the service of reassurance. Making someone feel good is what greeting cards do, what the worst kind of kitsch does. But not art. Great art never tells you to have a nice day. For that reason, among others (the rejection of *Fantasia* by the custodians of high culture is part of the equation), Walt Disney, in the 1950s, disavowed any interest in the kind of art endorsed by the critics. Despite his patent respect for Dalí and Thomas Hart Benton, both of whom worked at the studio, and his in-house art school for animators, he was interested in what pleased and amused the people who went to his movies. "If picture-postcard art moves people, then I like it," Walt told his eldest daughter in 1957. "If I'm corny, then millions of people in this country must be corny, too."

The statement is defensive and disingenuous, of course, but only a little. As a maker of mass art, he did care about the tastes and preferences of a vast multiregional, multigenerational, and multinational audience. And as an entertainer, a creator of comic characters, a teller of fairy-tale fables meant to resolve the conflicts encountered in the world of toil and trouble, he did not believe for a moment that art—his art, the picture-postcard kind—was obliged to be disturbing, challenging, unsettling. He believed instead that it ought to provide comfort and refuge from that world of woes he knew at first hand. His park was built behind a berm to protect it from the evils that daily beset humankind on all sides. It aimed to soothe and reassure. It aimed to give pleasure. Joy. A flash of sunny happiness. The small, sweet, ordinary, domestic emotions seldom implicit in the definition of aesthetic pleasure. The architecture of reassurance.

"All I want you to think about," Walt told his non-architects, "is that when people walk through . . . anything that you design, I want them, when they leave, to have smiles on their faces." Vitruvius once admonished architects to follow three principles of good building: commodity, firmness, and delight. Walt Disney left the business of making the building stand up properly to others. Commodiousness was a property the buildings at Disneyland possessed by virtue of the fact that you could generally accomplish inside them what their outsides suggested you could; it was a by-product of a methodology grounded in pictorialism. But what the first Imagineers set out to create afresh at Disneyland was a new architecture of pure Vitruvian delight: the architecture of reassurance.

Disneyland is domestic in flavor, even when the places simulated are public plazas and civic buildings (Fig. 76). Shrinking Main Street to the dimensions of a ranch-house subdivision in some brave, treeless suburb of the 1950s contributes to the impression. But so do the feelings attached to smallish, pinkish, safe, and comfy spaces. They are not the big, histrionic emotions appropriate to public life: righteous anger, heated passion, the soaring elation of victory. Disneyland is about mild contentment and the overarching reassurance that there is an order governing the disposition of things. A detectable order that will take the visitor by the hand and lead him through an astonishingly varied array of ersatz places, back to the Main Street from whence he began. The feelings are domestic in scale, of an order of magnitude exactly commensurate with a

84 Designing Disney's Theme Parks

68. Main Street elevation, 400 block, east side, showing Penny Arcade. Herbert Ryman. Pen and ink, colored pencil, and felt-tip pen on paper. 13 x 46. 1954.
69. Color diagram for painting the 400 block, east side, Main Street, Disneyland. Anonymous. Opaque watercolor on brownline. 12 x 43. 1955.

⅝-, or ¾-, or ⅞-scale show window in a toy store. Yet magnitude is less crucial to those sensations of well-being than the notion of order itself. The ninety-five-piece Disneyland Playset sold for $9.77 in the 1961 Sears Christmas catalogue provided the lucky recipient with a series of plastic mats emblazoned with the plan of the park, drawn to scale, so that the tiny plastic stores and the castles and the frontier stockade could be positioned in just the right places. In childish play, and within the precincts of Disneyland proper, the perception of order was the best sensation of them all.

Order implies control and there is no question about Walt's abiding interest in being in control—of his business, of the content of his films, of the smallest detail of his park. His rage for order led him to regret until the end of his days that he had not been able to afford more land on the fringes of the Anaheim property: the litter of gas stations, ineptly "themed" motels, and fast-food outlets that sprang up along Harbor Boulevard was an affront to his sense of a guest's ideal prelude to Scene One at Disneyland. In Florida, he bought up twenty-eight thousand acres so that every approach to the Magic Kingdom came through an elegant landscape of curved roads that permitted brief, tantalizing peeks at the familiar icons of a Disney domain.

Stories are about order and control: first one thing happens and then another. So are poems and novels and films—and so is art, for that matter. At Disneyland, Walt translated that verbal and pictorial narrative into a material, spatial dimension. He made a city, or a series of cities, that told a story, as a king or his visionary architect might do in drawing up the master plan for a lovely pleasure garden. First comes the fountain. Then, the statue. And then, the castle (Fig. 77). In a modern era of speculative, laissez-faire architecture, with each segment of the urban mix conceived by a different intelligence, each with a different case to plead, Walt's park looked radically different. Some were reminded of Versailles. Versailles for middle-class Americans in plaid Bermuda shorts. Others saw the iron hand of dictatorship, repression masked in smiles and mouse ears.

The charge of sinister intent is the risk art often runs when it sets itself apart from the operative norms of its time. And, although Walt Disney espoused corn over art, Disneyland was clearly a countercultural artifact—a work of art—despite the little emotions and the smiling willingness to please. Cities didn't smile. Neither did architecture, serious architecture. But in marked distinction to Los Angeles in 1955, the buildings of Disneyland were meant to be seen at close hand by pedestrians, whose cars had been consigned to a distant parking lot, forgotten for the day behind a tall earthen wall. Disneyland was pretty. Blatant competition between store and store was banished. The scale of the place was homelike, as unlike the corporate skyscraper and the hulking mall as could be imagined. If the product being sold at Disneyland is not really shoes or soap or civic betterment but contentment and pleasure, there might be profit, too, in unmasking the faults of urban America—its dullness, tawdriness, confusion, its overbearing swagger. And substituting harmony, mild adventure, safety, and

70. Interior of Main Street shoe salon, Disneyland. Harry Johnson. Charcoal, crayon, and chalk on paper. 13 1/2 x 28. 1954–55.

71. Proposed "Art Festival" for Center Street intersection on Main Street, Disneyland. John Hench. Opaque watercolor, repainted in acrylic in 1994. 22 x 37. 1963.

72. The various Center Street schemes—this Center Street with "hippie" artists is in the Magic Kingdom, Walt Disney World, Orlando, Florida—illustrate the process of revising and "plussing" the detail in the parks; over time, the street furniture becomes more elaborate. Herbert Ryman. Charcoal on paper. 17 x 30. 1969.

order—the order of art; the art of reassurance: the architecture of Disneyland.

Main Street Memories

For all its architectural inducements to follow the script, Disneyland was still a place that celebrated choice. The park resuscitated the act of choosing one route or destination over another by eliminating the unpleasant consequences: there were no bad neighborhoods lurking around the next corner and Frontierland was just as much fun as the land next door. But during Scene One—the ritual procession through the ticket gate, under the railroad station, and down Main Street—the layout of Disneyland allowed for no deviations from the master narrative. Everybody made the same trip from the station into town, the same long walk that the newcomer from somewhere else had to make back in 1900. The act of entry was a rite of passage telling the stranger to shake off the customs of that other place—the formless sprawl of Los Angeles out beyond the parking lot, the town two or three stops back along the railroad tracks. Here, on this spot, the day started afresh, with a new set of rules. And the first of the admonitions built into the fabric of Disneyland was this: Arise and walk! Walk, all together now, straight down Main Street from the train.

There were a couple of buses, a fire engine, and a horse-drawn trolley on the thoroughfare, primarily for atmosphere. They weren't built to carry crowds because Main Street was for pedestrians. Lookers in windows. Sniffers of aromas: chocolate from the candy shop, coffee, and fresh-baked rolls. People who strolled and

73. The quality of detail increased as new parks were built. This is apparent in a view of Town Square, Magic Kingdom, Walt Disney World, looking toward City Hall. Ernie Prinzhorn. Pen and ink on paper. 22 x 34. 1968.

fingered the merchandise and savored the glint of gold-leaf letters on a polished window pane (Fig. 78). If the castle drew the eye toward the Hub at the end of the street, the gaily colored awnings and the goods on display in the shops provided wonderful excuses for lingering here instead and enjoying the walk.

By forcing his guests to walk along Main Street, by banishing the automobile from his domain, Walt was suggesting that something was amiss in the car-mad culture outside the park. Although family tourism in the two-toned Chevy and the new Santa Ana freeway were both crucial to the success of Disneyland, the park offered a utopian alternative to the ongoing erosion of city centers by cars. With the exception of an Autopia ride designed to equip the drivers of tomorrow to cope with freeway driving, Disneyland in the 1950s advocated public transportation overtly and passionately. There were trains of all ages and sorts, boats, stagecoaches, and, before the decade was over, an advanced monorail system designed to be a prototype for eventual use in real-world cities (Fig. 79). As compensation for the loss of the go-anywhere freedom attached to automobility, the fixed-route vehicles at Disneyland offered atmosphere. Machinery that huffed and puffed or, conversely, didn't make a sound. Smokestacks. Steam. A conventional chassis dressed up in a sleek carapace of space-age plastic. The picturesque disguises worn by the elements of the mass-transit system amounted to horizontal wienies, or rewards for the good behavior of motorists willing to become pedestrians and passengers.

There was a close correlation in Walt's mind between walking, shopping, and make-believe scenery because L.A. had already learned to give pedestrians cinematic rewards for parking their cars. In the 1940s and early 1950s, the city finally resigned itself to its fate: Bullock's department stores commissioned Welton Becket and other California firms to redesign the shopping experience, so that motorists could literally drive into the store and park within steps of a given selection of merchandise. But Walt's favorite weekend haunts, built a decade earlier, had adopted a compensatory strategy to get drivers out from behind the wheel and make them eager to walk. The Farmer's Market of 1934 was a let's-pretend Midwestern farmscape, identified by a trademark windmill at curbside (Fig. 80). Crossroads of the World on Sunset Boulevard, completed in 1936, was a collection of boutiques housed in a half-timbered Elizabethan

74. Color reference chart for World Bazaar shop exteriors, Tokyo Disneyland. The World Bazaar is Tokyo's adaptation of Main Street, U.S.A. Susan Morales. Pencil and tempera on board, with acrylic overlay and attached labels. 20 x 40. 1981.

88 Designing Disney's Theme Parks

75. Proposal for Main Street Motors showroom, southeast block, Main Street, Disneyland Paris. Dan Goozee. Acrylic on board. 27 x 40. 1988.

village, a lighthouse, a ship, and an ersatz California presidio (Fig. 81). Other businesses tried the same ploy with great success. "Restaurant Row" on La Cienega Boulevard ran the gamut from a hot-dog stand operating out of a giant plaster-over-chicken-wire frankfurter to sit-down establishments that looked like grass shacks, castles in Spain, and colonial inns.

"Motion pictures have undoubtedly confused architectural tastes," wrote California architect Richard Neutra in 1941. "They may be blamed for...half-timbered English peasant cottages and 'mission-bell' type adobes, Arabian minarets, [and] Georgian mansions on 50 x 120 foot lots with 'Mexican Ranchos' adjoining them on sites of the same size" (Fig. 82). Although Neutra's target was the incoherent blob of Los Angeles suburbia that was oozing its way across Orange County toward Anaheim, following the path of the highway, he could just as well have been describing Walt's first plans for a little park adjacent to his backlot property. For Main Street is a movie set, a section of backlot foolery in which, behind the false facades, interior walls rarely correspond to the exterior dimensions of a given structure and the upstairs offices are nothing more than names painted on the windows for show. Walt talked about building an actual TV production facility immediately adjacent to the shopfronts for filming programs with historical settings. But in the absence of the television studio, Main Street still amounts to an elaborate setting for an unscripted drama enacted by the pedestrian and his fellow guests. It is a movie that runs inside the consciousness of the actors, a story about the wondrousness of pressing one's nose to a store window, of rubbing elbows with one's fellow creatures, of taking a walk in a place that bathes the senses in unalloyed charm.

The movie is "The Walt Disney Story," his own roseate memory of the good old days, when he was young and found the store windows of Marceline as dazzling as the bazaars of the Arabian Nights. The Santa Fe and Disneyland train was there because he remembered the whistle in the night, calling a sleepy child to dreams of romance and adventure. The railroad was there because he had built its predecessor in his own backyard to remind him of those golden memories. Disneyland, this most public of places, advertised incessantly on TV, was the private pleasure garden of a benevolent monarch, the autobiography of the little boy who heard the whistle calling, took the long journey to California, and made the movies that define the lands adjacent to the Hub. All of Disneyland is Walt Disney but the most personal, idiosyncratic part of the autobiography written there

76. Main Street sketch for Disneyland showing a residential district in the spot where the Castle would eventually rise. Dale Hennesy. Pencil on paper. 16 x 40. c. 1953.

in buildings, streets, and sidewalks is Main Street, U.S.A.

Because he was trying to recapture his memories intact, the list of Main Street businesses Walt recited like a litany to his designers was full of places that seemed, at first blush, to have little or no entertainment potential. He wanted a butcher shop in his streetscape, for example, and a pharmacy, and all the buildings required to sustain the civic health of real towns: a post office, a police department, City Hall, and a newspaper office. Some such establishments—the drugstore is a good example—were included in the final plans as little museums of old equipment under the sponsorship of corporations engaged in similar enterprises. Others, like City Hall, were turned to a variety of administrative uses. The butcher shop actually contained a restaurant. In the 1950s, however, before the majority of the stores had become one continuous mall stocked with Disney merchandise, Disneyland struggled to maintain a tenant list of shoe stores and other specialized apparel shops not because people came to the park to buy loafers and underwear but because the Main Street Walt remembered used to have them.

Memory is the reason Main Street is small in scale. A whole headful of recollections can fit under a perky pair of Mouseketeer ears and to the pilgrim, the old hometown always seems to be much smaller than it used to be. The miniaturization of the buildings identifies the locus of memory and reverie: the visitor has strayed unwittingly into somebody else's life story. Memory shrinks the past and sweetens it, too, until history becomes something small and precious and private. Main Street feels so intimate because it is a corner of Walt Disney's psyche, shared with his guests.

Main Street Urbanism

But unlike memories, Main Street is not quite frozen in time. Indeed, the era Disney picked was one of wholesale change. In it, electricity has just been invented. The odd automobile appears among the horse-drawn trolleys. Modern civilization is just around the corner of the cross street, halfway down Main, that Walt called Center (for which a Chinatown district was once contemplated). Main Street, U.S.A. trembles on the brink of progress and from this vantage point, the future looks bright and beautiful. Until 1964, when Imagineering incorporated the concept into a Carousel of Progress created for the General Electric display at the New York World's Fair, the official souvenir "fun" map of Disneyland designed by Sam McKim showed something called Edison Square, just off the Hub on a street running back behind Main, along its right flank (Fig. 83). Concept paintings for the district by Herb Ryman and Sam McKim show a neighborhood made up of town houses set cheek-by-jowl around a traffic circle. The houses were divided into clumps of four or six, each one representing the distinctive style of an American city in the Edison era: St. Louis, Boston, Chicago, and so forth (Fig. 84). Behind the facades was a series of sit-down shows and walk-through exhibits that demonstrated how technological wizardry and electric power had changed the American home and would continue to do so in the future. Main Street was the nexus of change, the benchmark against which the forward march of progress was to be measured.

For years, Walt was haunted by the idea that Main Street ought to stand for something other than his own memories. Some big idea. A construction fence that stood on Town Square throughout the park's inaugural decade had peepholes that revealed, instead of actual work in progress, paintings and 3-D photographs representing a group of attractions planned to occupy the whole area to the east of Main Street, between the square and the Hub. In addition to his work on Edison Square, Herb Ryman sketched elaborate plans for a Liberty Street, featuring architecture from the thirteen original colonies and a show enacted by life-size automata representing the American presidents. This was the big idea Walt wanted.

Like Edison Square, Liberty Street was subsumed into the package of Disney surprises unveiled at the 1964 World's Fair, where a walking, talking, Audio-Animatronics® Abe Lincoln with plastic skin startled America by rising from his chair and, on electronic cue, delivering a speech. In Florida's Magic Kingdom, Liberty Square, based on the drawings prepared for Disneyland, eventually became the setting for the robot-inhabited Hall of Presidents. But the script and some of the actual recordings seem to have been completed much earlier, in 1960, under Walt's direct supervision. At that time, the plan still called for a colonial village off Disneyland's Main Street, to demonstrate exactly how progress worked by setting up a contrast between the handmade

77. Comparative study of heights of Disney castles for Anaheim (the smallest), Orlando (also adapted for Tokyo Disneyland), and Disneyland Paris (not built in this form). Ahmad Jafari. Marker on brownline. 26 x 22. 1986.

EDL. FANTASYLAND CASTLE
ELEVATION 1/8"=1'-0" 3/12/86

goods sold in the silversmithery and the cabinetmaker's shop and the machine-made goods in the turn-of-the-century emporium. With the introduction of other times and places, Main Street would have acquired new, public significance as a marker in historical time.

A third zone scheduled to be carved out alongside Main Street in 1956, 1957, and 1958 was the never-actually-built International Street, the distant ancestor of EPCOT's World Showcase (Fig. 85). The concept here seems to have been a contrast between the American village, abustle with commerce and perfumed with a faint whiff of gasoline fumes, and the architecture of other countries, whose assorted thatched roofs and Ionic columns were of somewhat less recent vintage. The facades were ingeniously arranged so that from a vantage point halfway down the block, the viewer could see France by looking south and Denmark by turning in the opposite direction. Or Spain and Germany across the street, and so on, through fragmentary glimpses of Italy, England, Switzerland, and Japan.

When Walt's successors came to build their Disneylands in Japan and in France, Main

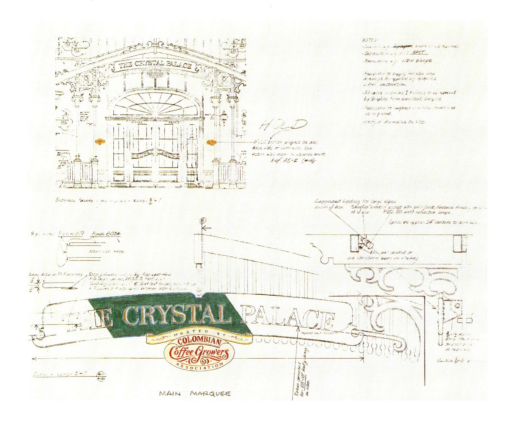

78. Color study for shop marquee, Main Street, Magic Kingdom, Walt Disney World. John Drury. Gouache, marker, pencil, and colored pencil on blackline. 19 x 24. 1984.

79. Tomorrowland monorail trains, Disneyland. John Hench. Opaque watercolor on paper; repainted in acrylic in 1994. 29 x 40. 1959.

Street presented special challenges. Thanks to the media, the whole world knew the American West, the space program, and the Disney characters. And, despite its colonialist overtones, Adventureland had sound ecological credentials: it was the place where generations of young visitors had first learned to care about nature and the preservation of animal life. But Main Street was another matter. It seemed too closely tied to Walt and his boundless faith in postwar progress to translate readily into the 1970s, 1980s, and 1990s. In Florida, where the object was to build Disneyland as it ought to have been built in the first place, with more money and better technology, there was no thought of banishing Main Street from the Magic Kingdom. But it cried out for some creative plussing. To accommodate the larger numbers of guests projected by market research, the entry passage needed to be wider. So, in order to give the desired impression of enclosure, the buildings were extruded vertically (Fig. 86). This meant that Walt's little Main Street grew up overnight, into a tall, lanky, almost-full-scale city, distinguishable from the genuine article by a greater density of decorative frou-frou, heavier moldings casting deeper shadows, and spots of intense color set off against a wedding-cake-white infrastructure—all local adaptations to the intense sunlight of central Florida (Figs. 87, 88).

In Japan, Ryman's drawings show the Imagineers wrestling with a rainy winter climate and with the question of whether Main

80. The Farmer's Market was the inspiration and namesake for an outdoor restaurant at the Disney-MGM Studios Theme Park at Walt Disney World, Florida. This is a view of the simulated Sunset Boulevard with the Farmer's Market. Andy Sklar. Pen and ink, watercolor, and opaque watercolor on paper. 20 x 26. 1991.
81. The entrance kiosk for the Disney-MGM Studios Theme Park is styled after L.A.'s Crossroads of the World. Sparkie Parker. Pen and ink, acrylic, and paint samples on blackline. 24 x 14. 1988.

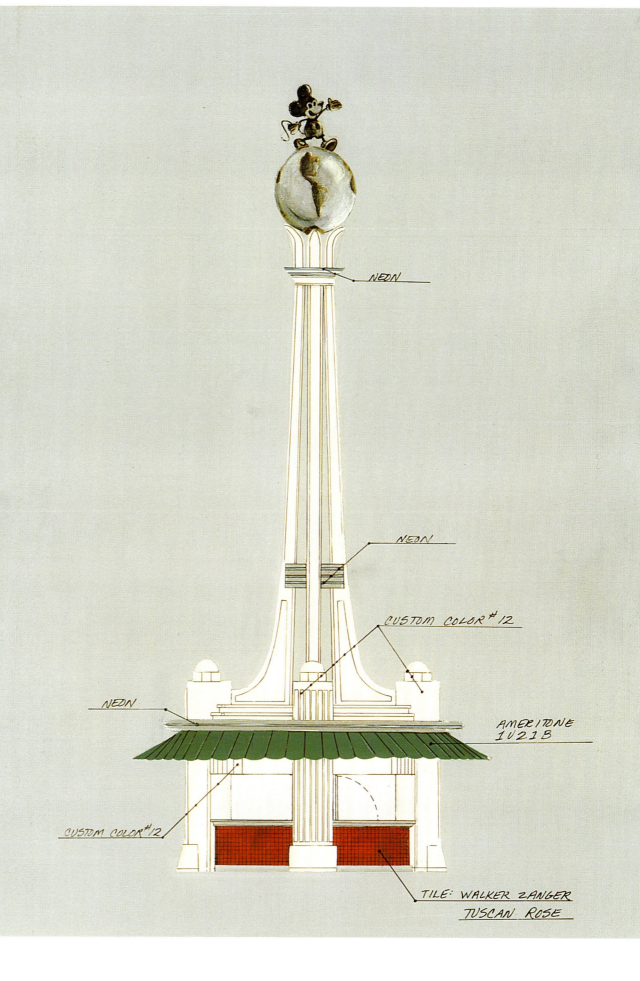

96 Designing Disney's Theme Parks

82. Mineral Hall and Cantina, Frontierland, Disneyland. Sam McKim. Pencil, opaque watercolor, and watercolor wash on brownline. 14 3/4 x 35 3/4. 1956.

Street, U.S.A. ought to go native and become a little Ginza. Some of the renderings depict a modern, multilevel shopping street, ablaze with neon, and roofed over with a glass shed that frames a distant view of the castle in an opening shaped like the profile of a traditional oriental temple (Fig. 89). After Disney's Japanese partners made it plain that they wanted a park as much like the original as possible, the roof of World Bazaar began to resemble a giant train shed or an iron-and-glass exhibition hall at a World's Fair of the 1890s, in keeping with the streetscape underneath, which was, for the most part, Victorian-American, with a half-block of Art Deco facade thrown in for good measure (Fig. 90). The Deco coffee shop of the 1930s introduced the possibility of real change to a Disney Main Street for the first time. Main Street was no longer a fixed position in time against which progress could be measured, nor was it that bright, shining moment when modern times began. In Tokyo in 1980, it was terrain through which history had marched with the passage of time, from long ago to only yesterday, before World War II changed America and Japan forever.

According to Eddie Sotto, Main Street's show producer at EuroDisney (now Disneyland Paris), in France everything was up for grabs again. Imagineering set out to reinvent Main Street according to the aesthetic and psychological needs of a European audience on a continent where every existing pleasure park had already copied Anaheim's entry motifs. Part of the appeal of the original Main Street is a perceived quaintness, Sotto argues, but it's hard to out-quaint Europe. His solution was to push Main Street in new directions. Walt's Main Street was caught in the grip of technological novelty but it never would grow up to be Los Angeles: his walkable Main Street was an unambiguous diatribe against the loss of intimacy, the alienation, and the uncontrolled growth of the contemporary city of the car. But Sotto was intrigued with a townscape that changed and matured. In the beginning, he thought the Paris Main Street ought to describe the moment when Europeans first became conscious of what America looked like by going to the movies. From gangsters and slick cars and Keystone cops and urban energy, the concept gradually toned itself down to a kind of Walt-like innocence when it was decided to use silk-screen versions of the Florida elevations as the basis for the new Main Street (Fig. 91).

Even at that, however, Paris was Main Street with a difference, as large and strident as Florida's, but infinitely more complex in design. Sotto's team larded the facades with extra millwork, drew pictures of a Main Street clogged with poles to carry electric cables, and even proposed an elevated train, riding on a fretwork of iron that nearly obscured the pretty facades behind the trestles. When these ideas were rejected—too bumptious, much too unlovely—they settled for a forest of gaudy billboards, catering to a French retro view of American consumerism, and stores whose interiors showed visible signs of remodeling as customer demand for newfangled products increased (Figs. 92, 93). Houses based on the "painted ladies" of San Francisco that European tourists longed to visit sprouted shops on their lower floors (Fig. 94): in this version of the familiar

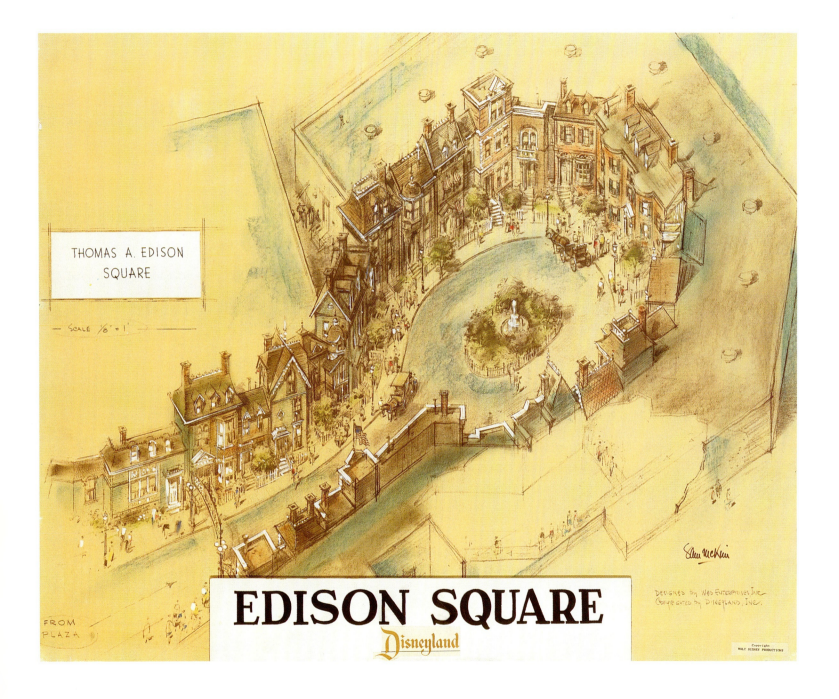

83. Planned Thomas A. Edison Square addition to Main Street area, Disneyland. Sam McKim. Colored pencil and gouache on brownline with pasted label. 26 x 32. c. 1957.

script, commerce has firmly taken command.

Additive, cluttered, and overdecorated with icons drawn from ads in popular magazines of the period, Main Street became a kind of pictograph for urban change. In one of the covered passageways behind Main Street at Disneyland Paris, built to protect shoppers from inclement winter weather, the story of the Statue of Liberty is told. The statue is a point of linkage between France and the United States in the 1880s but it is also the first tier in the layers of time Sotto and his collaborators applied to Walt's old Main Street like so many coats of makeup on an aging Parisian courtesan. This village is becoming a city. Flash forward twenty or thirty years. The old bicycle shop will soon reopen as an automotive showroom. Everything is in flux. The original Main Street, U.S.A. was built to stave off unwelcome change but Main Street Paris has lost that dewy flush of New World innocence. Like Paris proper, this Main Street knows a thing or two about what it means to be a real city, mature and wise, and subject to the caprices of history.

Mixing documentary realism with Hollywood fluff, one of Sotto's models was 20th Century-Fox's spun-sugar confection of a set for *Hello, Dolly!* But he also looked at books of photographs of Gilded Age interiors and catalogues from British firms that supplied tile and hardware for rehabilitating nineteenth-century warehouses into trendy flats. The objective was an environment that worked on two levels. The close-up shot would be rich, museumlike, full of detail, adult. The long shot—the local color—would be festive, bright, and altogether sufficient to the needs of the casual passer-by. But, like the builders of Main Streets elsewhere, Eddie Sotto also recognized the need to correlate the long, slow camera pan with the tight close-up (Figs. 95, 96). Seen from Main Street, the castle is the distant dream. The trick is to make it absolutely attainable by means of a wealth of tangible details in the foreground that lead, step by step, toward what once seemed to be only a mirage, a piece of painted backdrop, a cheap Hollywood camera trick. The Imagineer-designed Disneyland Hotel astride the entrance to the Disneyland Paris helps to make the connection clear by repeating the forms of the castle in a vocabulary of neo-Victorian shapes (see Fig. 98). Domesticated and overembellished with visual riches calibrated to the taste of the commercial

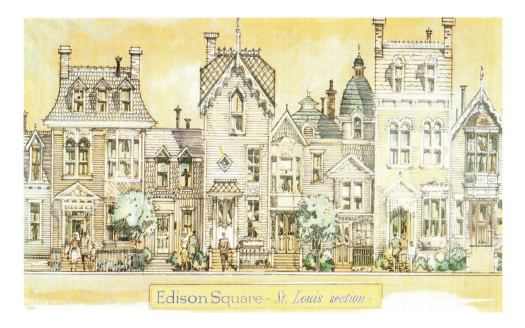

84. Saint Louis section, Edison Square, Disneyland. Sam McKim. Pen and ink and opaque watercolor on paper. 12 x 23. 1956–58.
85. Model for International Street, Disneyland, c. 1956.

traveler who has just stepped off the train at the Main Street station, the hotel nonetheless puts something of the far-off castle right here, at the head of the street. It constitutes the crucial middle distance between here and there.

In the 1950s, plans were floated for a hotel at Disneyland, to complete the streetscape of small-town America. In the 1960s, because the site was remote from major population centers and large enough to warrant an extended visit, themed hotels were integral to the plans for the Florida complex. By providing overnight accommodations and other amenities for tourists, Walt was also able to dispense with the urban blight that free enterprise had brought to Anaheim, in the form of cardboard motels and flashing signs for EATS. But the most interesting byproduct of the Florida hotels was the intrusion of Disney theming into real-life experience. At the Contemporary Hotel or the Polynesian Village, guests slept and brushed their teeth in a place that pretended to be something—some place, some time—other than what it was (Fig. 97).

The themed resort and not the gate became the point of entry to a Disney fantasy that continued beyond a single day of fun. In Paris, the Disneyland Hotel draws Main Street past the berm, past the railroad tracks, and into a complex of pathways and gardens that leads to a real train station and thus to Paris (Fig. 98). Builders of malls and the restored urban settings where T-shirts and scented soap are sold under the banner of "festival retailing" had already appropriated Main Street, U.S.A. for their own uses: pseudo-Main Streets are a fact of life in the global shopping village. Main Street at Disneyland Paris merely acknowledges the fact that an evanescent wisp of memory, a simulated movie set, a toy train village too large for its box has now stolen past the edges of Disney's assorted worlds and into the troubled heart of the dying city.

Cowboys, Artificial Rivers, and Plastic Hippos

The quadrant of Disneyland to the left of the

86. Main Street, Magic Kingdom, Walt Disney World. Collin Campbell. Acrylic on board. 27 x 48. 1969.
87. This study for the tall marquee on the front of the corner drugstore, Main Street, Magic Kingdom, Walt Disney World, shows the greater height of the Florida buildings and the use of rich, three-dimensional detail. The hot, flat light of Florida and wider street influenced these aesthetic choices. Harry Webster. Pastel and pencil on paper. 24 x 20. 1969.

Study of Drugstore Corner
Main Street Shops at Walt Disney World
Florida. U.S.A.
HJWebster 12.6.'69

102 Designing Disney's Theme Parks

BORDEN MAIN STREET ICE CREAM PARLOR

MAGIC KINGDOM—WALT DISNEY WORLD

88. Main Street elevation with Borden Ice Cream Parlor, Magic Kingdom, Walt Disney World. Ernie Prinzhorn. Silkscreen print. 27 x 37. 1969.

Hub—the whole western half of the park—is given over to the excitement endemic to liminal places where nature and civilization are competing for hegemony, with the outcome still in doubt. In Adventureland and Frontierland, the city has the barest toehold in the wilderness. What architecture there is is crude, temporary stuff for the most part, lacking both monumentality and finish. The three-deck Mississippi steamboat with its tracery of railings and black smokestacks banded in gold is the only plausible wienie in sight (Fig. 99). The rest is, or was, in 1955, a schematic rendering of pictures from a boy's book of derring-do (Fig. 100): a rickety log fort, the dusty board-and-batten street from a thousand Western second features, grass huts, native spears, and a tatty colonial outpost in a jungle where Humphrey Bogart and Katherine Hepburn would have found themselves at home (Figs. 101, x).

Verbal descriptions of Disneyland written in 1953 and 1954 link Frontierland (a.k.a. Frontier County) to the more highly developed plans for Main Street and to the ongoing miniatures project. One center of interest, therefore, was bucolic and pastoral: Granny's Farm, which was going to be stocked with a whole menagerie of live, dwarf farm animals. The other was the rootin' tootin' cowboy West. In the earliest documents, Frontierland is said to represent "a period of about 1840" by means of a slightly older rendition of Main Street, a Knott's Berry Farm village with the full cast of buildings needed to reenact the Hollywood myth of the West: the marshal's office, assay office, stage depot, general store, and the saloon (Fig. 102). Walt's own ideas of what that

89. Proposal for covered shopping concourse, World Bazaar, Tokyo Disneyland. Herbert Ryman. Marker on board. 19 x 24. 1976.
90. Unexecuted design for the entrance to World Bazaar, Tokyo Disneyland. Herbert Ryman. Marker on board. 19 x 24 1/4. c. 1976.

104 Designing Disney's Theme Parks

91. A 1969 silkscreen print of Main Street, Walt Disney World, served as the basis for the design of Main Street, Disneyland Paris, with its elevated trolley line (never built). Eddie Sotto. Brownline printed on translucent acrylic, over silkscreen print of Main Street, Walt Disney World. 21 x 30. 1987.

frontier town ought to look like came straight from the movies in the first place. When he described the ornate saloon he wanted for Frontierland, for example, Walt referred his artists to the recent Doris Day Technicolor musical, *Calamity Jane*. Deputized for duty at Disneyland's Golden Horseshoe Saloon, Harper Goff was startled to find himself copying the very saloon he himself had just designed for that Warner Bros. production in 1953.

Goff was also responsible for modeling the Jungle Cruise on a movie—specifically, *The African Queen* (1951). One of the park's unique and noteworthy rides, the Jungle Cruise was first envisioned as a "River of Romance" excursion through the Everglades and down the Swanee. By the beginning of 1953, it had been diverted to the jungles of South and Central America. But Harper Goff's drawings for the river, the foliage, the dock, the awning-topped vessels, and the Victorian boathouse with a rooftop observation tower, completed in September 1953, leave no doubt that the ride finally constructed at Disneyland was meant to let the passengers star alongside Bogart and Hepburn on their harrowing trip into film immortality (Figs. 103, 104).

In many ways, the Jungle Cruise defined what Disneyland was all about. It was a cinematic experience, an art director's pipe dream composed of curves and well-placed switchbacks that hid one part of the set from another and so preserved the illusion. It was ad hoc landscape architecture, conjured up almost overnight by the nurserymen who had worked on the grounds of Walt's house. And it was a vast, complicated experiment. After the park

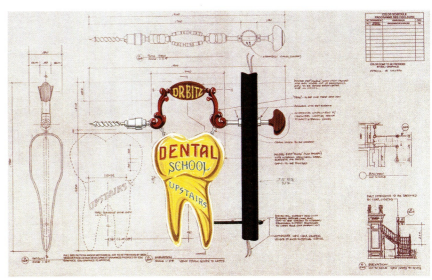

92. Interior arcade for shopping district, Disneyland Paris. Eddie Sotto. Pen and marker on paper. 23 x 26. 1986.
93. Main Street signage becomes progressively denser and more detailed: dental school signboard for Main Street, Disneyland Paris. Louis Lemoine. Gouache and pencil on brownline. 15 x 20. 1991.

Catherine Wagner. *"Molly Brown" Sidewheeler; Frontierland, Disneyland Paris, Marne-la-Vallée, France*. Collection CCA.

was a success and sophisticated refinements could finally be undertaken, landscape designer Bill Evans began to speak of "casting" vegetation for appropriate sections of Disneyland, so that the smallest detail of plant life would support the overall theme. But 1955 had found Evans and his brother a step ahead of the bulldozers clearing the route for the freeway system, scrambling to rescue any poor tree that could disguise the flat, unrelenting emptiness of what was supposed to look like a jungle come July.

While walnut trees growing on the property were being replanted upside down, with their roots now doubling as jungle vines, discussion turned to what Saturday-afternoon explorers would see from the safety of their boats. Zookeepers cautioned against using live animals. There were the usual problems of fencing and feeding to be reckoned with, and most of the exotic species that quickened the imagination were shy and nocturnal, unlikely to appear on cue to pose for the passage of the boats. And without hippos and crocodiles, the passengers were apt to notice that their boat was making a squiggly circuit of nothing at all. What Adventureland needed was a good, reliable zooful of mechanized animals that would attack every passing vessel, day after day, month after month, and never eat a tourist. Adventureland needed the Dancing Man with scales and ferocious teeth, Disneylandia rebuilt at life size.

Of all the things the critics found wanting at Disneyland in the 1950s—too few drinking fountains, too-high ticket prices, long lines at the Jungle Cruise—what they hated most were the phony animals that popped up out of the

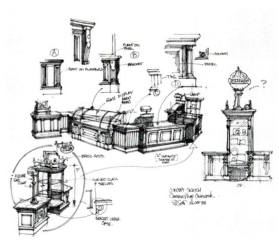

94. Southeast block, Main Street, Disneyland Paris. Joan O'Brien. Acrylic on blackline with ballpoint pen and lettraset. 15 x 31. 1990.
95. Main Street shop interior with automata, Disneyland Paris. Eddie Sotto. Acrylic and chalk on brownline. 29 x 33. c. 1987.
96. Designs for the cabinetwork in the Main Street camera shop, Disneyland Paris, reflect the influence of catalogues published by firms specializing in restoring historic buildings. Eddie Sotto. Marker on board. 16 x 20. 1988.

108 Designing Disney's Theme Parks

97. Proposal for the themed Polynesian Hotel at Walt Disney World, Florida. Welton Becket & Associates. Watercolor and ink on board. 24 x 36. 1970.

turbid green waters of a man-made Amazon (or Nile, or Mekong: the continent changed every time the boat rounded a curve) and wiggled their ears, wrinkled their snouts, raised their trunks, or bared their pointy teeth to the delight of the other passengers. Poet John Ciardi called Disneyland "Foamrubbersville" after the ersatz creatures he saw everywhere and novelist Julian Halevy, in the pages of the *Nation*, decried the fact that the Jungle Cruise wasn't the real thing. "The overwhelming feeling that one carries away is sadness for the empty lives which accept such tawdry substitutes," he lamented after steaming back to Harper Goff's dock. "On the riverboat, I heard a woman exclaim glowingly to her husband, 'What imagination they have!' He nodded, and the pathetic gladness that illuminated his face as a papier-maché [sic] crocodile sank beneath the muddy surface of the ditch was a grim indictment of the way of life for which this feeble sham represented escape and adventure."

Almost as offensive to high culture as the notion of replication—or the possibility that the audience might enjoy *The African Queen* and the Jungle Cruise more than a genuine safari—was the use of modern, inartistic materials to create crocodiles controlled by a system of underwater chains and switches. The original plastic and fiberglass animals on the Jungle Cruise fooled nobody, of course, but allowed anyone who wished to feel properly menaced the occasion for savoring that possibility. But as the technology of Disney's automata improved over the years, so did the drive to make the park into a more authentic approximation of its constituent illusions, a better, more

98. The main entrance to the Disneyland Hotel, Disneyland Paris, is also the entrance to the theme park. Jim Michaelson. Blueline. 30 x 53. 1988.
99. Bird's-eye view of Frontierland, showing Mississippi riverboat "wienie." Herbert Ryman. Brown ink and colored pencil on tissue. 21 x 39. 1954.

110 Designing Disney's Theme Parks

100. Frontierland fort, Disneyland. Frontierland restates Main Street in a Wild West idiom. Sam McKim. Pencil on paper. 20 x 39. 1955–56.

101. This charming study for a canoe ride in Florida's Frontierland captures a romantic, *Boy's Life* version of the American West. Art Riley. Acrylic on paper. 13 x 30. 1967.

artful representation of make-believe. The critics eventually got the realism they wanted, albeit in a place dedicated to improving on reality through the best available technological means.

In the space of forty years, the waterfront bazaar of Adventureland thus evolved from a series of musical-comedy grass shacks to a street that included fragments of ornate earthen facades plucked from the pages of the *National Geographic* to a knowing meditation on colonial cities where the original European-derived conventions of the imperial era have been overlaid by the corrugated iron and crude technology of the early twentieth century (Figs. 105–108). Frontierland, in the meantime, abandoned the simplicities of an image premised on cowboys and Indians and the one-horse town from some Saturday matinee for the complexities of a frontier that encompassed the adobe architecture of the Southwest, the boomtown, and, in Paris (where movies have made the French connoisseurs of the Wild West), a cattle ranch, the lonely mansion of a strike-it-rich opportunist, and a Plains Indian tepee stuffed with copies of museum-quality artifacts (Figs. 109, 110). As the camera's scrutiny of the Third World, flora and fauna, and historical sites has made an aura of authenticity harder and harder to achieve, the Disney parks have been forced to stay a jump ahead, in order to preserve the basic premise: that this is a movie, enjoyable on the same terms. That it's not a real crocodile, folks. But one whose sole purpose in pseudo-life is to entertain. To let you imagine what it might be like to be a movie star. Or the character the star impersonates. Either, or both.

The ultimate movie ride is also the newest Disneyland attraction, the Indiana Jones™ Adventure, opened in 1995 on the first curve in the river past the Jungle Cruise dock. The story

102. Pendleton Mills woolen shop, Frontierland, Disneyland. Like the Main Street stores, these board-front shops were readily tailored to the corporate image of potential lease-holders. Sam McKim. Pencil on paper. 19 3/4 x 36 1/8. Late 1954–early 1955.

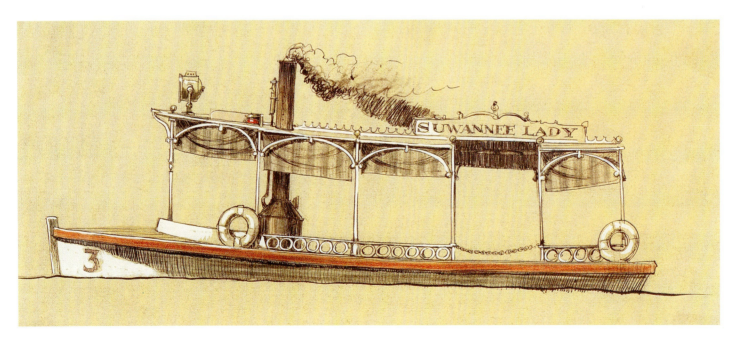

103. This fanciful Victorian design for a dock for Jungle Cruise boats has finally been fully realized in a new, two-story pre-show waiting area at Disneyland. Harper Goff. Pencil and colored pencil on brownline. 23 x 28. 1954.

104. Boat design for the Jungle Cruise attraction, Adventureland, Disneyland. Harper Goff. Opaque watercolor, pen, and conté crayon on cardboard. 10 x 22. Undated.

line comes from the popular series of films produced by George Lucas: once again, our intrepid archaeologist is off on a mission of discovery, tested at every turn by villains, snakes, and the ingenuity of ancient architects who tried to build plunder-proof repositories for the wealth secreted in their tombs and temples. The setting now is such a temple in the Lost Delta region of India, which, since it doesn't exist, cannot be faulted for inaccuracy (Fig. 111). But it seems real, anyway: an evocative composite of Mayan and Cambodian details, lost in an impenetrable jungle of Disney foliage, swathed in Indy's jerry-rigged scaffolding, and brought into temporal alignment with the rest of Adventureland (and *The African Queen*) by repeated references to the 1930s and the ragged end of empire. Technologically, this is the most advanced of the dark rides, with a computer-controlled passenger vehicle capable of movement in any direction (Fig. 112). But it is also the most architectural of all the Disney attractions, telling its story and achieving its dramatic impact through a carefully orchestrated sequence of interior and exterior spaces (Fig. 113).

The actual ride lasts for moments. Getting there, however, entails a long, complicated trek from the jungle into the ruins, through narrow passageways, along tottering corridors, up and down steep staircases, through chambers topped with domes, brightened by crumbling frescoes, or obscured in shadow (Fig. 114). Maps posted on the walls offer false directions. Suspense builds because, in contrast to the rest of the park, with its wienies and concern for absolute clarity, here the structure aims to

105. The Adventureland shops of Disneyland display an amazing architectural diversity. Authentic vernacular architecture is juxtaposed with buildings of colonial derivation, loosely based on Western prototypes. John Hench. Watercolor, chalk, and pen and ink on brownline; repainted in acrylic. 1994. 21 x 37. 1962.

106. A pollution-control device for the roof of the Adventureland restaurant at Disneyland shows that necessity is the mother of architectural invention. Han Woo Lee. Pencil on paper. 18 x 24. 1992.

confound, confuse, and stretch one's perceptions of the length of the trip into the inky heart of Indiana Jones's secret temple. Because the journey takes place indoors (and outside the berm, eventually), architecture *is* the attraction.

Columns, sculptural decoration, and mysterious inscriptions carry a story line that unfolds in space and time as the guest stumbles on, alternately squeezed into too-small spaces and isolated in too-large ones. The building is both the story and the means of telling it. When a robotic Indy finally appears to shout directions to each carload of fellow explorers, he seems profoundly redundant because his current crop of associates has already figured out the maze of ruins for themselves. They found their own separate ways into this mess— and they can find their way out again. The effect is like actually negotiating the frightful city Walt replaced with Main Street, U.S.A. in 1955—the place where danger lurked around every corner and the precise location of one's destination was always in doubt. In Adventureland in 1997, the urban experience became a metaphor for the jungle. Or vice versa.

One of the first major additions to Disneyland was New Orleans Square, a demi-land carved out of the park in 1963 as a transitional zone mediating the juxtaposition between Adventureland and Frontierland. The major attractions in New Orleans Square relied heavily on the new, lifelike Audio-Animatronics® figures—the distant offspring of the Dancing Man and the plastic crocodile— developed by Imagineering for the Disney-built corporate pavilions at the 1964 World's Fair. The Haunted Mansion, finally opened in 1969, was full of robotic ghouls observed from ride vehicles that swiveled as they moved forward, putting the passenger in the position of a moving camera that looks first in one direction and then in another. The selective or managed gaze would have permitted more efficient storytelling. But divided responsibility, time pressures, and a growing awareness of the intrinsic power of architectural space conspired to foil plans for a complex story about the Blood family, a jilted bride, and vows of eternal vengeance.

Instead, former animator Marc Davis's conception prevailed and the Mansion became a plotless fun house, a series of mildly frightening episodes, each complete in its own right. Doors belly out under the pressure of a ghostly rage confined within. Corridors recede into infinite distance. The paisley pattern on the wallpaper resolves itself into so many ferocious bats, preparing to swoop. But as the "doom buggy" winds its way up into the attic, past the vestigial bride, the scene shifts to a cemetery, outside the Mansion. The terror arises as much from the violation of the dramatic unities, the abrupt turning inside out of the building, as from the graveyard tableau itself.

In the nearby Pirates of the Caribbean, a boat ride departs from the dungeon of some island fortress and again, suddenly, it is outside, gliding past a New Orleans café at nightfall, down a waterfall, and then adrift somewhere in the Caribbean, outside and inside and underneath a sacked and burning town (Fig. 115). Each place is utterly convincing in its own right: the charred timbers smell of smoke and the flames crackle and hiss. By switching the point

107. Bird's-eye view of Casbah Square, Adventureland. Christian Hope. Watercolor, pen and ink, and colored pencil on paper. 20 x 26. 1993.
108. The show building exterior of the Indiana Jones™ Adventure, Disneyland, also shows the mixture of historic styles and ad hoc additions that makes this section of the park visually rich and evocative. Tony Mendoza. Marker and opaque watercolor on brownline. 18 x 24. 1991.

of view spasmodically from interior to exterior, however, the movie metaphor is deepened and amplified. Instead of the bookish, linear narrative of Main Street, the Mansion opts for the cinematic jump cut. Continuity and reassurance are first established and then abruptly denied, for an emotional effect that floats free of narrative and hovers in the air like the disquieting scent of a burning city.

The exterior of the Mansion was a bone of contention at Imagineering for almost a dozen years. Sam McKim and Ken Anderson both did preliminary work on the fabric of the building, emphasizing its ruinous character, while Walt kept insisting that any structure in Disneyland had to be clean and perfect: the customers expected nothing less (Figs. 116, 117). In the meantime, several search parties were dispatched to enclaves of the antebellum South to work up ideas for New Orleans Square. The first delegation arrived in the city in February 1957, as Anderson was completing his written description of a tottering "ghost house" in the Charles Addams tradition. The second, led by John Hench and Herb Ryman, came back with snapshots of the French Quarter from which the latter's evocative studies of courtyards and cafés were derived.

The album of pictures is significant because it marks the victory of documentary accuracy over romantic pictorialism. While New Orleans Square is every bit as lovely and sad as the watercolors of Ryman and Dorothea Redmond could make it, the elevations come straight from the study photographs (Fig. 118). Even the definitive design for a spanking new Haunted Mansion, completed by Marvin Davis

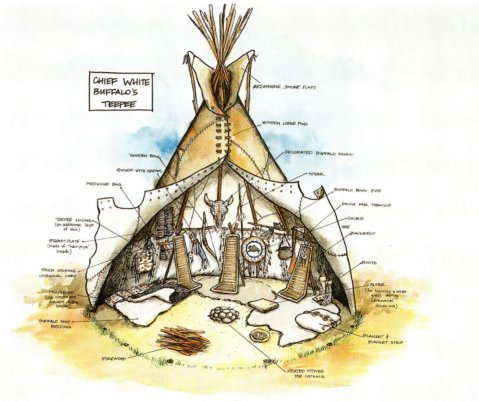

109. This study for a Western cookout barn, Disneyland Paris, adds a Midwestern, domestic component to the Wild West of Disney's Frontierlands. Katie Olson. Acrylic and colored pencil on board. 19 x 40. 1989.

110. This design for a tepee walk-through attraction, Disneyland Paris, draws on Europeans' intense and sophisticated interest in Native American artifacts. Maggie Parr. Watercolor and marker on blackline. 14 x 18. 1993.

116 Designing Disney's Theme Parks

111. Wall map, Temple of the Forbidden Eye, for interior of the Indiana Jones™ attraction, Disneyland. In this ride, architecture is the attraction. Chuck Ballew. Colored pencil, acrylic, and ink on blackline. 35 x 48. 1994.

in November of 1961, draws on a real Baltimore landmark for the ironwork, columns, and chimney pots (Figs. 119, 120). Walt was justified in telling the mayor of New Orleans, who paid a call at Disneyland to see how the West Coast version of his city was coming along, that it was going to be exactly like the real thing—only cleaner.

Walt Disney died in 1966, before the interiors of the French Quarter attractions could be finished. But during the tenth-anniversary edition of his Disneyland show, broadcast on January 3, 1965, he introduced the plans and the plusses, beginning with all the things completed since 1955: the monorail, the submarine ride, and the 150-ton, seventy-foot artificial tree built in Adventureland in 1962 to accommodate a Swiss Family Tree House based on the recent movie about the Robinson family. Then Walt took his viewers on a tour of coming attractions represented by elegant scale models, each one introduced by a proud Imagineer: Marc Davis and the picture gallery for the Haunted Mansion; Claude Coats with the town the Pirates of the Caribbean would plunder and torch; "Johnny" Hench showing off a model for the Plaza Inn, in which historic-house Victoriana with all the trimmings has superseded the slapdash historicism of the old Main Street (Fig. 121). Mary Blair presented a foam-core mock-up showing how It's a Small World (from the New York World's Fair) was going to look in Fantasyland. But Walt talked about some things himself. New Orleans Square, for instance, where a shopper could get happily lost for an hour or so in a tangle of "very intriguing" little streets (Figs. 122, 123). And the Enchanted Tiki Room in Adventureland, where space-age electronics made mechanical parrots talk and sing (Fig. 124). Where columns and pediments sang, too. Where architecture played music and vibrated to the driving rhythm of the drums.

His first reliable, full-scale automata, the Tiki birds had been an ongoing feature of Disney's television show for several years. His

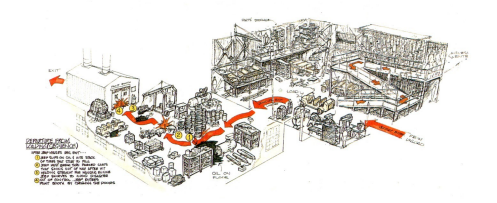

112. Ride layout for the Indiana Jones™ attraction at Disneyland, showing the passenger loading area. Dan Gluck. Marker on board. 14 x 31. 1989.

current interest in robotic birds, however, stemmed from the idea of putting a Chinatown district on or near Main Street. Imagineers Bruce Gordon and David Mumford have pieced together the tangled story of the Chinese restaurant on Center Street that was supposed to have had a talking dragon, birds in cages, and a Confucius robot to entertain guests during the meal. In the meantime, John Hench had been taking a course in restaurant management at Walt's behest and when the Chinese eatery was abandoned in 1960, found himself working on a dinner show for Adventureland instead. The idea was that the meal would last only as long as a show performed by birds, flowers (bought off-the-shelf from a supplier who sold plastic decorations to restaurants and bowling alleys), and South Seas carvings, all powered by gusts of compressed air controlled by a fourteen-channel magnetic tape, or by the same Audio-Animatronics® technology that would later make Lincoln talk and the pirates pillage (Fig. 125).

Pacific island culture was a major fad of the 1960s, touched off by Hawaiian statehood ceremonies and confirmed by Thor Heyerdahl's sailing adventure, *Kon-Tiki*, and Elvis Presley movies set at Waikiki. Polynesian food was perfect for the Disneyland experiment, according to Hench, because it was so new: except for Trader Vic and Don the Beachcomber, "nobody had definite ideas about how a Polynesian meal should proceed." So no one, presumably, would be shocked to hustle through a dinner timed to a chorus of singing machinery. But, while the Tiki Room at Disneyland still uses restaurant chairs for seating, and

113. Preliminary study for the foyer outside the labyrinth, Indiana Jones™ attraction, Disneyland. Topper Helmers. Marker on blackline. 23 x 30. 1991.

114. A color study for the ride load-unload area, Indiana Jones™ Adventure, Disneyland, shows the use of space to create feelings of anxiety and to support the illusion that the visitor has walked deep into the ruins of a real temple. Jenna Frere. Acrylic on black board. 36 x 43. 1994.

Imagineering the Disney Theme Parks 119

115. Interior set for Audio-Animatronics® figures, Pirates of the Caribbean attraction, Disneyland. Marc Davis. Opaque watercolor and pen and ink on brownline. 20 x 33. 1965.

a coffee service station in the middle of the room is the stage for the fountain finale, the dinner-theater concept was discarded at the last minute and the place opened instead as a quirky, mysterious show.

The audience filtered in and sat down around the outside of a hollow square, facing inward. The lights went down. Bits of interior decoration—birds on perches, baskets of giant orchids—began to croon. A fountain rose out of the floor in the center of the room and added to the chorus. Then the figures carved into the wooden posts opened their mouths, rolled their eyes, and chanted (Fig. 126). Lintel statues drummed. The lights went out. Outside the windows, lightning flashed and rain pelted down in torrents. Then the storm passed. The doors flung themselves open. The Tiki hut fell silent. And the audience filed back out into Adventureland. The building was the show; architecture as high drama. That's all there was.

Fantasyland

Along with Main Street, Fantasyland was the part of Disney's park that got the most attention in the planning stages. Like Main Street, it held deep personal significance for Walt: the amusements in Fantasyland alluded to the full-length animated features that were his unique contribution to movie-making. *Snow White* and *Peter Pan* and *Alice in Wonderland* were real films, not cartoon shorts, and Mickey Mouse, a holdover from the days when the studio made short subjects full of gags, only acquired a permanent home in Disneyland in 1993, with the opening of Mickey's Toontown.

116. Proposed front and side elevations for the Haunted Mansion, New Orleans Square, Disneyland. Sam McKim. Watercolor and crayon on brownline. 19 x 34. 1957.

117. Proposal for the Haunted Mansion, New Orleans Square, Disneyland. Sam McKim, painting on a copy of a Ken Anderson rendering. Watercolor, opaque watercolor, and ink on photostat. 16 x 19 3/4. 1958.

118. Detail of a building, New Orleans Square. Dorothea Redmond. Gouache and pencil on blueline. 10 x 14. 1965.

122 Designing Disney's Theme Parks

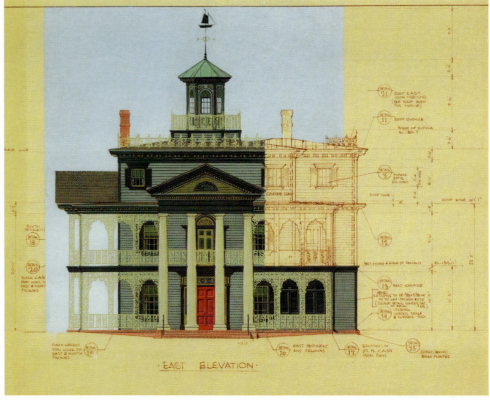

119. South elevation, Haunted Mansion, New Orleans Square. Marvin Davis. Pencil on paper. 24 x 21. 1961.
120. Color diagram for painting the Haunted Mansion, Disneyland. Anonymous. Gouache and pencil on brownline. 19 x 23. Before 1963.

The features, on the other hand, were solid accomplishments in Walt's own eyes, and worthy of commemoration in a land of their own.

Familiar to children all over the world, they were also full of highly marketable icons. But it was no easy task to build a place that took advantage of public affection for Disney's animated classics. The lovable characters were mice and dwarfs and puppets and baby elephants, hard to represent in three dimensions and wildly inconsistent in scale. Apart from the ubiquitous castle for living happily ever after in, there was no single, obvious architectural signature of the Disney filmography, either (Fig. 127). Fantasyland presented problems architecture had never been asked to solve before. So, if the art directors and the architects held sway elsewhere, Fantasyland rapidly became the preserve of the animators.

Claude Coats, who had done backgrounds and color styling for *Fantasia*, *Dumbo*, and the other early features, also worked on most of the original rides for Fantasyland. And he saw a direct relationship between inspirational watercolors commissioned by Disney to set the tone for the fairy-tale features, the models built after them, and the character of Disneyland. Coats attributed the overall scale of Fantasyland and the vaguely Bavarian courtyard behind the castle to the children's book illustrator Gustaf Tenggren, whose popular books influenced the once-upon-a-time look of several Disney films on which he worked. Just as Walt had wanted to move Ward Kimball's train station to the park, so the animators working on Fantasyland tried (and failed) to find a

121. Imagineer Claude Coats, a Disneyland "ambassador," and Walt Disney discuss a model for the Pirates of the Caribbean attraction during filming of a TV show, November 1964 (top left).

122. Walt Disney displays a model of New Orleans Square, c. 1964–65 (top right).

123. Café for New Orleans Square. Marc Davis. Watercolor with pen and ink on paper. 16 x 19. 1963 (bottom).

124. Bird's-eye view of the waiting area outside the Enchanted Tiki Room, Disneyland. John Hench. Opaque watercolor on brownline. 30 x 34. 1963.

suitable venue for a Tenggren-designed puppet theater from *Pinocchio*. If they could have managed it, Fantasyland would have looked exactly like a Tenggren watercolor, Coats thought. A Tenggren watercolor with interiors by Albert Hurter, the genius behind the highly animated inanimate objects—an organ, a kitchen pump, a collection of clocks—that made the on-screen houses of Geppetto and the Seven Dwarfs so appealing (Figs. 128, 129, vi).

The chronic cash shortage mandated another solution in 1955. The chief structural components of Fantasyland were prefabs, disguised as a uniform series of medieval tents, decorated with pennants and ribbons to match King Arthur Carrousel in the middle of the space. But the dark rides within these buildings, which depicted the interiors and exteriors needed to tell the stories of Snow White, Mr. Toad, and Peter Pan, had very little in common with the much-admired Tenggren-Hurter style. Instead of the rounded corners and cozy, highly wrought atmospherics of the early animated features, photographs of the rides show canvas flats painted in a modern, stylized shorthand, a fleeting squiggle of the brush across a rough rectangle signifying the elaborate carving of a mantelpiece Hurter would have rendered in hypnotic detail. The broad strokes were good theater—and a lot cheaper than three-dimensional scenery. The mine cars and pirate ships moved so quickly that passengers had no chance to linger over detail anyway; they had to grasp the meaning of a given setting in the blink of an eye. But the quasi-Cubism of the flats was also a style being practiced at the Disney studio in the 1940s and 50s.

Although histories of animation often fault Disney for a relentless drive toward a monolithic realism that put the studio out of synch with experimental work being done in the period by UPA and other, smaller studios, realism was not the trademark of the Disney product during the park's formative years. Short subjects and features alike displayed considerable variety, especially in the design of backgrounds. One source for the flat, abstract treatment of the surroundings in which fully rounded characters operated was Mary Blair, the gifted stylist who accompanied Walt's party to Latin America in 1941 (see Fig. 149). Several films on which she subsequently worked—*The Three Caballeros* (1945), *The Adventures of Ichabod and Mr. Toad* (1949), and *Alice in Wonderland* (1951)—use strong geometric patterns for backgrounds, with foliage or architecture indicated in a cursory way by elegant linear designs drawn over the color fields.

Salvador Dalì, who also worked for Disney briefly in the 1940s, used similar devices in the fifteen seconds of film he completed during his stay in Burbank. *Alice*, the most surrealist and Daliesque of the Disney features, actually identified hallucinatory illusions via abstraction: the world of England and sunshine and kittens is as cuddly as any scene in *Snow White*, but once our heroine falls down the

125. Study of interior nave, the Enchanted Tiki Room, showing robotic birds. The performing parrots were Walt Disney's first fully realized examples of three-dimensional animation. John Hench. Opaque watercolor on brownline; repainted in acrylic in 1994. 18 x 23. 1963.

TENOR

BARITONE

BASS

126. Study for animated war god column, Enchanted Tiki Room. The building itself performs and sings. Marc Davis. Watercolor and ink on paper. 16 5/8 x 13 1/4. 1963.

rabbit hole, an interlocked grid of discordant background color bisected by an energetic line signifies the unreal. In the dark rides at Disneyland, this distinctive shorthand style for backgrounds proved both practical—fast and cheap—and important for maintaining the complex illusion that one was careening through the English countryside in a Disney cartoon about the fabulous Mr. Toad.

The gestalt of shape always figures in Disney architecture—how circles and towers make the viewer feel. But the notational style of the 1950s often tells the audience exactly how to interpret a given building, too. Bruce Bushman's working drawings for the Casey, Jr. attraction illustrate the point (Fig. 130). Casey, Jr. is a small-scale railroad that operates within the confines of Fantasyland, overlooking miniature replicas or models of Toad Hall, Geppetto's workshop, and the other buildings seen in the Disney animated features. Like the mine train in Frontierland and the monorail in Tomorrowland, this railroad restates the core themes of Disneyland in another guise. The world of the Western. The world of science fiction. And now, the world of animation. Bushman's line sketches are whimsical, fun, and clearly just drawings, not recreations of some real-world place. Everything is a little too tall or not quite straight, tipsy and skewed, as though both train and station could toot away down the track without human agency (Fig. 131). And the Casey, Jr. station was built to the exact specifications of the drawing, a wackier, happier version of Ward Kimball's depot, as though the sketch had escaped into real life and taken root, without a straight line in evidence (Figs. 132–134).

Storybook Land, the garden of miniature trees and shrubs below Casey, Jr. where the little houses stand, is considered by some to be Walt Disney's last will and testament to Disneyland, his template for what the whole of Fantasyland should have looked like had the money not run out. The little houses—Toad Hall, the cottages of the Three Little Pigs, Peter Pan's London, the castle of Cinderella's prince—were fiberglass stand-ins, models for full-scale buildings to be erected later (Figs. 135, 136). And the structures themselves were models, built in the Burbank model shop after sketches by Ken Anderson (Fig. 137). Sometimes the model makers got actual blueprints from the draftsmen back at the studio, but they were so out of scale and so peculiar looking that the craftsmen generally "eyeballed" the buildings instead. For there was a vast distance between a film set, a baronial hall, and a cartoon version of same.

When the park opened for business in July of 1955, Storybook Land did not. Canal Boats of the World gave tours of dirt and bare grass until the buildings could be properly eyeballed into alignment with the relative size of the nearby train and mated with a suitable array of tiny plant life. Finally, with much attendant hoopla, the remodeled boats began to glide past the new background scenery of Storybook Land in 1956. The Mouseketeers from Disney's afterschool TV show—Darlene, Bobby, Sharon, and Lonnie—were on hand for the festivities. On the *Mickey Mouse Club*, the backgrounds were blatantly bogus, stiff constructions of painted canvas that enhanced the day's activities but remained subordinate to them. The Mouseketeers were meant to be the center of attention, as they danced and sang. The scenery was, well—scenery. The entrance to a mine. A ranch. A kitchen made of brushstrokes and broad swaths of color applied to geometric shapes that did little more than suggest the outlines of tables, wooden beams, or fencing. It was cartoon scenery at the farthest end of the aesthetic spectrum from the houses of Storybook Land, with their real copper roofs and stained glass windows and brass hinges.

In 1956, all the dark rides looked like the *Mickey Mouse Club* and Casey, Jr. But Casey chugged and puffed his way through a Storybook Landscape conceived in a different style, in which backgrounds were just as important as foregrounds, and there was no clear distinction between what the viewer half-noticed in passing and what lay at the center of the field of vision. In Storybook Land, the tiny architecture seemed so real, so complete, so right, that the viewer looked profoundly wrong for the space. Out of scale. Unreal. Or not as real, in any case, as the little Toad Hall.

Buildings and 'Toons

In the late 1980s, as the venerable Mickey Mouse approached his sixtieth birthday, it was noted with some embarrassment that the chief corporate spokesman for the theme parks had no home of his own inside Disneyland. There was no cunning little Mickey house next door to Toad Hall. The reasons are varied. Walt tried and failed to find a permanent clubhouse or tree house for the *Mickey Mouse Club* inside the berm in the early years, when the Mouseketeers were at the height of their popularity

127. Studies for castles in Fantasyland, perhaps interior sets for the Peter Pan Flight, Disneyland. Claude Coats (?). Pen and ink on tissue. 18 3/4 x 23 7/8. 1955.
128. Concept sketch for a Storybook Gardens attraction, Tokyo Disneyland. The cute, cuddly storybook style of the early Disney animated classics remains wildly popular in Japan and has exerted a strong influence on the architecture of Tokyo Disneyland. Mona Koth. Acrylic on board. 30 x 40. 1992–93.
129. An *Alice in Wonderland*-themed shop for Fantasyland, Disneyland. Bruce Bushman. Colored pencil on brownline. 17 1/8 x 22 1/8. 1954.

128 Designing Disney's Theme Parks

130. Early proposal for the Casey, Jr. Circus Train ride, Fantasyland, Disneyland. Bruce Bushman. Colored pencil on brownline. 19 x 24. 1954.

(Fig. 138). But the best explanation seems to be that Walt was tired of the mouse, that he equated Mickey with the old black-and-white cartoon days, before the advent of the animated features showcased in Fantasyland. At Disneyland, Mickey, Minnie, Donald, Goofy, and the other Disney stars of the cartoon era were always treated like visitors. They rode in parades and shook hands on Main Street but at night they went home, to an imaginary toontown somewhere near the old Hyperion Avenue studio.

As Mickey made the change from cheeky rodent to club mascot, smiling ambassador of good will, and cheery T-shirt emblem, he became more appealing to children. When kids came to a Disney park, they wanted to meet Mickey. For the anniversary year, the solution was a temporary Birthdayland at the Magic Kingdom in Florida. The long-term answer was Mickey's Toontown, or Main Street, U.S.A. for old cartoon characters, with a city hall, a row of downtown shops, a trolley, a train, a clock tower wienie, and a sedate residential suburb all built in a slightly lopsided, screwy style that reflected the antic energy of the cartoons once made to be shown between the halves of the double feature (Fig. 139). What that cartoon city might have looked like was explored in the 1988 movie hit, *Who Framed Roger Rabbit*, a Steven Spielberg production in which the cartoon royalty from several studios came back for a last hurrah. The first of the lands to be constructed wholly outside the berm, on a narrow crescent of property at the top of the old Disneyland map, Mickey's Toontown was an effort to rethink the relationship between

131. Casey, Jr. locomotive, Fantasyland, Disneyland. Bruce Bushman. Pencil on paper. 12 x 18. 1955.
132. Ticket booth/station for Casey, Jr. ride, Fantasyland, Disneyland. The station is a cubist version of animator Ward Kimball's backyard depot. Bruce Bushman. Pencil on paper. 19 x 24. 1955.

architecture and fantasy, between animation and the theme park (Fig. 140).

Joe Lanzisero was in charge of conceptual development for Mickey's Toontown. A practicing animator until he became an Imagineer in 1987, Lanzisero brought that perspective to his new job. And while the notion of a cartoonist building an attraction would not have been a peculiar one in the 1950s, when it was standard operating procedure for self-made park "architects" to come from the animation department, things had changed considerably by 1991, as the Toontown project got underway. During the EPCOT era, the architects got the upper hand: their task had been to create two sets of conventional, monumental buildings in Florida, one based on new corporate office park design and the other on existing historical landmarks. The result was felt in plans for additions and alterations to the other parks. Instead of story, imagination, and emotion-laden atmosphere, the process now appeared to be driven by the need to build actual sock-'em-in-the-eye landmarks—substantial, memorable buildings.

The redesign of Anaheim's Fantasyland, undertaken piecemeal in the 1970s and completed in 1981–82 when the area was closed and gutted, replaced the old flat-fronted prefab facades with richly three-dimensional blow-ups of the little buildings in Storybook Land. Mr. Toad's Wild Ride was now inside a magnificent new Toad Hall superstructure, bristling with chimneypots and coats of arms, and even the ride experience was altered by the substitution of three-dimensional props for much of the old painted scenery. Snow White fled from the witch inside a splendid castle. And Pinocchio became the subject of a brand new ride, housed in a perfect Tenggrenesque workshop that was dark but absolutely unterrifying. The whole thing was as sweet and cute as a freckle-faced four-year-old licking a lollipop. As such, the character of the New Fantasyland has had a strong appeal for the designers of Tokyo Disneyland: in Japan the cuteness factor or *kawaii* amounts to a cultural obsession, fed by plans for Fantasyland enhancements that leave no item of interior decor unadorned and no exterior un-Tenggrened (see Fig. 128).

Hyperrealism and scrupulous fidelity to the background art for Disney features marked one viable approach to the architecture of animation. But Joe Lanzisero noted that the backgrounds in Mickey cartoons of the 1930s and 1940s seldom seemed "cartoony" enough for Mickey's Toontown (Fig. 141). Putting cartoon characters in dull, straight-edged, believable places had given them an emotional reality that was unique to the Disney corpus. But he was more interested in the stylized, attitude-laden backgrounds of Mary Blair and Eyvind Earle because Mickey's Toontown was not a mere background. Despite the opportunity to have the kids' photos taken with Mickey, Toontown was the show, the entertainment, the thing that people came to see. Like a Blair background, it needed to speak for itself in color and shape. The houses needed architectural personalities consistent with the characters who lived there: goofy for Goofy, of course; solid and sunny for Mickey; fussy, frilly, and pastel-toned for Minnie (Fig. 142). But lacking any real guidance from the movies themselves, how do you build a cartoony house?

Lanzisero went back to the basic principles of reassurance, to the correlation between shape, gesture, and feeling—in this case, the simple, cartoon repertory of circles and angles, sag and stretch, stop and go. Ex-animators now studied houses as they once studied the way a duck's tail can convey impatience. Buildings struck attitudes, like Donald and Mickey did, but they didn't make faces: the Toontown team agreed that structures would look like frozen statues if they exaggerated the facial expressions that all buildings seem to have. And Mickeys' Toontown was made to be seen in motion, as guests explored the rooms of the

133. Frontierland station at Disneyland, styled after Ward Kimball's Grizzly Flats depot.

134. Casey, Jr. station, Disneyland, 1989.

Imagineering the Disney Theme Parks **131**

houses and shopped in the little Hub where the trolley turned around.

When the business of building Mickey's Toontown finally began in earnest, the show designers did the first rough drawings in the happy, bulbous shapes of a 1940s or 1950s Mickey, and the architectural group made it all real by checking for compliance with codes and making sure there was room inside for the intended human functions (Fig. 143). The image, to the Imagineers, was infinitely more important than the process. Architecture was a means to an end. The crunch came on the site. Contractors and architects knew how to do things in a certain way and elsewhere in the park, a window casing, even if it was a window for Toad Hall or a Wild West saloon, had some counterpart in the builder's catalogue. Fantasyland had legitimate right angles. But such was not the case in Mickey's Toontown (Fig. 144).

The usual architectural plans had been drawn by the unusual expedient of making models from the sketches, photographing the models to scale, and then tracing off an elevation. Conventional two-dimensional plans proved useless in the field, however. Eventually, Lanzisero had to carry models to the worksite in Plexiglas boxes so that the unusual angles and shapes could be studied in three-dimensions by the framers and plasterers who were struggling to duplicate the plans (see Fig. xii). Often, art directors and workers arrived at on-the-spot solutions, after the former had literally drawn guidelines for difficult details on the plywood substructure in spray paint or marker. Marty Sklar, Vice-Chairman and Principal Creative Executive of Walt Disney Imagineering, is quoted as saying with some pride that 70 percent of the work on the parks is done in the field. It is a mark of honor, a sign that the original creative process still works. At Mickey's Toontown, the figure was closer to 90 percent.

The cinematic approach to architecture succeeds or fails with the first establishing shot. Being outside the berm gave Lanzisero a built-in means of framing the observer's first perceptions of the place by the use of a sunken entry. The road to Mickey's Toontown dips under Disney's peripheral railroad track, temporarily blocking the vista. A clump of signs—for a 'toon Rotary and other service clubs—signals the existence of a town. But the bizarre streetscape comes as a pie-in-the-face surprise, when it finally reveals itself on the uphill slope beyond the underpass. The establishing shot in this cartoon adventure is of the slam-bam variety, like the opening of a vintage Warner Bros. chase cartoon (see Figs. 140, 141).

The location of Mickey's Toontown in the "backstage" area of Disneyland also meant that Anaheim became part of the view. Although all the town's large buildings were lined up opposite the entry to block the horizon, hotels and signs still peeked over the roofline and spoiled the illusion. In the model stage, the designers tried a series of cut-out buildings in the background, as abstract as any Mary Blair composition, but the flat architectural symbols fought with the three-dimensional intensity of the built architecture in the foreground. The solution was a picture of what the landscape of suburban Toontown ought to look like, or a set of visual intrusion flats that mimic the puffy hills of the comic pages and parody the Hollywood sign with a parade of alphabet-soup letters that spell out the word TOONTOWN (Fig. 145). The painted flats behind Mickey's Toontown are poignant reminders that

135. Construction of the Pinocchio village in Storybook Land, Disneyland, visible from Casey, Jr. tracks.

136. Toad Hall, Storybook Land, Disneyland.

137. Walt Disney and model maker Harriet Burns confer about the Seven Dwarfs' cottage for Storybook Land, c. 1956.

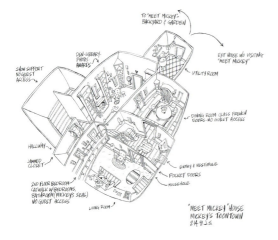

Fantasyland began with the art of animation and with just such flats, flashing by in the darkness and telling a story by means of shape and color alone.

It's a Small World after All

In geographic terms, the closest major attraction to Mickey's Toontown is the Small World boat ride, just past the railroad tracks ('toons live on the *wrong* side of them!), on the back edge of Fantasyland. In terms of stylistic innovation and a radical approach to the social construction of architecture, Mickey's Toontown can be seen as a 1990s version of what was once Pepsi-Cola's pavilion at the 1964 New York World's Fair—It's a Small World, also dubbed "The Happiest Cruise in the World." At Disneyland today—and more especially in Tokyo and Paris—passengers set sail from a building encrusted with kinetic rotors and pinwheels, spinning away against a Louise Nevelson-like construction of flat, fragmentary geometric shapes which, when scrutinized more closely, turn out to be references to famous architectural landmarks of the world: the Eiffel Tower, the Leaning Tower of Pisa, the dome of the Taj Mahal (Fig. 146). Inside, in quasi-darkness, guests see several hundred identical child-dolls in varied national costumes dancing in dreamlike settings that employ the same kind of notational symbols to identify their places of origin. But whether they pose in front of a pyramid or an onion dome, the smiling figures all look just alike because, in the words of the song that plays incessantly throughout the voyage, "It's a small world after all!".

Pepsi had approached the Disney organization in search of a ride in the spring of 1963, dangerously close to opening day. Pepsi had agreed to sponsor a display publicizing UNICEF, the United Nations Children's Education Fund, and now, suddenly, with third- and fourth-generation Audio-Animatronics® figures for the Ford, General Electric, and the State of Illinois pavilions misbehaving in every spare corner assigned to Imagineering, Walt agreed to bail out Pepsi. Messengers were sent back to New York with blueprints for a huge, L-shaped building in hand. At that point, however, nobody—including Walt—knew what was going to be inside (Fig. 147). The attraction finally opened at Flushing Meadow with a totally undistinguished billboard facade, similar to the Fantasyland prefabs at Anaheim. Only Walt Disney's name in big red letters guaranteed that it would be worth coming in for a look.

The ride proper was a collaborative project. Marc Davis worked on sweetly funny details that enlivened the trip—a trio of Dutch geese that quacked in time to the music, a five-year-old Cleopatra. Claude Coats laid out the path of the global river that carried the boats. Rolly Crump worked on the animated toys scattered throughout the scenery, as well as the 120-foot Tower of the Four Winds, incorporating fifty-two separate mobiles, that stood outside and hinted obliquely at the unusual sights to be seen inside the bland industrial shell. A giant sculpture that met building codes, it was reminiscent of the work of Jean Tinguely. Neither representational in its details nor part of the one-world narrative of the ride, it was an

138. Cutaway view of Mickey's House, Mickey's Toontown, Disneyland. Until Toontown was built, Walt Disney's best-loved character had no permanent home in any of the theme parks. Jim Shull. Pen and ink on board. 19 x 24. 1991.

139. Toon Town Hall clock tower, Mickey's Toontown, Disneyland, is another urban "wienie," helping to clarify the space of the new land. Rennie Marquez. Colored pencil on paper. 19 x 16. 1991.

Catherine Wagner. *Minnie Mouse's Kitchen; Mickey's Toontown, Disneyland, Anaheim, California.* Collection CCA.

abstract composition that was endlessly fun to look at. A puzzle. A wonderment. A glorious folly.

The abstraction of the exterior was matched on the interior by the national and regional environments in which the dolls spun and twirled like Crump's mobiles. The dolls themselves, with their snub noses, big heads, and tiny features, came directly from a series of Hallmark note cards designed under the Walt Disney label by Mary Blair in the 1940s (Fig. 148). One set used country themes tied to the release of *So Dear to My Heart* (1949). Another was based on places Blair visited during her Latin American junket with Disney. What the subjects had in common was intense, sometimes dissonant color, simple shapes, and children with the huge heads of infants. It's a Small World inherited Blair's Modernist approach to form and color along with her cute-as-a-button figures. It's a Small World is the International Style applied to the task of storytelling and painted in psychedelic colors.

Blair is usually credited with the color scheme for the ride. But as her other projects for the theme parks show, this color stylist's job went far beyond the decision to use families of saturated reds—ranging from oranges through violet to cerise—in "hot" regions of the Small World (Fig. 149). Her deployment of specific mood-setting colors in large, unmodulated areas, often intensified by the complementary shades of graphic overlays, amounted to a working definition of flower-child "mod" design in the 1960s and was enhanced by the specific repertory of forms to which that color was applied. So the reflecting pool in front of a

140. The entrance to Mickey's Toontown was carved out under the berm and the peripheral railroad tracks. Don Carson. Dr. Martin's dye on paper. 15 x 32. 1992.

141. Toontown Square, Disneyland: another Main Street complex—for 'toons only. Rennie Marquez. Colored pencil on paper. 14 x 40. 1991.

142. This early concept study for Mickey's Toontown revolves around a series of distinctive character houses. It is Main Street domesticated. Scott Baker. Acrylic on board. 33 x 40. 1989.

143. Mickey Mouse's House, Mickey's Toontown. Linda Parker, on an elevation by Oscar Cobos. Acrylic, gouache, mylar, and lettraset on blueline. 20 x 30. 1992.

lavender and lime-green Taj Mahal is a lopsided rectangle that is also the chief constituent element of every other angular cutout in this little world, just as all domes and circles have egg-shaped profiles and all arches are taller than they are wide and slightly unsteady on their stork-like legs. The buildings seem to be collages, made of colored paper that comes in a standard set of colors and shapes. Not quite pictures of buildings but not quite buildings either, the settings of It's a Small World match the childhood theme with an environment that could have been made by an imaginative toddler equipped with blunt scissors, paste, and a couple of cardboard boxes.

The effect of Blair's treatment of place is to make one locale a lot like another in this Small World, and to make it plain that architecture is a kind of universal principle that changes only by degrees from Paris to Istanbul to New York City. The Museum of Modern Art's 1955 *The Family of Man* exhibition, a display of photographs of people from all parts of the world caught up in common moments of joy and crisis, had made a similar point with the human face as the iconographic constant. It's a Small World articulated the theme with a limited vocabulary of abstract shapes shuffled and rearranged to form the Great Buildings of the World. Or architecture as a form of late-Cubist collage.

In 1966, with the fair over, Small World moved to Disneyland, minus the Tower of the Four Winds, which proved too costly to

144. Minnie's Kitchen, Mickey's Toontown, Disneyland. Ginnie Barr-Ruscio. Marker and colored pencil on paper. 26 x 36. 1991.

138 Designing Disney's Theme Parks

145. Mickey's House at Disneyland, with visual intrusion flats blocking views of the signs and power lines of Anaheim.

disassemble. The ride was refurbished and lengthened. The housing was also slated to be replaced by something more monumental and whimsical than its original corrugated box. Adding a clock tower with Small World dolls that popped out on the quarter hour was the easy part, and a practical replacement for the moving tower. But a solution for the rest of the facade proved more elusive.

Rolly Crump remembers the crisis occasioned by the overall conception of the exterior: after two months of work, convinced that real-world architecture was not for her, Mary Blair went home to New York in despair, leaving her drawings to the model makers. The result, however, is the planar grid still in position today, a miscellaneous collection of rectangles fitted together like the segments of a Piet Mondrian painting or the windows and supports expressed on the face of a New York skyscraper by Gordon Bunshaft (see Fig. v). Blair's later sketches for other Small World facades are actual collages made of squares of transparent plastic film glued to a backing; the presence of the medium is apparent in the see-through segments and the flat puzzle pieces that fall into place across the fronts of all of them (Fig. 150). Her master facade is a visual intrusion flat without the Toontown sign. The shapes hint at temple fronts and minarets but act like a curtain, screening off a panorama of world architecture simplified and harmonized under the aegis of internationalism. This is an architecture of squares and grids and rectangles, like the all-but-identical facades of modern office buildings in Los Angeles, Orlando, Tokyo, and the new edge cities around Paris.

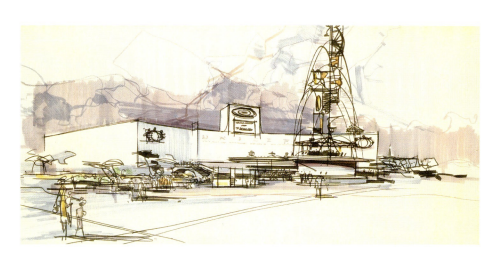

146. Color study for repainting the facade of It's a Small World, Disneyland. Jimmy Pickering. Acrylic, marker, and gold pen on blackline. 18 x 24. 1992.

147. Design for the Pepsi building at the New York World's Fair in which Disney's It's a Small World attraction was located. Herbert Ryman. Marker on paper. 18 x 40. 1963.

Cities of Tomorrow

Tomorrow has a distressing habit of catching up with daydreams about it. Or the daydreams prove wildly wrong. Either way, building a simulated future is a risky business. The New Tomorrowland—one in a long sequence of new and improved models—unveiled at Florida's Magic Kingdom in February of 1995 acknowledges the futility of the endeavor (Fig. 151). Orlando's Tomorrowland is a 1920s and 1930s version of the future, or the fantasy future that was once imagined by the visionaries who built the 1939 World's Fair. Tomorrowland in Paris, called Discoveryland, is a tribute to European genius couched in terms of the future wonders predicted by Jules Verne and H. G. Wells at the turn of the century (Fig. 152). But there is more to these retrospective tomorrows than timidity, economics, and the need to placate French critics already enraged by this latest example of American cultural hegemony. In the case of the Magic Kingdom, the design team led by Eric Jacobson found itself in hot competition with the day-after-tomorrow futurism of EPCOT, just a monorail ride away. They were also faced with the recurring charge that the Disney future worlds are cold, impersonal, and rather forbidding places, not the magical gadgetland of robotic appliances and pleasure trips to outer space envisioned by Walt Disney in 1955.

So Jacobson and his colleagues made their Tomorrowland into a funky, retro version of Mickey's Toontown or Main Street, a simulated community with a Chamber of Commerce and a Power and Light Company housed in a WPA-out-of-Peter Behrens-style turbine building. The Avenue of the Planets is ablaze with bright, warm color. The tall white rocket ship that once anchored the Disney Tomorrowlands has been replaced by a gyrating Astro Orbiter that owes its spirit of semiserious fun as much to Rube Goldberg as to NASA (Fig. 153). Walt Disney's future is there, too, in the revised and updated Carousel of Progress, a tribute to Walt's steadfast belief that with a little luck, a big corporate investment in research and development, and the consumer's continuing avidity for new household products, tomorrow was bound to be just terrific. In this latest Tomorrowland, the words of the old Carousel of Progress theme song ring a little hollow. But they didn't in 1967 when the Carousel was new. "There's a Great Big Beautiful Tomorrow!" chanted the thirty-two Audio-Animatronics® figures who demonstrated how electricity had improved the American family's standard of living since the electric fan replaced the hand-powered paper kind. Next to the Small World anthem, it was the most popular song in Disneyland in 1966 and 1967. Wow! Wasn't the future wonderful?

Built for the 1964 World's Fair—the last fair, perhaps, to take the concept of progress seriously—and sponsored by General Electric, the Carousel of Progress was the embodiment of old, unexecuted plans for an Edison Square adjacent to Main Street. At Edison Square, the visitor would have entered a presentation on the domestic improvements wrought by electricity through a series of house facades from c. 1898, when the story began. At the World's Fair, the same idea was treated in a

148. A Hallmark note card designed by Mary Blair for the Walt Disney Art series, c. 1948.
149. Stylist Mary Blair at work on It's a Small World attraction, Pepsi-Cola pavilion, New York World's Fair, c. 1963.

Imagineering the Disney Theme Parks 141

150. Facade concept design for It's a Small World, Magic Kingdom, Walt Disney World. Mary Blair. Collage with colored plastic film. 15 x 20. 1969.

different format; interiors from various eras from 1898 through the late twentieth century were recreated on segments of a central circular platform around which six moving theaters slowly revolved (Figs. 154, 155). The common factor was the home.

When the show came back to Disneyland for an extended run, it was installed in a building that resembled a flying saucer barely tethered to earth by the swoop of a slender boarding ramp. In 1965, Welton Becket's firm had prepared a series of drawings suggesting ways to integrate the support pylons for the monorail system with a dynamic new look for Tomorrowland; the new Carousel of Progress building, as the centerpiece of the refurbished future, was inspired by those Becket renderings (Fig. 156). But the exhibits inside the Carousel were less dramatically futuristic. Instead of the space-colony imagery of the exterior, they looked back to Edison Square and the character of the average American home.

In New York, after the audience left the rotating theater, they were invited to visit just such homes in a town called Medallion City. Medallion City was a mock-up of an ideal all-electric subdivision of 1964: the future had already arrived, it seemed, and awaited the pleasure of the consumer at the nearest appliance retailer (Figs. 157, 158). In Anaheim, the finale was buoyantly utopian. The audience boarded a moving "speedramp" to Progress City, a 115-foot-wide diorama with fourteen hundred working street lights, twenty-five hundred moving vehicles, and more than forty-five thousand structures so detailed that the interiors were finished even when they were

151. Nighttime on the Avenue of the Planets in the "New" Tomorrowland, Magic Kingdom, Walt Disney World. Steve Anderson. Computer-generated color printout highlighted in acrylic. 29 x 46. 1992.

152. Entrance to Videopolis, Discoveryland, Disneyland Paris. Michael Marquez. Acrylic, pen, and watercolor on paper. 15 x 22. 1988.

not fully visible from the outside. According to a 1967 report issued by WED Enterprises, "the overall design of . . . Progress City is based on a concept developed by Walt Disney for the Experimental Prototype Community of Tomorrow, EPCOT, which he had planned for . . . Florida."

With Progress City, Walt had clearly left the theme park behind. He was ready to build a real city with an airport, a nuclear power plant, a greenbelt full of schools and churches and split-level homes, an industrial park where General Electric could test new rocket engines, and, in the center, a thirty-story hotel from which was suspended a transparent canopy sheltering the downtown area (Fig. 162). And an amusement park, of course. The plans for the "scenic cyclorama" of Progress City show a radiant layout, a garden city of residential cul-de-sacs set in greenery unspoiled by the rumble of traffic. Cars have been replaced by electric carts and various forms of rapid transit that converge noiselessly on the center (Figs. 159, 161). Trucks enter the city through underground passageways; unseen and unheard, they discharge their cargo in a vast common basement corridor (Fig. 160). Up above, all is rational, beautiful, and calm. Planes and factories keep their distance from houses and schools. The circles and ovals of the ground plan suggest a place with a center, or heart—a true community. Or a place something like Disneyland, wheeling placidly around a central hub as the music softly plays. Welcome to Progress City, where the lyrics come to life and there will always be "A Great Big Beautiful Tomorrow!" thanks to Walt and his Imagineers.

Tomorrowlands

If Disneyland as a whole—its spatial reassurances and human scale, its concern for providing visual pleasure, its walkability and fanatical cleanliness—was a critique of Los Angeles and the modern city, then Tomorrowland was supposed to be the spot where solutions to urban problems were dramatized. A place where Walt could try to articulate a future so compelling that his guests and their children would want to go home and make it all come true, down to the moving sidewalks and the dancing fountains. But Tomorrowland almost didn't happen. Late in 1954, that part of Disneyland was still empty. There were moody drawings for monorails whooshing through a city comprising odd, spherical and elliptical buildings raised on stilts (Figs. 163, 165). But there were no actual monorails and no buildings at all.

The last themed area to be constructed (often before the more prosaic working drawings were finished), Tomorrowland's lack of content was disguised on opening day by lots of balloons. For the next decade, it limped along as a collection of miscellaneous details: a clock that told the time anywhere on earth, the sets used for Disney's 1953 version of Jules Verne's *20,000 Leagues under the Sea*, a rocket ship, a midget freeway system, and a clutch of off-the-shelf trade-show exhibits on the wonders of chemistry, aluminum, and modern plumbing (Fig. 164). The poor relation in the happy family of lands, Tomorrowland's architecture consisted of a double row of assorted boxes that shunned the heroic geometry of the

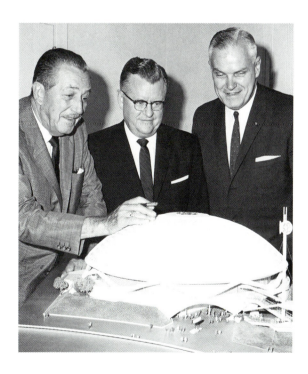

153. Model of Astro Orbiter for Walt Disney World. Steve Anderson. c. 1992–93.
154. Walt Disney examines a model of the General Electric Carousel for the New York World's Fair, designed with the help of Welton Becket. The pavilion was not built precisely as illustrated, but the design later served as the basis for the Disneyland version.

High Modernist skyscraper in favor of the roadside modernism of the vernacular. Tomorrowland was modern mainly by virtue of its aesthetic poverty: it had the fewest decorative details of any part of Disneyland. But the stark geometry of the commercial shed, as Robert Venturi would later observe, could be redecorated at will. And this was a great advantage in a place that was constantly changing in a vainglorious effort to keep up with a future that would never stand still quite long enough to solidify into meaningful architecture.

The Massachusetts Institute of Technology-designed Monsanto Home of the Future was the first effort to provide a building commensurate with Walt Disney's dazzling dreams of the future but still feasible to construct using advanced technology and the latest experimental materials (Fig. 166). Erected in 1957 at the gateway to Tomorrowland, it was a strange, cruciform structure made of modular fiberglass components bolted to a concrete base or stalk. Four lobate wings cantilevered out into space like the petals of a strange Martian flower, inviting unflattering comparison with the traditional, boxy shapes of tract housing. Each wing opened itself on two sides with a curtain wall of glass, so the house resembled a giant TV set showing the mullion grid of a Manhattan skyscraper on its only channel, as an elegant test pattern of line. The Monsanto home was the International Style humanized, scaled down for human consumption, curved into friendly shapes, and

155. Proposed exterior for the General Electric Carousel Theater, Disneyland. When GE's Disney-designed attraction moved to California from the New York World's Fair, the exterior was reworked to enhance the fading futurism of Tomorrowland. Collin Campbell. Acrylic on board. 32 x 46. 1966.

156. Hypothetical design for a New Tomorrowland, Disneyland. Morganelli (?) for Welton Becket & Associates. Charcoal and pencil on board. 15 x 19. 1965.

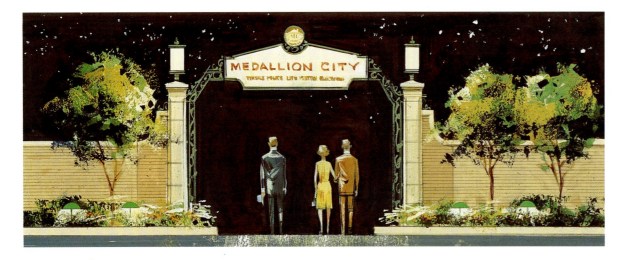

rescued from severity by a showroom's worth of push-button phones, lighting panels, pole lamps, low-profile sofas with built-in end tables—and an Atoms for Living Kitchen by Kelvinator. It was the first real indication that Walt harbored ambitions to build a place where the children who came to his park might some day really live.

The several new Tomorrowlands of the 1950s and 1960s were all serial experiments in real-world urbanism. The first New Tomorrowland had its grand opening in June of 1959 and the main attraction was the first working monorail in the United States. The second New Tomorrowland, in 1967, would add a peoplemover system suitable for business districts and exterior ceramic murals resistant to pollution and vandalism (Fig. 167). With rare exceptions—the nuclear submarine ride added in 1959; a constant fascination with space flight and how to make architecture look like NASA's moonshot hardware—the incessant improvements all aimed at providing workable blueprints for change: for improving the circulation of people and goods, for making houses easier to run and maintain, and for creating memorable public spaces that would be an unfailing pleasure to use. In the early 1960s, Walt's inner circle of Imagineers ("imagineering" is surely the ultimate Tomorrowland word, redolent of rocket fuel and derring-do) remember the founder lugging books on city planning around with him and muttering to himself about traffic, noise, and neon signs.

Both his office bookcase and the studio library contained multiple copies of architect Victor Gruen's 1964 *The Heart of Our Cities*,

157. Entrance to Medallion City, General Electric pavilion, New York World's Fair. Sam McKim. Opaque watercolor and ink on blueline. 11 x 17. 1963.
158. House for Medallion City, General Electric pavilion, New York World's Fair. Sam McKim. Opaque watercolor and colored pencil on blueline. 11 x 18. 1963.

a study that proposed remedies for an "urban crisis" the author described in chilling detail. The reason for the crisis was the decay and disappearance of the ancient city center under the influence of cars and suburbs and media, like television, that made face-to-face contact irrelevant. When the center eroded, the sense of community usually vanished along with it. But equally pernicious was the "subcityscape" of commercial cacophony Gruen equated specifically with Los Angeles; his diatribe against the blight of billboards on Ventura Boulevard sounded like Walt's perpetual complaints about the signs on Harbor Boulevard, outside Disneyland.

In his own work as the creator of Southdale in Minnesota—the first enclosed, indoor shopping mall—Gruen had already addressed the problems of how to invent a viable social center for the automotive suburb and how to manage and control the competitive instincts that drove merchants to deface their stores with the graphics of supersalesmanship. Southdale, which was built as Disneyland was being completed, was a Main Street for a new suburb that lacked one, having many of the same characteristics that made Walt's streetscapes so appealing. For example, Gruen championed the interests of the pedestrian at Southdale. He reassured the frazzled shopper with open, lively, readable interior spaces and codes that harmonized the facades of stores, to stave off visual fatigue. In the absence of an organized political structure, he fostered a sense of place by providing urban amenities in the form of public sculpture, artist-designed benches, and fountains.

159. Aerial view of a residential suburb for the City of the Future (Progress City) model, Carousel of Progress, Disneyland. Herbert Ryman. Opaque watercolor with varnish on board. 6 x 8. 1966.

160. Transportation Center for Future World, EPCOT (unbuilt Experimental Prototype Community of Tomorrow city in Florida). Herbert Ryman. Opaque watercolor on brownline. 24 x 51. 1966.

Gruen's ideas were already well known before his book appeared, as were his recent projects of the late 1950s and early 1960s, including Midtown Plaza in Rochester, New York, which had been built around a Small World-ish Clock of All Nations, from which dolls in the style of Mary Blair's emerged on the quarter hour. Like Progress City, Midtown Plaza also had a service concourse at the basement level for deliveries. And most of Gruen's published diagrams of ideal cities are, like the New Towns envisioned in Disney's Carousel of Progress, based on a Corbusian radial plan, with pods of activity that pinwheel outward from a cluster of downtown skyscrapers. Except for its thoroughly Disneyesque name, Progress City could have been Gruen's own master plan. And no one was very surprised when Walt wandered into John Hench's office one morning in the early 1960s and proposed that the two of them go ahead and build it, at full scale, on a twenty-eight-thousand-acre plot in central Florida. "Johnny," Walt asked with a gleam in his eye, "how would you like to work on the city of the future?"

Project X

Walt had acquired the land as a direct result of his participation in the 1964 New York World's Fair. Robert Moses, the powerful urban planner and master builder who ran the fair, wanted Walt to open Disneyland East on that site after the festivities were concluded. Independent study by the company concluded that such a park would indeed be feasible, but only in a warm-weather location readily accessible by car. Florida was the obvious choice. Land was still cheap in parts of the state that did not sport glitzy new beachfront hotels by Morris Lapidus. As his agents began buying up parcels of scrub and swamp around Orlando, Walt began wondering exactly what to do with a blank slate roughly twice the size of Manhattan.

It was a foregone conclusion that what the reporters had begun calling Disney World would contain another Disneyland or its "equivalent": Walt said as much in a televised press conference with the governor of Florida in November of 1965. But the new versions of Main Street and Frontierland and the rest were only the money machines necessary to underwrite something different. Not another Tomorrowland, exactly: "At the pace we're going," Walt conceded, "tomorrow would catch up with us before we got it built." Something else. "We've done a lot of thinking about a model community . . . a city of tomorrow," he added. But it had to be real—realistic. He didn't "believe in the extreme blue-sky stuff that some of the architects do." Because, after all, "people want to live like human beings," and whether he was ready to lay it all out or not, he wanted to build a place where his customers could live.

Back in Anaheim, meanwhile, John Hench and his colleagues were plussing Tomorrowland again. In a series of meetings attended by Walt in 1964, they had introduced a concept called "SpacePort," the core of a New Tomorrowland scheduled for completion in 1967. The idea later devolved into an indoor roller coaster, the Space Mountain attraction at Walt Disney World. But the planning concept—a multilevel transportation hub or port—became the center-

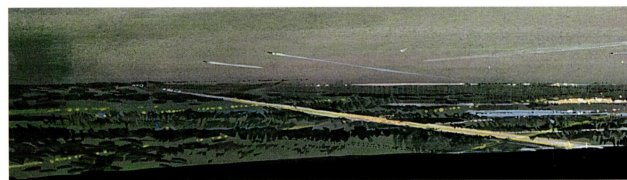

161. Car of the future, General Electric pavilion, New York World's Fair. Sam McKim. Chalk on black matboard. 13 x 20. 1963.

piece for Project X, Walt's name for the top-secret Florida city. Hench called the hypothetical buildings he conjured up for SpacePort "cartilaginous," (Figs. 168, 169) an elegant way of describing a sinewy, flexible system of beamways and cantilevers connected at nodal points that were not quite buildings in the traditional sense. It was an architecture closely related to a series of the 1965 Welton Becket proposals associated with this most recent transformation of Tomorrowland (see Fig. 156). Herb Ryman's renderings picture the same hub buried under the thirty-story skyscraper (a masted, self-possessed structure, like Becket's Capitol Records building of 1955) in the middle of Disney's new city (Fig. 170). From the Becket-influenced SpacePort, too, comes a sense of organic, prehensile components stretching themselves out from the center of their own volition in a web-like configuration that is part grid—geometry, logic, straight edges—and part living creature.

If Disneyland's SpacePort and Progress City fertilized Project X, the relationship was not entirely reciprocal: the city planners, the EPCOT team, labored in secret in a special room at the studio designated for the purpose. The so-called Florida Room had sixteen-foot ceilings and padded walls for pinning up plans, and it was the lair of Marvin Davis, who had returned to Imagineering to do for the boss what he had done more than a decade earlier during the planning stages for Disneyland, when Walt was struggling to see what the vague ideas in his mind would look like on paper. Eventually, after Walt's death, Davis drew up the master plan for Walt Disney World. But in 1965, his assignment was the hypothetical city, which was shortly dubbed the Experimental Prototype Community of Tomorrow, he says, because Walt thought the acronym sounded about right (Fig. 171).

Davis thinks, however, that by the time he was moved into the Florida Room, Walt had already suffered a major setback, reflected in the lukewarm attitude toward architects he projected at the 1965 press conference. According to Davis, Walt had taken his ideas on urban planning straight to his friend Welton Becket because the notion of building a city seemed a good deal more daunting than building a stage-set version of one. One of the largest producers of commercial architecture in the country, the Becket firm was then in the throes of creating Century City, the important town-in-town development rising on the former 20th Century-Fox lot in West Los Angeles, near Beverly Hills. Given the firm's backlog of experience, Walt hoped that his visionary dreams for Florida could find concrete form in Becket's office (Fig. 172).

But Becket did not design EPCOT. Marvin Davis believes that Becket's presentation book, delivered three months later, may have disappointed Walt and convinced him to give the project to Imagineering after all. That Becket book is lost, but existing 1965 sketches for some visionary environment—the drawings incorporated into the New Tomorrowland in 1967 (see Fig. 156)—cannot be assigned to any specific Disney project. But if they are pages from the rejected EPCOT brochure, the reasons for Walt's chagrin are obvious. The drawings are picturesque, even thrilling, but do not describe a place where the human beings to

162. Skyline background for Progress City model, Carousel of Progress, Disneyland. Herbert Ryman. Opaque watercolor on board. 5 x 40. c. 1965–66.

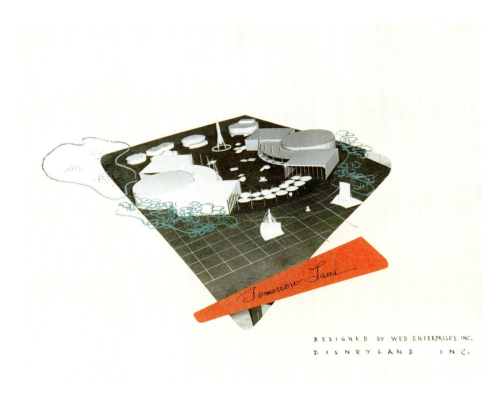

whom Walt alluded in his press conference would have chosen to live in the 1970s. Created by non-architects to entertain visitors to the Carousel of Progress, Progress City had begun to look more like that place—the one Walt always saw when he closed his eyes. Once upon a time, Marvin Davis and the proto-Imagineers had translated Walt's mental pictures into Disneyland. Maybe they could do it again.

So, locked in the Florida Room, Davis made maps with green backgrounds alluding to the greenbelt concept (Fig. 173). There were maps of residential subdivisions, light-industry zones, and shopping districts; maps showing the intricate circulation of traffic, under and around the city; and maps of the underground hub, beneath the thirty-story hotel (Figs. 174, 175). His assistant, George Rester, drew the skyscraper hotel that grew sheerer and sleeker in each successive version (Fig. 176). Using leftover designs for the International Street never completed at Disneyland, Collin Campbell and Herb Ryman showed how the blocks of buildings around the Hub could become a kind of world boutique. And, with those plans and renderings and paste-ups arranged for best effect on the walls around him, Walt made his EPCOT film to recruit the potential partners he hoped would one day occupy the factories and offices of his city of twenty thousand happy souls. The set looked just like the Florida Room and he rehearsed the pitch before select groups of friends. The actor Walter Pigeon came. Art Linkletter. Welton Becket and his two young sons. Disney pointed to his maps and talked and wondered. Did this sound like a city you'd like to live in, he asked?

163. Overview of Tomorrowland, Disneyland. Anonymous. Collage with colored paper, ink, photostat, ink, and watercolor. 17 x 21. 1954.
164. Entrance pylon and canopy, Richfield Autopia, Disneyland. Herbert Ryman. Photostat of drawing. 14 x 26. 1955.

The EPCOT presented in the movie was a utopia, a model for solving "today's city problems . . . through proper master planning." But it was a highly selective vision of the city, pictorial rather than political in character. Walt worried about the impersonal feeling of urban America, for instance, and the effect of chaotic, uncontrolled environments on human behavior, but he never openly expressed an interest in slum clearance, poverty, unemployment, pollution, and racial unrest. Although these symptoms of the urban malaise of the 1960s are implicit in his descriptions of EPCOT—where everybody works and retirees are not welcome; where jobs are at one's doorstep; where his company later experimented with innovative new modes of waste disposal, water purification, and energy conservation—the city in the film is more like a movie set, suffused with feeling, sentiment, and mood. It is a series of circular maps and sections that project a strong rhetorical image of wholeness, unity, and embrace, of harmony, safety, and underlying order.

The voice-over speaks of new technologies arising from the private sector (the EPCOT industrial park, that is; "a showcase of industry at work") as the answer to the ills of America's older cities. But EPCOT was not one of them. Built afresh, far from the troubled landscapes of Watts and Harlem, EPCOT illustrated "the need . . . for starting from scratch on virgin land." There is a calculated, new-made innocence about the EPCOT renderings shown in the film. Painted in splashes of vibrant golf-course green by the veterans who had once sold Disneyland to indifferent investors, the pictures

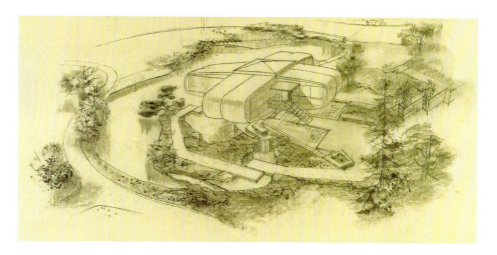

165. Proposed Land-Sea-Air Building for Tomorrowland, Disneyland. Anonymous. Colored pencil and chalk on brownline. 18 1/2 x 20 5/8. 1954–55.
166. The Monsanto Home of the Future in Disneyland. John Hench. Pen and ink with charcoal on paper. 20 3/4 x 53 1/4. 1957.

of Walt's New Town were as seductive as they were beautiful (Fig. 177). Factories looked properly industrial, with their towers and stacks aglow in the darkness. But they were clean and eerily deserted, as if to suggest their unobtrusive silence. Houses were showpieces, grouped in amiable kaffeeklatsches around fortuitous lakes. Sealed away in its fifty-acre dome, the inner city had been sanitized for the protection of a generation of skittish suburbanites who never went downtown any more.

EPCOT after Walt

Walt Disney died of lung cancer in the hospital across the street from his studio in December of 1966. In the Florida Room, the work on EPCOT went forward with a fresh intensity: the city of the future was Walt's last, best dream and the planning team was determined to see it come true. Marvin Davis remembered the glory days back before the Florida Room, when the project was still headquartered in an obscure cubbyhole at WED and Walt came by at least three times a week, brimming with excitement, to reposition the pieces of his giant Florida puzzle: the Magic Kingdom park, the hotels, the city. On Wednesday, the apartment buildings would be here and the factories over there. On Friday, as often as not, they'd be reversed. On Monday mornings, after a weekend of tinkering with the maps, Walt would bustle in with a fresh set of ideas, drawn on paper napkins the staff surreptitiously plucked out of the wastebasket after he left. "He designed the whole traffic flow around EPCOT on a little napkin," says Davis.

167. Study for a redesigned entrance to Tomorrowland, Disneyland. Herbert Ryman. Opaque watercolor on paper. 33 x 50. 1965.

168. The beginnings of "cartilaginous" architecture—seen in this sketch for a General Motors Adventures in Science complex at Disneyland—are clearly related to Welton Becket's earlier plans for a "new" Tomorrowland. John Hench. Opaque watercolor on board. 22 x 45. 1959.

169. Overview of a redesigned Tomorrowland for Disneyland. Herbert Ryman. Opaque watercolor on board. 30 x 40. 1967.

Right: Catherine Wagner. *Avenue of the Planets; New Tomorrowland, Magic Kingdom, Walt Disney World, Orlando, Florida.* Collection CCA.

"But EPCOT [itself] was Walt's target. It was the real wienie. . . . To Walt, the wienie was the good part."

But Walt's brother called the meetings now and Roy Disney was troubled by the notion of building a city, with all the headaches that entailed. What did a movie studio know about water and sewer lines, municipal government, running a fire department? If Magic Kingdom employees were to be the inhabitants of EPCOT, didn't the city run the risk of becoming another Pullman, Illinois? A fractious company town? When Davis and his colleagues showed how they intended to implement Walt's plans, they met with a sad, simple answer. "Marvin," said Roy Disney. "Walt's dead." And so was the city known as EPCOT. But EPCOT, the theme park, stayed in the pipeline. First came Disneyland East—the Magic Kingdom—taller, bigger, better. Then a series of resort hotels to encourage visitors to make a vacation of it, to extend theming to the hours when the rest of Walt Disney World was closed for the night, and to protect the edges of the property from unwanted intrusions. And finally, EPCOT, whatever that might one day turn out to be (Fig. 178).

The hotels were, in a way, the last vestige of Walt's plan for a true residential community.

170. Overall view of downtown district in Progress City model (Disneyland), showing surrounding greenbelt, central skyscraper, and multilevel transportation center. These elements would all reappear in Walt Disney's plans for building a real, functioning city to be located in central Florida. Herbert Ryman. Watercolor, pen and ink, and pencil on board. 20 x 22. 1966.

Imagineering the Disney Theme Parks 155

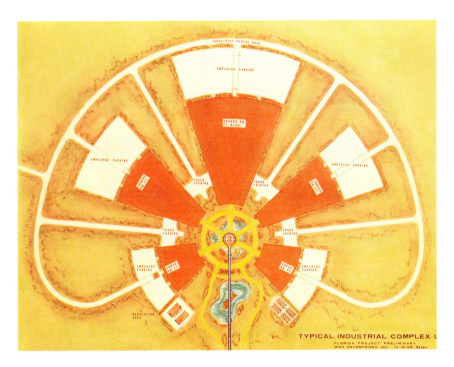

171. Marvin Davis with site plans for EPCOT Center, Walt Disney World (top left).

172. Marty Sklar (left) and Welton Becket (center) pace off the Disney property in Florida (top right).

173. A diagrammatic view of a typical industrial complex within "Project X," prepared for Walt Disney's filmed presentation of his plans for a Florida new town. Marvin Davis. Colored pencil, watercolor, and felt pen on brownline, pasted to cardboard. 39 1/2 x 53 1/2. 1966 (bottom left).

174. Site plan for "Project X," the Florida city, showing the city center and transportation hub. Marvin Davis. Collage with watercolor and colored pencil on photostat. 40 x 46. 1966 (bottom right).

Families stayed for days at a time in environments designed to foster a collective fantasy of being shipwrecked on a sunny Polynesian island, for instance. Or a fantasy of stopping for the night in a city that looked exactly like up-to-the-minute cities ought to look—clean, fresh, brightly lit, and perky, decorated in brilliant, modern primaries set off against stark white surfaces—and hopping off a monorail in the soaring atrium lobby of one's hotel (Fig. 179). While only the Contemporary Resort and the Polynesian Village were actually built at that time, the plans called for a ring of similar themed hotels all around the edge of Disney World, acting as a kind of buffer zone between Florida, the highway, and the cares of the everyday world—and the Magic Kingdom. The hotels carried a little of the magic into quotidian reality: toothbrushing, watching TV, and shaving in the morning all took on a kind of glow when the walls were hung with simulated bamboo and a bedside table straight from the pages of a decorating magazine rose gracefully out of the floor on a single plastic leg (Fig. 180).

Originally, there were to have been five hotels ready for opening day in 1971: the Asian,

175. Aerial view of "Project X" shopping district, with a much older view of Disneyland's unbuilt International Street reused as an avenue of boutiques. George Rester rendering, painted and modified by Herbert Ryman. Pen and ink and watercolor on brownline with tape. 43 x 51. 1966.
176. Thirty-story centerpiece hotel for Experimental Prototype Community of Tomorrow. George Rester. Opaque watercolor, colored pencil, and pen and ink on plastic sheet over colored board. 53 1/2 x 35 1/2. 1966.

158 Designing Disney's Theme Parks

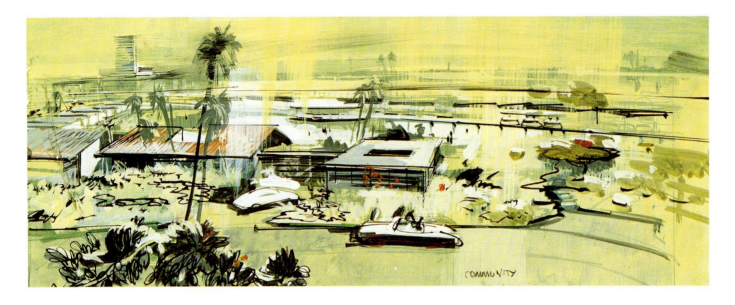

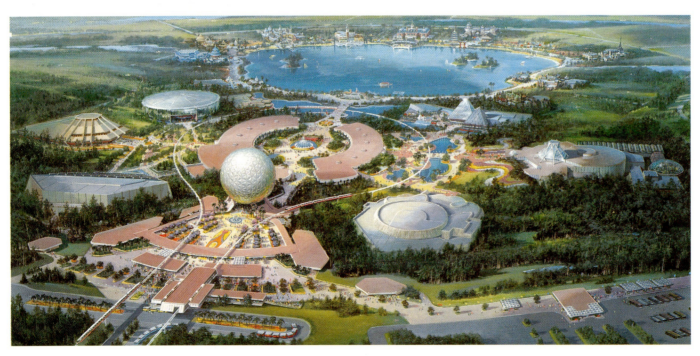

177. A residential quarter of Progress City served by the monorail system. This Disneyland project clearly influenced plans for the Florida property. Herbert Ryman. Opaque watercolor, pen, colored pencil, and varnish on board. 8 x 19. 1966.

178. An aerial view of EPCOT Center in its post-urban, theme-park phase. Clem Hall and Bob Scifo. Acrylic on board. 33 x 58. 1981.

the Venetian (Fig. 181), the Persian, the Contemporary, and the Polynesian Village. The idea was to provide a taste of world architecture and atmosphere, as a World's Fair did. So Disney World became an international version of the old Disneyland "fun" map, arranged in concentric circles with Fantasyland make-believe at the heart of the matter, ringed by a series of standard tourist fantasies at the boundaries. Going to Hawaii. Vacationing in Venice. Sending back postcards from some impossibly distant capital in the Orient. Living a life of glamour, luxury, and sophistication, like the people in magazines did. It was a map of the real places in the world that had already been transformed into quasi-fantasy by Hollywood, paperback books, and the collective imagination.

Herb Ryman's studies for the shopping district in EPCOT city used the same romanticized places arranged in a circle of perfumed pleasure around the business center (Figs. 182, 183). And the idea was taken up again in the World Showcase section of the post-Walt EPCOT, opened in 1982. Picture-postcard snippets of Venice and Paris; Shakespearian half-timbering; a Canadian railroad hotel; a bit of Independence Hall; pagodas, dragons, and roof tiles all wheel around a lagoon (Fig. 184). And the visitors move counterclockwise around that circuit, shopping and dining in an enormous, roofless mall.

When it became clear that the nations depicted would or could not sponsor full-blown, World's Fair-style pavilions, shopping and eating foreign food—and watching the occasional film—became the principal activities at World Showcase because merchants, airlines, tourist boards, and export industries picked up the slack. As originally designed, however, most of the venues were intended to provide adventures keyed to the culture and geography of the country in question. The German pavilion was to have featured a trip down the Rhine, for example. Plans for the Japanese compound included an Audio-Animatronics® time-trip describing Japan's involvement with the West. But thanks to sponsorship problems, the Japanese show was transferred to Tokyo Disneyland in 1983 and many of the other entertainment features of the pavilions were either built in attenuated versions or scrapped.

Without them, World Showcase became a very classy mall with the Piazza San Marco (in reverse) recast as a Potemkin village in which Italian leather and glass and heaping plates of fettucini Alfredo were sold. The facades were just facades; Italian restaurants often put a Leaning Tower of Pisa or a shapely gondola on the neon sign, and these facades were signs, too, albeit of a fancier sort (Fig. 185). Facades were glorified shop windows—whereas, at the Polynesian Village, the visitor went inside, deep backstage, and lived out a make-believe adventure as a bona fide member of the cast. From the minute the alarm clock went off in the morning until she drifted off to sleep at night to the beat of native drums, life itself was a dark ride. A perfect beach, man-made and manicured hourly. Tahitian toast at the breakfast luau. Torch dancers in grass skirts at the floor show. A Polynesian bed in a Polynesian bedroom with a balcony overlooking the beach.

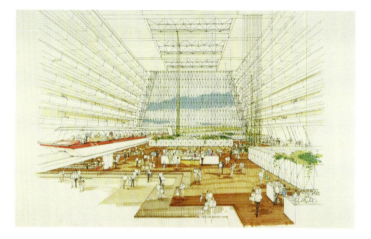

179. Atrium and shopping concourse, Contemporary Hotel, Walt Disney World. R. Kaminski for Welton Becket & Associates. Marker with pen and ink on board. 28 x 34. 1969.
180. Proposed deluxe guest suite for Polynesian Village Resort, Walt Disney World. John DeCuir, Jr. Watercolor and pencil on board. 21 7/8 x 40. 1970.

The Becket firm designed the first pair of themed hotels, the Polynesian and the Contemporary, and prepared presentation drawings for the rest. But it is clear that Becket did so with considerable assistance from Imagineering. There are Becket renderings for the public spaces and the elevations, for instance, and some Becket-commissioned research paste-ups, using photos of objects in museum collections to develop a repertory of Polynesian decorative motifs. And it is also clear that, in the design of wallpaper, menus, carpeting, and other specially-made materials used in the hotels, the artists at Imagineering took their lead from these sources.

But the majority of the sketches for guest quarters were prepared by John Decuir, Jr., Dorothea Redmond, Mary Blair, and other Disney artists (Fig. 186). They dealt with the close-up aspects of theming and chose the off-the-shelf items best suited to preserve the agreed-upon illusion. Becket, for his part, worried more about the prefabricated room modules being built nearby by U.S. Steel and the framework into which they would be slotted, like so many drawers in a Polynesian bureau veneered in faux bamboo (Fig. 187).

Yet the division of labor between Welton Becket and Imagineering was never clear cut. Becket was hired because Walt reasoned that real architects ought to build real buildings—and Becket's hotels, like the 1953 Beverly Hilton, had set the industry standard for high drama coupled with a cost-effective management of service spaces. Before his death, however, while he was making the rounds of companies targeted to set up research facilities

181. Proposed Venetian Hotel for Walt Disney World, Orlando, Florida. Welton Becket & Associates. Watercolor on paper. 24 x 36. 1970.
182. Proposed Spanish Quarter, International Shopping Center, World Showcase, EPCOT Center. Herbert Ryman. Pencil and watercolor on paper. 20 x 42. 1966.

at EPCOT, Walt led side expeditions to inspect John Portman's new atrium hotel in Atlanta, the Plaza in New York, and the Doral in Miami. The atrium idea found its way straight into Becket's A-frame design for the Contemporary (although, according to Marty Sklar, the firm at one point threatened to withdraw from the project on aesthetic grounds if the Disney people insisted on running their monorail through the lobby, as Walt had wanted (Fig. 188). Marvin Davis, who served as liaison officer between Becket and Imagineering, worked to minimize the shoebox sameness of modular construction methods by exterior theming. Early Becket plans for the Polynesian Village show another giant A-frame, with palm trees, but the hotel complex as built dispersed the room units into lower longhouses scattered about the site. After revision by the Disney artists, landscaping performed much of the theming function, and the cozy intimacy of a mock native village was maintained by the small scale of the individual buildings.

The Becket hotels preserved Walt's concept of EPCOT as a wellspring of new corporate technologies for the twenty-first century. U.S. Steel, in partnership with WED and Welton Becket & Associates, set up an on-site plant to manufacture 1,450 "unitized" guest rooms, self-supporting modules capable of being stacked three high without external structural support (Fig. 189). The rooms were framed in steel, and came equipped with wall finishes appropriate to the theme, carpeting, furnishings, and a bath.

183. Aerial view of EPCOT Center, showing hotels, Magic Kingdom, and circular shopping center.
Carlos Dimiz. Colored pencil on brownline. 29 x 60. 1974.

As each unit was completed, the hall door was locked. The next time it was opened was when the room had been hoisted into position and plugged into the water and electrical systems. Prefabricated buildings were nothing new: Walt had used them in Disneyland. The innovation in Orlando was the use of new, lightweight materials for interior walls and fixtures. Previous modular hotel rooms weighed up to thirty tons apiece. The Disney World units weighed only six tons.

But doing things the old way was cheaper in most cases than experimenting with new ones; friction developed between the manufacturer and the client and the hotel project was scaled back to two resorts. Guests lived there, for a day or two, in idyllic conditions. The grass was green. No cars were needed here: buses and monorails ran straight to the park. The infrastructure, should the guest have cared to learn about it, was the best American industry had to offer. This was the EPCOT city of Walt Disney's dreams—or as close to it as his corporate heirs would come until the 1990s, when, without the direct participation of the Imagineers, the Disney Development Company began building city-like housing complexes in Florida. In the meantime, around the ornate lobbies of the themed hotels, including the new entrance hotel at Disneyland Paris and the Grand Floridian at Walt Disney World, hovered the last faint traces of Medallion City and Progress City and "Waltopia," the EPCOT that never was.

Future World

The EPCOT Center that opened in 1982 was something different. The footprint was different, for one thing. The heart-shaped map with the axial corridor to the Hub was gone, replaced by a figure-eight pattern of tangent circles (Fig. 190). The circle at the back of the site is World Showcase, with eleven fragments of distinctive national architecture disposed around a man-made lagoon. The circle at the front is Future World, and here, eight (originally six) corporate pavilions are arranged around the outer rim of a vast plaza, articulated on its inner edge by two paired arcades laid out (like those at Disneyland's Tomorrowland) in a manner reminiscent of Bernini's colonnade at Saint Peter's in Rome.

The strongest vertical on the standard "fun map" plan for a Disney park had always been

184. Entrance to the Italian pavilion, World Showcase, EPCOT Center. Bob Scifo. Acrylic on board. 40 x 35. 1979.

185. Italian pavilion, World Showcase, EPCOT Center.

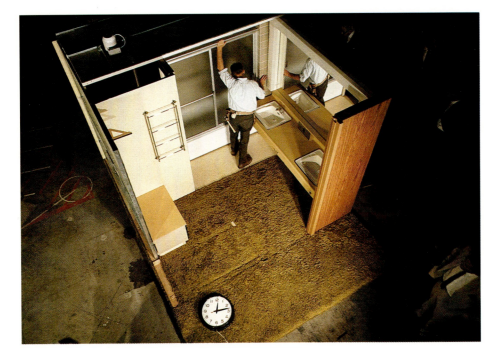

186. Typical guest room, Contemporary Hotel, Walt Disney World. Dorothea Redmond. Watercolor on paper. 13 x 16. 1969.
187. Modular hotel room under construction in Disney World's U.S. Steel on-site factory, 1971.

the castle, at the end of a planned vista on axis with the point of entry. At EPCOT, the wienie is an enormous sphere, 180-feet tall, set down at the entrance to the first circle, blocking the axis, but translating the two-dimensional circles of the plan into a three-dimensional motif that defines the future in terms of portentous, uncompromising geometric shapes. Both the design and the placement suggest a World's Fair: the gleaming white Perisphere from New York in 1939 and Buckminster Fuller's soaring bubble of a geodesic dome that served as the American pavilion at Expo '67 in Montreal. EPCOT is a permanent fair, with the picturesque cultural stuff in the back, in the metaphorical past, and the corporate future up front, where it counts. Walt loved fairs, of course. Victor Gruen had urged city planners of the future to incorporate them into fabric of the community. In central Florida in the 1970s, a fair was the next best thing to a city.

Anticipation and speculation about EPCOT were keen throughout the decade. Publicity made it apparent the park with the peculiar-sounding name was going to be, well, different. It was not another Disneyland. Publicists encouraged visitors to come to EPCOT in a meditative frame of mind, to learn, to be inspired. After Vietnam and the Kennedy assassination and the failure of the Great Society, inspiration was a suspect commodity. Disneyesque optimism was in short supply, too. Walt's old ideas about EPCOT city were dredged up by the reporters who had heard him describe it in 1965 and 1966. But pictures of the model doled out to the media didn't look much like that city (Fig. 191). There was no

188. Monorail emerging from the lobby of the Contemporary Hotel, Walt Disney World. George McGinnis. Watercolor on paper. 29 x 37. 1969.

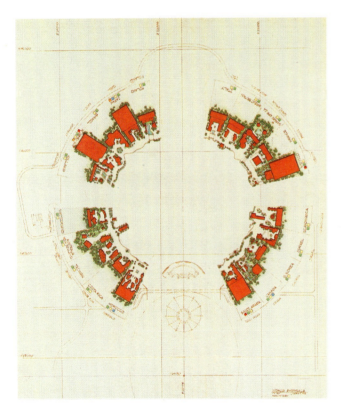

more discussion of twenty thousand souls in permanent residence there. And the guys posing with the models weren't Walt. They were fellows named Marty Sklar and John Hench and they represented the anonymous, corporate Disney that had decided, after much soul wrenching, to build a prudent, feasible EPCOT (Fig. 192). Or to do what could be done.

Imagineers who worked on EPCOT still talk about the "rented pencils." So massive was the project and so short the time allocated to the work that almost every big architectural firm in California was pressed into service when the crunch came, doing the elevations and the technical drawings for the contractors. But the underlying concepts for the buildings of Future World, and the presentation drawings from which the process began, came from Imagineering, albeit in a fitful way, much influenced by the sponsorship issue. Tony Baxter tells of months of work developing a crystalline shape for a pavilion the planners hoped to use for a discussion of ecology. The shape arose from a consideration of themes or backstories related, sometimes subliminally, to both natural and architectural metaphors: greenhouses, biosphere research, tall trees, the Emerald City of Oz (Fig. 193). When the design was finished, however, Disney could not find a company ready to promote ecological concerns in the late 1970s, despite an ongoing national energy crisis. So the building was shelved, temporarily as it turned out. Only at the last minute, just before EPCOT was scheduled to open, did design aspects of the one-time ecology pavilion resurface to symbolize imagination and creativity under the aegis of Eastman Kodak.

In the case of General Motors, the overarching idea—motion—and the willingness to participate were there from the beginning, so much so that the basic conceptual work was left to the in-house office charged with building General Motors displays at fairs and trade shows. The result was one of the more obvious pavilions in the complex: the building looks just like the tire on a late-model Chevrolet (Fig. 194). But most of the structures in Future World also describe their contents through their architectural signatures. One building resembles a giant wave, to carry out an ocean theme. Soil conservation and agriculture are illustrated inside what seems to be an example of earth-sheltered architecture. The energy pavilion is topped with pivoting solar collectors. The result is a kind of talking architecture, so many Venturian "ducks" quacking away in the then-current corporate vernacular of curtain walls and reflective glass (Fig. 195).

The most disappointing thing about EPCOT is talking architecture which seems to say, in effect, that the future already happened, some time in the late 1960s. One of the consistent hallmarks of Disney architecture is its refusal to be avant garde: reassurance, on the contrary, means using the familiar conventions of real-world architecture—and then "plussing" them until the audience has to smile. That was the strategy adopted in Future World. The normative model was the new office park of the 1960s. It was California's Stanford Research Park with high-tech labs set like simulated jewels on the velvet greenery of a corporate campus. Or the business district of an edge city somewhere in Silicon Valley, where a canted

189. Modular hotel room being inserted into its framework, Walt Disney World, c. 1970–71.
190. Site plan for World Showcase, EPCOT Center, showing placement of national pavilions. Harper Goff. Colored pencil on brownline. 32 x 38. 1978.

Catherine Wagner. *Swan Hotel, Tower of Terror, and Spaceship Earth* (from left to right); *EPCOT, Disney-MGM Studios Theme Park, Walt Disney World, Orlando, Florida.* Collection CCA.

facade and an entry canopy shaped like a flying saucer distinguished one corporate entity from another. Or an urban skyscraper with a roofline modeled on the finial of a Chippendale breakfront to project a suitable "image," tortuously related to the products, pretensions, or even the logo of a given company. Future World pinned its tomorrows to the fitful dreams of corporate America and thus to a vision of the future that stretched no farther than next year's annual report. In 1982, the patented quaintness of World Showcase came as something of a relief after a future conceived in terms of big, modern, geometric containers that contrived to look all alike, despite their desperate efforts to seem unique and different.

Today, ironically, Future World has begun to grow quaint and funky, like a string of love beads and a pair of bell bottoms rescued from the attic. Like the New Tomorrowland in the Magic Kingdom, it represents the good old days, when the future that fizzled out still seemed to hold some promise. Because they concentrated on the future Walt foresaw in the 1930s, 1940s, and 1950s, the Tomorrowland team had more exciting material to work with. The would-be plussers of Future World draw on a more modest heritage of auto showrooms and office complexes, the roadside detritus of the International Style.

Into this world, according to Barry Braverman, who oversaw the EPCOT Design Studio, recent plussing has tried to bring a new sense of urbanism. The plaza at the center of Future World was an empty, forbidding space, formal and cold. Signage, color, and light have been added to simulate the electric sensibility of the Ginza. Piecemeal change amounts to a part of the new EPCOT narrative: in real cities, says Braverman, the future is always implicit in small alterations made to the existing infrastructure on a daily basis. Yet tomorrow, for many Americans today, is a ranch in Montana, a final flight from urban life. And that is the greatest irony of all. On the verge of making EPCOT more like the real city it was always meant to be, it has become irrelevant, puzzling, and strange. Going to Future World in 1997 is not much different from visiting one of the foreign places arrayed like rare curios in a museum around the shores of the adjacent lagoon.

Inside the Berm—and Outside

The Disney parks are the best-known vernacular landscapes in the world. In the 1950s, little kids taped "fun maps" of Disneyland to their bedroom walls and prayed: a whole generation of Americans grew up believing that they'd almost rather go there than go to heaven. The victorious athletes who, in a masterful series of TV spots, tell the world that now they're goin' to Disneyland confirm the stereotype. So do the sick children whose last wish is to see the Magic Kingdom. A trip to a Disney park is like going to heaven. A culmination of every dream and hope. A summation of an American life. The ultimate

191. Panoramic vista of the Theme Center, EPCOT Center. John DeCuir, Jr. Acrylic on board. 36 x 80. 1975.

vacation. No wonder that academic moralists, so quick to judge the heart's desires of others, so quick to label someone else's dreams as nightmares, despise Disneyland and all its far-flung colonies. In 1992, a French intellectual called the new Disney park rising on her native soil "a cultural Chernobyl."

Before Disneyland Paris ever opened, she saw nightmare visions, a "horror of cardboard, plastic, atrocious colors, solidified chewing-gum constructions, and idiotic folk stories that come straight out of cartoon books for fat Americans." But as the Japanese backers of Tokyo Disneyland realized when they insisted that their park be as much like the Anaheim prototype as possible, Disney's lands are American places. The French alternative is a vacation in Nice or Provence instead. And everybody has the choice, of course. The Disney parks are mass cultural fantasies, dreams shared by lots of other people, standing in the same line you are. The alternative is a dream all your own.

The critic for whom all pop culture is inauthentic and crass, the by-product of grasping capitalism, is probably never going to like Disneyland. And the critic from whom the preoccupations of American mass culture over the past half-century—the TV Westerns of the 1950s, exploring the conflict between institutions and individuals; the Cold War tensions played out in the space race of the 1960s; the battle for the custody of earth's green spaces; the preservation of the city—elicit only contempt won't care much that the icons of the Disney parks were located on precisely those sore spots in the national psyche. Nor that these icons embodied, in an engrossing new medium, the themes of a half-century's worth of thought, debate, and worry. That Disneyland needed to create an architecture of reassurance in the first place meant that the issues raised by the iconography of the park were, at some level, profoundly disquieting.

The one aspect of the world's Disneylands that has met with cautious approval from the critical bloc is the architecture. Although in some circles "Mickey Mouse" has become a synonym for "plastic" (almost invariably, haters of Disney parks insist that the buildings must be made of cardboard, plastic, and other cheap and/or non-traditional materials), the company is quick to pass out copies of complimentary comments by Robert Venturi, Peter Blake, James Rouse, and others willing to concede a scrap of merit to Main Street, U.S.A. and the early plans for EPCOT.

In 1964, the futurist Ray Bradbury, an early defender of the plastic crocodiles in Adventureland who later consulted with Imagineering on the design of the Spaceship Earth attraction inside the geosphere at EPCOT, insisted that Disneyland has "already solved . . . most of the problems that beset Los Angeles."

Bradbury was onto something. The history of Disneyland makes it abundantly clear that Walt Disney saw the park as an alternative to things he didn't like about L.A., including automobility, suburban sameness, and the lack

192. John Hench and Disney consultant Ray Bradbury plan the Theme Center for EPCOT Center, late 1970s.

of a memorable civic center. But there were things he liked very much about the city and intensified within the confines of the berm. Fantasy buildings, shaped like derby hats and hot dogs, that suggested what a malleable, pictorial medium architecture could be. Resonant period styles, like California Mission and the movie-star Colonial manner of the early Welton Becket. Landscaping as a part of the operative Hollywood fantasy that made L.A. bloom like an oasis in some Rudolph Valentino desert of the soul. Icons: the Art Deco tower outside Crossroads of the World and the pseudo-Midwestern windmill at the Farmers' Market. Walt collected them all, like so many toy buildings on a railroad layout, and re-arranged them in his park. Inside the berm, the things he liked reshuffled themselves into a series of coherent streetscapes in the blessed absence of the things he didn't. That was, after all, the advantage Walt Disney had over Los Angeles. In Disneyland, Walt was in control. In Los Angeles, it was every builder and merchant and politician, every driver and shopper and pleasure-seeker for herself.

James Rouse, keynoting a Harvard conference on urban design in 1963, called Disneyland "the greatest piece of urban design in the United States today." His own historic development districts, in which architecture of the urban past has been recycled for recreational shopping by extracting narrative themes from industrial sites, points to one important way in which Disney architecture has influenced the changing American city. Seaside, Florida (1981), Disney's own Celebration, and the rash of other newly minted upper-middle class communities of walkable streets and neo-Victorian porches seem to have pulled off an idiosyncratic merger between Disney's Main Street and Progress City. The New Urbanism of Elizabeth Plater-Zybeck, Andres Duany, and

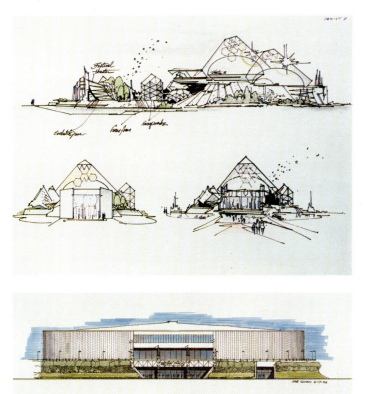
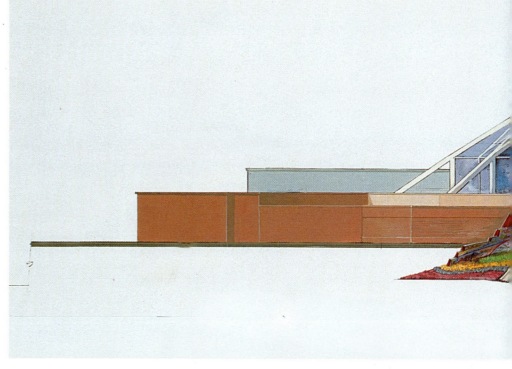

193. A crystalline building (Imagination pavilion) for Future World, EPCOT Center. Dan Goozee. Marker and colored pencil on board. 20 x 26. 1979.
194. Redesigned General Motors pavilion, EPCOT Center. Abe Quiben. Marker on blackline. 18 x 29. 1994.

Peter Calthorpe is a prettier, less corporate version of the 1965 and 1966 plans for the unbuilt EPCOT. Thus, in terms of its effect on real-world architecture, Rouse may have been right when he dared to use the terms "Disneyland" and "urban design" in the same sentence.

What is less often noted about Rouse's speech, however, is the rest of the paragraph, where he went on to note that Disneyland is not a city, but an amusement park, albeit the best of all the modern pleasure gardens: "It took an area of activity—the amusement park—and lifted it to a standard so high in its performance, in its respect for people, that it really has become a brand-new thing." The new thing—the thing that is not a city but is, indeed, something new—is what intrigues the millions who make the pilgrimage to a Disney park, in search of pleasure, largely undeterred by energy crises, recession, and the opprobrium of their self-anointed betters.

So what's new in the Disney parks? New attractions that comment on the city in new ways—most recently, the Extra TERRORrestrial Alien Encounter in which the future preys upon an unsuspecting present set in a convention center, like the one in your own downtown, back home (Figs. 196, 197). Being terrified is fun so long as you know that it will all be over soon, but the underlying notion that the future may be awful is a new concept for a Tomorrowland. The Tower of Terror at Florida's Disney-MGM Studios theme park is an old city hotel (Fig. 198). Hundreds like it, in downtowns everywhere, are waiting for the kiss of the wrecker's ball: it's the kind of place you skitter by, as fast as you can go. Unsafe. Unsound. The elevator plummets suddenly, out of control, like the future, with the aliens in charge. What's new in the Disney parks is often what's very old. The old questions persist, for example. What should the city

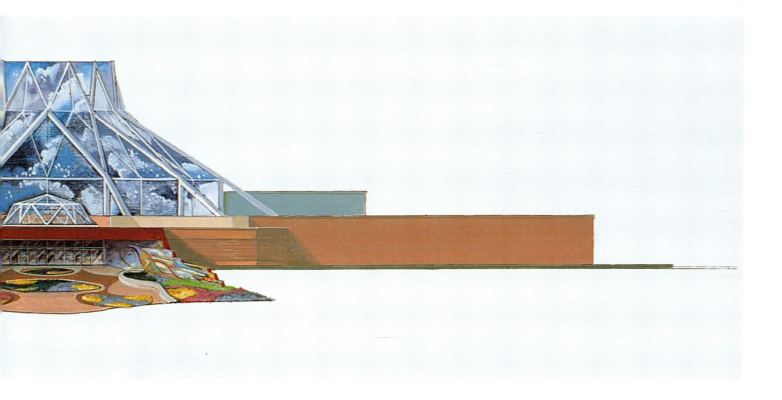

195. As finally completed, the Land pavilion, Future World, EPCOT Center, reflects the vogue for earth-sheltered construction.
Joe Rohde. Watercolor on blackline. 17 x 51. 1981.

look like? And who or what's in control?

Card Walker, the CEO of the Walt Disney Company when EPCOT was built, talks about Walt's determination to control the Florida site, where his utopia was going to rise. Planning the new city of the future depended on order, on someone taking charge of public spaces. Bob Weis, who laid out Hollywood Boulevard at the Disney-MGM Studios park in the image of Main Street, sees it as the very model for an orderly environment, marching in small, manageable steps toward the facade of Grauman's theater according to a rhythm set up by the facades of the buildings on either side of the street (Fig. 199). A green one, a curvy one, a good neon sign, a building that looks like a camera. Deco ladies on the cornice, over there, sculpted in aluminum. Outside the parks, says Weis, the Disney passion for order now translates itself into more exuberant public spaces, full of ladies and neon and interesting things put there for the visitor to discover. Control is order. And order means taking care. Making provision. Plussing the real world. That's what's new in the American city, thanks to the Disneylands, which are not cities.

Tim Delaney, the show producer for Space Mountain at Disneyland Paris, says that what's new about architecture Disney-style is that nobody thinks about architecture. Or cities. They think about dreams and fantasies. And when they come true, you have a mountain that's a building, or a building that's a dream (Fig. 200). What's new about Disney architecture says Tom Morris, creative director at Disneyland Paris, is that they don't necessarily start from those perfect, all-done renderings any more. For the Paris castle, they started with the details, the fragments that felt like a castle in this part of France (Fig. 201). Woods. Trees. The twist of Mont St. Michel, as it spirals up out of the water, like a vine. Eyvind Earle's

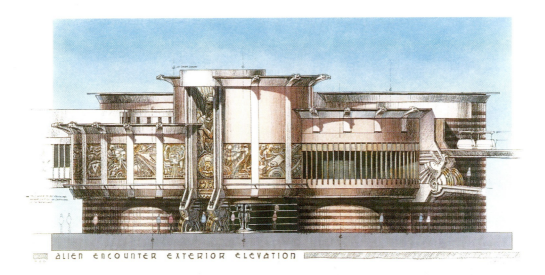

196. Proposal for exterior, Alien Encounter attraction, Tomorrowland, Walt Disney World (originally designed for Disneyland). Gil Keppler. Marker and crayon on blackline. 28 x 46. 1990.
197. Unexecuted "oppressed worker" caryatid for the interior of the Alien Encounter attraction, Tomorrowland, Walt Disney World (designed for Disneyland). Gil Keppler. Pen, pencil, and colored pencil on paper. 36 x 23. 1992.

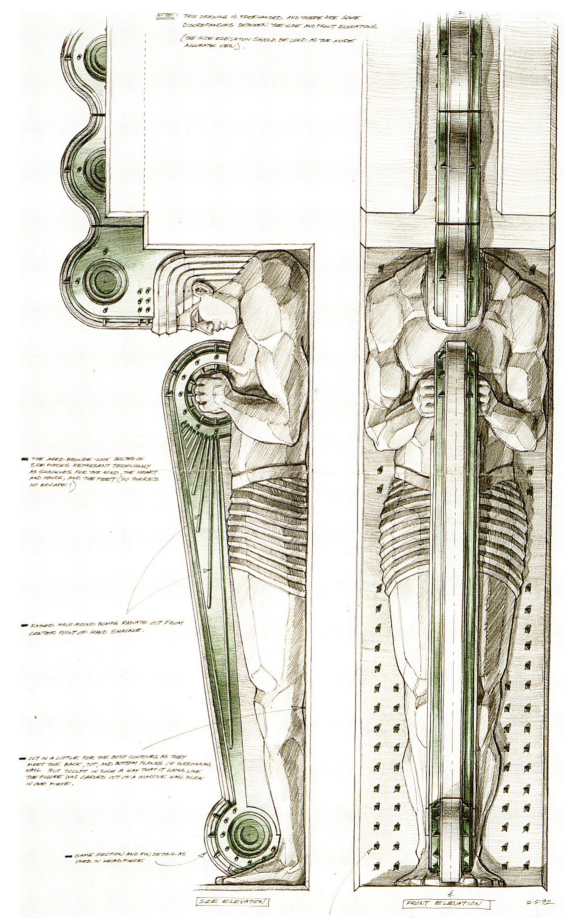

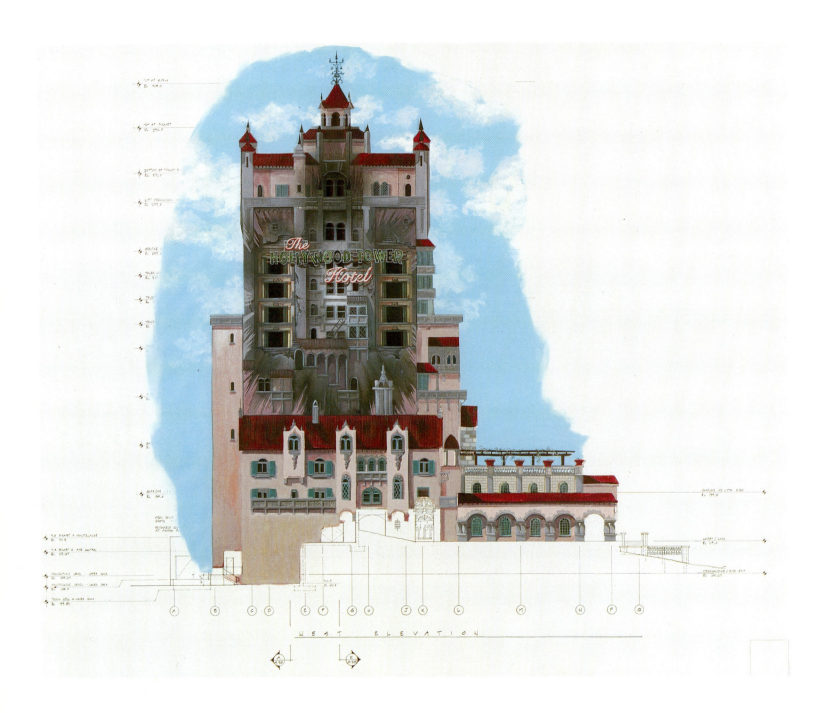

198. Hollywood Hotel, Tower of Terror, Disney-MGM Studios Theme Park, Walt Disney World. Suzanne Rattigan (colorist) and Coulter Winn (rendering). Acrylic on blackline with transparent overlay. 34 x 44. 1992.

long-ago drawing for the castle of the French princess in Disney's *Sleeping Beauty*. Puzzle fans can work all winter on the pinnacles of Ludwig II's castle, Neuschwanstein, bringing order out of a chaos of a thousand pieces. The pieces of the Paris castle came together in that same way, one part at a time. But the order came not from the outside—from a picture of some preexisting castle—but from the logic and the energy of the separate parts. After Walt, much of the creative energy of the theme parks was generated by the details. Plussing. A change in color. A new layer of ornament. The turret that suggests how it ought to be conjoined to a nearby patch of wall.

What's new about Disney architecture is a sense that Walt's berm can exist almost anywhere. Jan Sircus, Bobby Brooks, Tom Figgins, and Stuart Bailey, who worked on the new Disney Galleries in Las Vegas, midtown Manhattan, and other outposts far from any Disneyland ticket window, understand their real-world architecture as a commentary on the design of the parks. In these newest Disney stores, the threshold is the berm, isolating the visitor from the street or the mall, and inviting a theatrical suspension of disbelief. The berm, in retrospect, becomes a proscenium arch marking off a sort of little drama which is not, strictly speaking, about the mall. In Las Vegas, it's about Mickey and Minnie and the other Disney characters playing at being make-believe Romans, in a complex setting made up of columns: falling columns, trompe-l'œil columns, column parts, weighty columns upholding one tiny figurine, statues of columns. Like some crazed, space-age version of Giulio

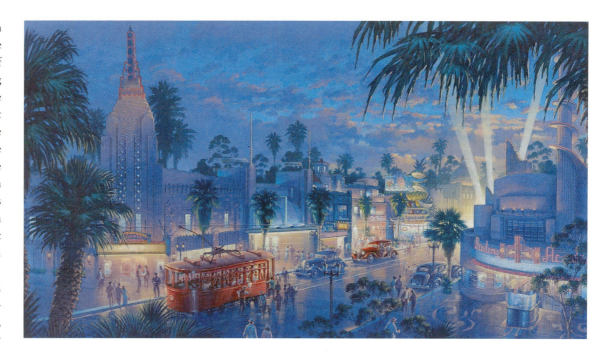

199. Sunset Boulevard at night, Disney-MGM Studios Theme Park, Walt Disney World. Brian Jowers. Acrylic, airbrush, and colored pencil on blackline. 26 x 33. 1991.
200. Space Mountain project, Discoveryland, Disneyland Paris. Tim Delaney. Acrylic on board. 30 x 58. 1993.

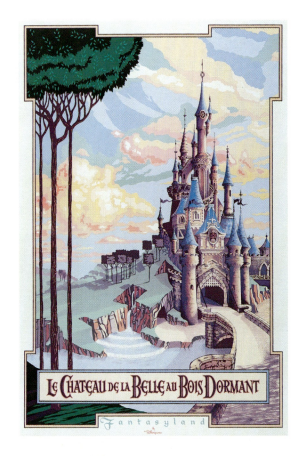

Romano's tumbling Palazzo del Tè, the shop seems to invite comparison with the classical vocabulary of Postmodernism and its ponderous, learned playfulness (Fig. 202). No, say the designers from Imagineering. We need to be clearer and more literal. We need to connect with people. To delight. To tell a little story starring the Disney characters. This isn't a museum or a monument. It's a Disney store (Fig. 203).

Being a Disney store, a themed hotel, a Disney park, imposes a burden on the architecture. It must be usable and utterly fantastical, all at once. It isn't enough to be a city or a place of business. It isn't enough to be Postmodern. Or chic. The operative aesthetic is too old-fashioned for that. Nineteenth-century culture prized imitation and illusion, or what Walt liked best about his miniatures. The culture of Disneyland comes from the pre-modern era, and Walt was a showman in the best traditions of the art of his turn-of-the-century boyhood, on Main Street, U.S.A. But those clever simulations embarrass us now, those bits of Italy and Art Deco L.A. They're plastic, cardboard, unreal. Twentieth-century Modernism looked for authenticity instead: Modernism made art out of the vernacular and exalted the functional. Just as Disneyland did, ironically. The stores on Main Street sell Disney products. You can spend the night fast asleep in a hotel disguised as a monorail station. Disneyland isn't a city: too much reality would ruin the illusion. Too much illusion, conversely, would ruin the reality—and that never happens. Disneyland is a dream and a place. No place. Utopia. A not-a-city. A city of dreams.

201. Disneyland Paris poster with Sleeping Beauty's Castle. Tracy Trinast and Tom Morris. Silkscreen print. 45 x 30. 1992.
202. Interior of Disney Gallery, Las Vegas.
203. Mickey Mouse display case for the Walt Disney Gallery project, Main Place, Santa Ana, California. Ed Roberts. Marker and pen on paper. 9 x 11. c. 1994.

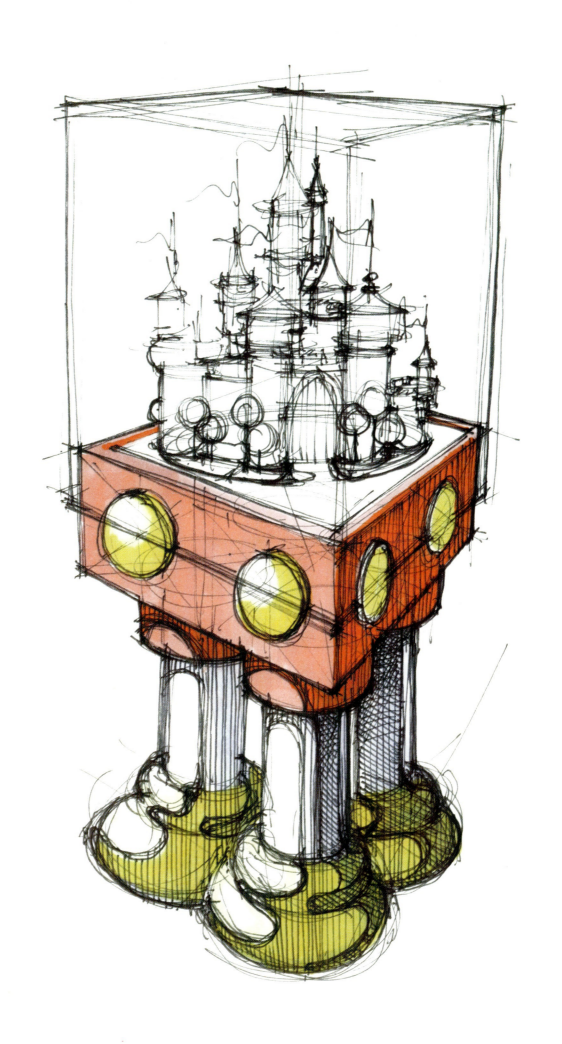

MAKING IMAGINATION SAFE IN THE 1950s

DISNEYLAND'S FANTASY ART AND ARCHITECTURE

Erika Doss

Catherine Wagner.
It's a Small World;
Fantasyland, Disneyland,
Anaheim, California.
Collection CCA.

"Their happiness castle," announces the full-color, full-page advertisement in a November 1957 issue of *Life* magazine (Fig. iv). A well-groomed family of four, all beaming huge mouthfuls of Gleem-scrubbed teeth and all sporting the latest Sanforized Casual Wear fashions, stands in front of Disneyland's Sleeping Beauty Castle and the entrance to Fantasyland. Dad holds the two ecstatic children—one boy, one girl—aloft in his arms, an Eastman Kodak Pony 35-mm camera prominently centered on his chest. He and the kids gleefully gaze skyward, the children's arms stretched out as if to clutch an escaped Mickey Mouse balloon. Mom faces the camera more directly. One arm reaches out to pat her young son, and the other, embellished with fake pearl bracelets and a white plastic handbag, is absently bent at her waist. Towering in the background, the turreted castle anchors this casual yet clearly staged picture of familial togetherness, and buttresses the aim of the entire advertisement, as the text illuminates:

Fantasyland is such fun! What family could resist the magic of happiness that brightens Disneyland like sunshine! That is why Walt Disney's Magic Kingdom is called 'the happiest place on earth.' Visitors leave their troubles behind. This Disneyland peace of mind can be enjoyed all through the year with the new Family Accident & Sickness policy developed by the North America Companies (INA). Like the famous INA Homeowners and Tenants policies that add so much to home protection, it is a *package policy* . . . Ask your INA agent about our program. It is a foundation for the happiness castle that healthy young families are building for their future!

If guests felt the compelling need to guarantee their "Disneyland peace of mind," the ad also notes that an "Information Center maintained by INA and their independent agents" on Disneyland's Main Street, U.S.A., was just the place to go.

Published a little over two years after Disneyland's Anaheim opening on July 17, 1955, this advertisement obviously plays to one of America's main obsessions in the 1950s: the affirmation and sustenance of family life.

iv. Advertisement for Insurance by North America (INA), from *Life*, November 18, 1957.

Disneyland, of course, was envisioned from the start as a place for families, an amusement-park extension, as historian Russell Nye observes, "of the backyard outing or family picnic." Walt Disney himself, disgusted with the "dirty, phony" carnies he had frequented with his young daughters in the 1930s and 1940s, vowed that Disneyland would be built as a "family park where parents and children could have fun together." In postwar America, he observed, "family fun" was as "necessary to modern living as a kitchen refrigerator." Yet, how was it that fantasy, and hence Fantasyland, came to fit within that familial vision? How did an architecture of truly fantastic dimensions—the Sleeping Beauty Castle being merely the centerpiece to an entire amusement park jam-packed with magical and make-believe settings—come to represent an architecture, and an entire national mindset, of security and reassurance? What, indeed, was the meaning of fantasy for Disneyland's artists, and Disneyland's audiences, in 1950s America?

Despite an abiding art historical reading of the 1950s as an era of ascetic and austere modernism, and similarly misguided assumptions of the decade's *Ozzie and Harriet* ordinariness, an undercurrent of myth and magic, of fantasy, pervaded both the fine arts and popular culture. In the world of architecture, this was blatantly realized in the mystically driven designs Frank Lloyd Wright conjured for New York's Guggenheim Museum (1946–59) and for the Beth Sholom Synagogue (1959) at Elkins Park, Pennsylvania. It was more subtly referenced in the light, airy, and spacious tract housing that architect Cliff May imagined for California's booming population, and heralded as his "Magic-Money Houses" (1953). In the world of art, it included the style of magic realism, a "dreamlike" aesthetic that characterized the work of scores of painters, including Salvador Dalì, as well as sculptors, graphic designers, and Disney animators. In more general cultural terms, the 1950s obsession with fantasy and the search for universal archetypes is evident in the postwar popularity of such books as Joseph Campbell's *The Hero with a Thousand Faces* (first published in 1949) and the dominance of Jungian psychology.

Fantasy—the bizarre, the eccentric, the grotesque, the unconventional, the unrestrained—filtered throughout 1950s America. But so, too, did impulses toward order, containment, and control. As cultural historian Warren Susman explained, post-World War II America embodied a dual consciousness of "abundance, opportunities, freedom, possibilities, and new sense of liberation" intermingled with anxiety, fear, and edgy disaffection. Susman's central 1950s icon for these "conflicting, yet mutually reinforcing" tensions was Disneyland, which he described as "a collective fantasy, an immense metaphor for the system of representations and values unique in postwar America." Postwar cultural obsessions with fantasy suggest a common search for alternatives, for new "possibilities." Yet, as Susman argued, postwar Americans were both attracted to and apprehensive about such "possibilities." Responsive to this conflicted "structure of desire," Disneyland's makers brilliantly manipulated this equation by creating a park where suspension of disbelief merged with order. Fantasyland, in particular, was constructed as an environment that synthesized public, postwar ideas about myth, ritual, and psychic redemption. Its architecture fused postwar enthusiasms for imagination, horror, hallucination, and magic with deep-felt desires for safety, security, restraint, and direction.

Fantasyland, of course, is only one of the "lands" that make up Disneyland, but it may lie closest to Walt Disney's earliest conception of the park as "Kiddieland," a place where parents could take their children, or children could take themselves, and enjoy hours of "'singing' waterfalls and fountains, pony rides, statues of the Disney characters, picnic areas, a roller coaster ride that would go over a simulated broken bridge." By 1955, Disney's dream of a safe and clean haven for American families had been extended to include Adventureland, Frontierland, Tomorrowland, and Main Street, U.S.A. But Fantasyland remained host to the greatest number of amusements most specifically oriented toward children, from the dark rides like Peter Pan's Flight, Snow White's Adventures, and Mr. Toad's Wild Ride—all fast-moving indoor rides set in spooky fluorescent-paint environments—to the outdoor flying and spinning rides such as Dumbo the Flying Elephant and the Mad Tea Party. For the faint of heart, Fantasyland also included tamer excursions and adventures aboard the Casey, Jr. Circus Train and the King Arthur Carrousel.

By 1959, Fantasyland also featured an Alice in Wonderland ride in which kids chased the White Rabbit in oversize, brightly colored caterpillar cars; a Storybook Land ride whose canal boats passed through the mouth of Monstro the Whale (of *Pinocchio* fame) and cruised past the miniaturized homes of the Three Little Pigs and the Seven Dwarfs; and the Matterhorn Bobsleds, a roller-coaster ride whose speedy sleighs careened in and out of the 147-foot glacial peak of the park's tallest attraction. And in 1966, It's a Small World opened, arguably the most popular (because it is the least frightening) of the Fantasyland rides among the preschool set (Fig. v). A twelve-minute boat ride that glides past hundreds of cheerful Audio-Animatronics® dolls representing the family of man, It's a Small World also features the park's catchiest riff, a treacly melody that lodges itself irrevocably in the brains of captive riders.

Most of Fantasyland's rides were specifically linked to the Disney movies that were also especially oriented to children, including the animated features *Peter Pan* (1953), *Snow White and the Seven Dwarfs* (1937), *The Adventures of Ichabod and Mr. Toad* (1949), *Dumbo* (1941), and *Alice in Wonderland* (1951), and live-action adventure films such as *Third Man on the Mountain* (1959)—the impetus for Disneyland's 1/100-scale version of the Matterhorn. Much as children who watch

Disney films often act out the roles of Cinderella or Maleficent the evil fairy (from *Sleeping Beauty*) at home, the rides in Fantasyland were designed to allow children to "step into" and become a part of their favorite animated films. Central figures in several rides were downplayed in order to allow their riders to "become" Snow White or Peter Pan. As Disney put it, "What youngster hasn't dreamed of flying with Peter Pan over moonlit London? Here in the 'happiest kingdom of them all,' you can journey with Snow White through the dark forest to the diamond mine of the Seven Dwarfs (Fig. vi); flee the clutches of Mr. Smee and Captain Hook with Peter Pan; and race with Mr. Toad in his wild auto ride through the streets of old London Town."

While mass culture critics bemoan Disneyland's emphasis on homogenization and its management of social control, they tend to ignore how Fantasyland's rides, in particular, accommodate play, magic, and intuition. As Miles Orvell argues, "Fantasyland occupies a special realm, a kind of unconscious or basement level for the mythos of the human realm, for it features the stories of fear, struggle, transformation, and conquest transposed to the level of the unconscious, of fantasy, of the fairy tale." Obviously, Fantasyland is the physical playground of Disney's celluloid, and consumerist, visions. But it also provides a temporal space where audiences may individually and imaginatively engage with and negotiate familiar myths and rituals on their own terms. They do so because, on the one hand, the rides are safe: kids don't fall out, or lose their fingers, or go mad. On the other hand, Fantasyland, like the fairy tales around which it is largely structured, contains "an emancipatory potential." As Jack Zipes maintains, "Even the mass-mediated fairy tales which reaffirm the goodness of the culture industry that produces them are not without their contradictory and liberating aspects. Many of them raise the question of individual autonomy versus state domination, creativity versus repression, and just the raising of this question is enough to stimulate critical and free thinking."

In the 1950s, then, the magical power of Fantasyland lay in its security and its entreaty to social subversion and cultural emancipation. Following a Freudian/Lacanian perspective, fantasy embodies the desire for integration, fusion, fullness, and accord in a world circumscribed by separation, dissolution, and alienation. In an American scene where tensions between abundance and anxiety were manifest, Fantasyland provided an arena in which those desires might be safely negotiated, sutured, and fulfilled. Like few other venues of mass culture in the 1950s (rock 'n' roll, perhaps), Fantasyland allowed and even encouraged the expression of desire by both children and adults. Even while it was also, paradoxically, couched in concepts of control and perhaps, guidance, Fantasyland proposed an alternative worldview from an obviously different socio-aesthetic environment. For American audiences searching for personal fulfillment, Fantasyland's countercultural potentiality (not promise) may account for its profound popular appeal from the 1950s to the present day.

Central to Fantasyland, and central to the entire park, is the Sleeping Beauty Castle (Fig. vii). Constructed of concrete blocks sculpted to look like quarried limestone and marble, decorated with royal blue turrets and golden spires, encircled by a rock-rimmed moat that is home to hundreds of swans, and entered by way of a working drawbridge, the castle rises just seventy-seven feet above the moat. It appears much taller because of the use of forced perspective: the blocks of stone near the top are significantly smaller than those at the base and thus create the illusion of soaring verticality. Such visual tricks were employed by Disneyland's makers (most of whom were, of course, filmmakers and movie animators themselves) throughout the park, from scaling down Main Street to $3/8$ths, or $5/8$ths, or $7/8$ths of its "true" size, to intimating the dramatic elevation of the Sleeping Beauty Castle.

The aesthetic intent of the Disney Imagineers was not to duplicate the real but to fabricate the ideal, creating in Main Street, U.S.A. a more intimate and "neighborly" small town, and in Fantasyland a setting where fairy tales were made even more wondrous. Writing in the mid-1970s, Umberto Eco denounced Disneyland as "a fantasy world more real than reality," assuming that its audiences, especially its American audiences, were incapable of making distinctions between the real and the "hyperreal." A more recent group of writers condemns Walt Disney World's consumerist contrivances, complaining that guests cannot separate the pleasure of the rides from the pleasure of the gift shops. Both critiques are far too sweeping in their stereotyping of Disney audiences as "passive consumers of entertainment" for whom rides and commodities, and hence fantasy and reality, are one and the same. Admittedly, Disney's theme parks are predicated on making money and at this they're doing extremely well (even Disneyland Paris recently reported its first annual profit). But, the gift shop price tags remind audiences (including children) of the realities of capitalism and, as critic Anne Norton observes, "Americans in Disneyland do not mistake it for reality. Rather, recognizing it as a representation of desire, they celebrate their collective capacity to produce a world more rational and more rewarding than that which Providence supplies them."

For 1950s Americans, the fantasy of Main Street was that it embodied what they wished small-town America could be (or could have been), as opposed to the suburban strip-mall reality they knew was waiting for them right outside Disneyland's parking lot. Similarly, Fantasyland rewarded its audiences with exciting and enclosed physical spaces, and odd and eccentric characters, which could be experienced on a safe and entirely temporal basis, in direct contrast, for example, to the kinds of real-world freaks and crazies photographed by Diane Arbus and Richard Avedon in the late 1950s and early 1960s. Fantasyland, of course, also made clear demarcations between the forces of good and evil (Snow White vs. the Wicked Queen, Peter Pan vs. Captain Hook, etc.), thereby heightening, perhaps, American desires for (or expectations of) moralistic simplicity in an age of increasing sociocultural and political complexity.

As the core of Disneyland, the Hub in front of Fantasyland's Castle radiates out into the avenues that lead to the rest of the park's lands. But the Sleeping Beauty Castle itself remains the primary visual hook that draws visitors through and down the axial conduit of Main Street, U.S.A. (Fig. viii). It is here that families congregate to watch the processions of characters and floats that make up Disneyland's daily parades, where visitors view the park's nightly fireworks spectacles, and where Tinker Bell, hoisted to the turret tops on a hidden line, sprinkles pixie dust in a live-action approximation of the opening credits of all-America's one-time favorite Sunday-night television show, *The Wonderful World of Color*. The park's televised dedication ceremony in 1955 concluded at Fantasyland, where Disney proclaimed, "Fantasyland is dedicated to the young and the young in heart, to those who believe when you wish upon a star, your dreams do come true," and then strolled across the drawbridge and through the gateway of the Sleeping Beauty Castle.

The castle is the park's most prominent "wienie"—Walt Disney's own term for the magnet, or marquee, that architects and urban planners use to attract and then disperse pedestrian mobs in a variety of directions. Crowd flow and directional pull were crucial to Disney's vision of a well-ordered and harmonious park. Convinced that a preponderance of choices (where to park, walk, eat, shop) and a lack of visual centrality made other theme parks (and indeed, most of the built environment)

physically tiresome and psychologically alienating, Disney's goal was to provide the illusion of total freedom in a carefully structured setting. As John Hench, one of Disneyland's primary project designers, put it: "Decision-making is very fatiguing. If you start wandering from one thing to another, not quite knowing what you want to see, you will wear yourself out." Or as Disney himself said: "The Hub gives people a sense of orientation. They know where they are at all times. And it saves a lot of walking."

Each of the Disney theme parks has a castle as its central landmark, from the Cinderella Castle at Walt Disney World in Orlando (which was copied at Tokyo Disneyland) to Le Château de la Belle au Bois Dormant at Disneyland Paris. The Sleeping Beauty Castle orients and guides guests at Disneyland in Anaheim. Fantasy architecture, in other words, reassures children and adults who might be overwhelmed by Disneyland's visual splendor and numerous sensual opportunities (walking, seeing, riding, listening, touching, smelling, eating), and nudges them toward specific pathways throughout the park. In an odd and ironic gesture, fantasy, family, and the relative security of guidance and control, all become intermingled and practically inseparable, especially in Fantasyland.

Like Fantasyland's various rides, the Castle references a specific Disney movie. In this case, the fairy-tale château suggests the cartoon palace animated in the wide-screen, Technirama 70-mm feature, *Sleeping Beauty*. In production throughout the 1950s, the movie was not released until 1959 because of Disney's almost total concentration on opening his theme park. Since Disney had been concentrating, too, on making live-action films (like *Davy Crockett* in 1955 and *Old Yeller* in 1957) and venturing into the world of television (with the ABC network's hit show *Disneyland* in 1954, which later evolved into *The Wonderful World of Color* on NBC), *Sleeping Beauty* marked the studio's return to lush and colorful

animation and fairy-tale fare. Layered in rich details and intricate backgrounds that Disney artist Eyvind Earle reproduced from early Renaissance paintings, including the enchanting miniatures of the Limbourg Brothers' *Les Très Riches Heures du Duc de Berry* (c. 1413–16), *Sleeping Beauty* is one of Disney's most decorative and luxurious cartoons. Its story line was somewhat flimsy, however, prompting one critic at an early showing to remark, "The characters talked about the story they were in, but didn't live it—the audience never felt it—it was never real."

The Sleeping Beauty Castle is similar, a jewel-like architectural shell that is the park's most memorable symbol but one that visitors mostly walk through on their way to "feel the fantasy" of Disneyland's other attractions. When the park first opened, *Life* magazine reported that "a model torture chamber" was planned as a lure inside the Castle. That would have given the building an unexpected, multidimensional character not unlike that in Jean Cocteau's surreal film *La Belle et la bête* (1945), in which a formerly ordinary mansion is transformed into a magical and horrifying castle where humans serve as candelabras and mirrors become mysterious time transporters. But in Disneyland's Castle, such "instrumentalization of fantasy" never actually occurred. Instead, the "Sleeping Beauty Castle Walk-Through" opened in April 1957, a modest attraction consisting of a few dusty dioramas of Briar Rose Barbie and Prince Philip Ken dolls, posed in scenes from the still unreleased movie and mounted in glass cages set into the castle's cement-stone walls. While the castles at Orlando, Paris, and Tokyo were designed to enclose shops (La Boutique du Château in Paris), restaurants (King Stefan's Banquet Hall in Orlando), and rides (the Mystery Tour inside Tokyo's Castle does feature a dungeon and a mechanical dragon and commands the longest lines in the entire park), Anaheim's castle was conceived merely as a comforting geographic landmark.

Even if the Sleeping Beauty Castle comes off only as a lavish bit of formalism, it remains the most extraordinary encapsulation of 1950s fantasy, an architectural pastiche of European styles blended with elements seemingly derived from magic realist paintings, World's Fair sculptures and pavilions, various commercial and vernacular environments, and outsider art. Herb Ryman's initial design for Disneyland (the "Anaheim Scheme"), drawn as an aerial view in 1953, shows the Castle as a dramatic and imposing structure pushed to the park's northernmost acres and surrounded by a steep and elaborately turreted rampart. By 1954, however, Ryman's plans had been greatly refined, with the Castle more centrally placed in the park and built in a style, as Disney lore has it, "inspired by the pinnacled Neuschwanstein castle in Bavaria."

Disneyland's Castle bears some faint resemblance to Ludwig II's late-nineteenth-century rendition of a monumental early-Gothic château, built atop the ruins of several older castles on a mountain slope in Hohenschwangau, Bavaria, given the historically false nomenclature "Neuschwanstein" in 1891. But the Disneyland structure is far more like the last of "Mad King Ludwig's" grandiose architectural schemes, a projected castle at Falkenstein near Fussen (Fig. ix). Insistent on building an eagle's nest retreat atop sheer cliffs, a hideaway where he might completely escape the goings-on of the Second German Reich (to which he had essentially abdicated Bavarian sovereignty in 1871), Ludwig II contracted with Prince Thurn-und-Taxis's chief architect,

v. Background design for the interior of It's a Small World, Disneyland. Mary Blair. Opaque watercolor on paper with printed pictures of flags. 25 x 35. 1965.

Max Schultze, to draw up plans for a new castle in Falkenstein. Schultze's 1884 model of a three-story late-Gothic edifice with numerous turrets, a front balcony, and a five-story watch tower, enclosed by a rock wall with low towers, and entered through a uniaxial gatehouse, is remarkably similar to Ryman's 1954 conception of the Sleeping Beauty Castle. While Disneyland's palace would be built on a somewhat squatter plan than the soaring scale Schultze proposed for Falkenstein, its tightly situated mass retained several of the Bavarian castle's essential ingredients, including the tall watchtower, the plentiful turrets, the towered wall, and the central gateway entrance.

Schultze's clay maquette of Falkenstein, along with numerous watercolor sketches he made of the castle's ground plan and interior rooms, have been on display since the 1920s in the König-Ludwig-II Museum in Herrenchiemsee. During the 1950s, hordes of Americans trekked to Germany, from occupying forces and their dependents to tourists aiming to get a taste of the cultural standards to which the United States, the postwar globe's economic and military leader, might also aspire. Ludwig's castles were landmark "must-sees" among the standard tourist packages assembled for tens of thousands of GIs stationed at bases from Bad Tölz to Baumholder, and for Americans from all over the States. Disney himself was certainly familiar with these examples of fantasy architecture from his extensive travels in Europe in earlier decades; apparently, a favorite spot was Tivoli Gardens, in Copenhagen. Moreover, from 1950 to 1954, Disney spent a good deal of time in England and on the continent overseeing the production of live-action films such as *Treasure Island* (1950). As plans for Disneyland burgeoned in the early 1950s, Disney dispatched designers to study amusement parks and tourist spots all over America, from Knott's Berry Farm in Buena Park, California to Greenfield Village in Dearborn, Michigan. But, like Disney artist John Hench, who studied art at the Sorbonne in the late 1930s, Disney also recalled those European architectural landmarks—and tourist attractions—that might fit with the mass-culture fantasy scheme he was imagining in Southern California.

Hench, who would greatly assist Disney in the development of the Anaheim park, was trained at the Art Student's League in New York and the Otis Art Institute in Los Angeles, joining the Disney studios as a sketch artist in 1939. Like the studio's other cartoonists, he attended night classes at the Disney Art School. Disney's was the first animation outfit to start its own art school (in 1932), prompted by the founder's own concerns that his staffers always improve and progress as *artists*, not merely as cartoonists, particularly as Disney himself had "earned widespread praise in intellectual circles for his innovative animated fantasies" throughout the Great Depression. Editorial cartoonist David Low, for example, championed him as "Leonardo da Disney" in a 1942 *New Republic* essay, remarking on his "artistry and extension of range" and "understanding of the meaning of observed movement." Also in the early 1940s, Russian filmmaker Sergei Eisenstein declared Disney's films "the greatest contribution of the American people to art," and art critic Emily Genauer commended *Fantasia*'s modern art alliances, writing: "One or two of [the animated segments] recall Kandinsky especially. There were several closely related to the surrealist Miró. And the opening night audience—many of whom, doubtless, raise up their hands in horror at abstract paintings—loved it."

Indeed, Disney was not only an artist but a modern artist. If late-nineteenth-century American culture emphasized the disjunction between civilization and savagery, and between art and passion, many twentieth-century American artists were determined to connect them via the integrative mode of modern art, characterized by its formalist predilections for dynamism, flux, paradox, ambivalence, montage, overlapping, and simultaneity, and its social aims of eliminating the previous culture's separated spheres. As historian Steven Watts writes, "Modernist impulses flowered everywhere in Disney's world of fantasy as his animation constantly blurred the line between imagination and reality to produce a wondrous universe where animals spoke, plants and trees acted consciously, and inanimate objects felt emotion." He adds that in Disney's early films "fluid perception, free-flowing fantasy, and a yen for simultaneous experience moved to center stage," and "a preoccupation with the dream state" revealed "a fusion of intellect and emotion, superego and id as warm fairy tales often encapsulated dark, nightmarish visions." While Disney himself never expounded upon his allegiance with Modernism, he was clearly committed to modern art's tenets of fusion and integration. And he expected the artists who worked for him to strive toward the same integrative aesthetic vision.

Hired at the Disney Art School to "raise the level" of the artistic skills among the studio's animators, Don Graham, an instructor at the Chouinard Art Institute in Los Angeles, taught night classes in "action analysis" and line drawing. His classes were essentially required of Disney studio artists like Hench, as were the series of guest lectures on the history of art and the ways in which Disney filmmakers might appropriate the modern styles of cubism, futurism, surrealism, and abstraction, which were given by art critic Jean Charlot in the late 1930s. But, as the studio pursued animated feature films such as *Snow White* (1937) and *Bambi* (1942), Disney also insisted that his artists make the characters "as real as possible, near-flesh-and-blood."

In other words, in typical modern art fashion, aesthetic distinctions between fantasy and reality were purposely confounded. As Hench remarked in a 1975 interview, "so-called 'reality' is more fantastic than 'fantasy.' Those two terms are not only interchangeable, they often overlap." Stating "I definitely feel that we cannot do the fantastic things based on the real, unless we first know the real," Disney directed his artists "to go to the source" and "study the real object." But he also demanded their imaginative manipulation (rather than duplication) of reality. As Disney staffers conceptualized the Sleeping Beauty Castle it is not unlikely, then, that they turned their gaze to "real" castles in Europe. Writer Ray Bradbury insisted, for example, that one of the spires atop the Sleeping Beauty Castle was "a duplicate" of the spire which Eugène Viollet-le-Duc "restored" to the Cathedral of Notre-Dame in the nineteenth century. Or, if they didn't see the castles as tourists, perhaps the Imagineers studied architectural fantasies from around the world in the pages of *National Geographic*, which Disney himself called a "truly invaluable research tool." But their gaze was almost certainly colored, too, by aesthetic impulses leading toward the blurring of distinctions between fantasy and reality.

One modern artist whose work was particularly embedded in that blurring was surrealist painter Salvador Dalì. Indeed, both Disney's and Hench's postwar aesthetic interests, and their subsequent ideas for the development of Disneyland, may have been shaped by their interaction with Dalì in 1946. During the 1940s, Disney temporarily gave up working on feature films and spent time

vi. Cottage of Seven Dwarfs, from the original interior set of a Fantasyland "dark ride" about Snow White's adventures. Ken Anderson. Tempera on board. 6 x 8. 1954.

vii. Disneyland castle under construction, Anaheim, California, 1954–55.
viii. Sleeping Beauty Castle in Fantasyland, Disneyland. Herbert Ryman. Colored pencil on brownline. 22 1/2 x 50 1/2. 1954.

creating short animated segments (some for the war effort) which were released in packages. In 1946, he decided that these packages could be enhanced by having "big-name artists" work on their production, and so he hired Dalì to generate the graphics for a short six-minute musical number called "Destino." Based on a Mexican ballad by Armando Dominguez, "Destino" was conceived as one of the Disney studios "Good Neighbor" packages, animated shorts focused on the "spectacle of the Latin American landscape" and compiled into movies like *Saludos Amigos* (1943) and *The Three Caballeros* (1945). Hench and Disney artist Bob Cormack were assigned to assist Dalì's story sketches and to shape the avant-garde artist's surrealist style into the kind of Disney omnibus that would appeal to a global public.

Dalì was already well known to that public, especially to American audiences. In 1924, André Breton defined surrealism as "pure psychic automatism," a fairly broad description encompassing the calligraphic formalism of Paul Klee, the frottage mannerism of Max Ernst, and the dreamlike pictures of René Magritte. Actually, Dalì's art was closer in style to that coined "magic realism" by Museum of Modern Art director Alfred Barr in 1942, who described it as the "contemporary art of painters who by means of exact realistic techniques try to make plausible and convincing their improbable, dreamlike or fantastic visions." Magic realist art, like Dalì's odd pictures of limp watches and hallucinatory landscapes, straddled straightforward narrative styles and more off-the-wall surreal styles by pushing realism to the limits but not over the edge and by emphasizing the imaginative and the implausible, not the impossible. Although it is taken for granted that Abstract Expressionism reigned as the dominant mode of modern art in post-World War II America, magic realism was a close contender as a creepy, off-kilter aesthetic that appealed not only to scores of artists but also to a public self-consciously caught up in, but not quite able to resolve, the ironies and tensions of postwar life.

To the average American, such art meant "Dalí," who first came to mass attention with an appearance on the cover of *Time* magazine in December 1936 and who thereafter dominated both the pre- and postwar press with his art gallery antics and "weird" paintings. The Time-Life empire, always clued in to public taste and desire, was particularly attentive to Dalí and extensively covered his every stateside movement, from art shows and ballet premieres to fairground spectacles. In their full-color coverage of his 1939 Julien Levy Gallery exhibition in New York, *Life* took a psychoanalytic stance in explaining Dalí to their millions of readers, concluding that in his picture *Sleep*, Dalí "painted the huge head to suggest a monster because in dreams man is free to indulge his passions and commit crimes. The little dog was Dalí's childhood pet and the houses are his 'little town of dreams'." Similarly, in their review of Dalí's *Bacchanale*, a 1939 ballet loosely based on "the Venusberg scene in Richard Wagner's *Tannhäuser*," *Life* described Dalí's "paranoiac performance" as "the psychoanalyzed nightmare of King Ludwig II of Bavaria, Wagner's mad patron, set to Wagner's music." Full of "sex and lovely girls," *Bacchanale* also featured nymphs, fauns, bacchantes, sinister-looking swans, and wildly painted surrealist sets of fairy-tale castles. *Life* reported that *Bacchanale*'s audience found the show "amusing, annoying, puzzling, and disquieting," which guaranteed, said the magazine, that the ballet would be "very successful."

While the links between Disneyland's fantasy architecture and Dalí's magic realist paintings—and the Bavarian castle sets, menacing swans, and "lovely girls" of his surrealist ballet—are compelling (Fantasyland, after all, also features big-headed characters, a dream-like atmosphere, scaled-down village settings, and a castle), the similarities between Fantasyland and Dalí's outrageous *Dream of Venus* attraction at the 1939 New York World's Fair are equally strong. Dalí's pavilion attracted huge crowds at the fair and an incredible amount of press, including this, again from *Life*:

Dream of Venus, the creation of famed Surrealist Painter Salvador Dalí, is the most recent addition to the still-growing list of amusement-area girl shows and easily the most amazing. Weird building contains a dry tank and a wet tank. In the wet tank girls swim under water, milk a bandaged-up cow, tap typewriter keys which float. In the Dry Tank a sleeping Venus reclines in a 36-ft. bed, covered with white and red satin, flowers and leaves. Scattered about the bed are lobsters frying on beds of hot coals and bottles of champagne. The outside of the building vaguely resembles an exaggerated shellfish and is ornamented with plaster females, spikes, and other dreamlike oddities. All this is most interesting and amusing.

Of course, Dalí's brand of magic realism appealed at the 1939 fair, and well into the 1950s, for deeper reasons than those of sheer amusement. Especially in postwar America, Dalí's eerie illustrations and installations corresponded to the same sorts of conflicted desires that Disney himself would seek to articulate at Fantasyland. The fact that Dalí was so incredibly successful in the public realm, receiving further acclaim for the dream sequences he designed for Alfred Hitchcock's 1945 movie *Spellbound*, certainly also appealed to Disney, whose entire postwar financial future would come to depend on the popular success of the Anaheim theme park.

Dalí spent two months working on "Destino" at Disney's studio in 1946, surprising everyone with his prompt, daily production of sketches and his friendly, "team-player" demeanor. The sketches he produced were characteristically Daliesque: arid landscapes scattered with melting watches, broken statuary, and odd fragments of classical architecture, or strange portraits in which figures metamorphosed into balls, turtles, ants, and dandelion puffs. Aiming to have his magic realist art reach "immense numbers of people," Dalí proposed that "Destino" blend live action and animation, much like the Disney feature *Song of the South*, which was released in 1946. Concentrating on a pair of modern dancers flitting across his surreal landscapes in search of true love, Dalí imagined his Disney project closing "with a baseball game ballet culminating in a magic temple of love floating in the sky." But, after about fifteen seconds of Technicolor film for this Disney-Dalí collaboration were produced, "Destino" was dropped. Disney archivist David Smith feels the project "got too far out for Walt," but as plans for Fantasyland began to foment, Dalí's artistic presence at the studio, and his widespread popular appeal, influenced Disney's creative directions.

In fact, the studio's animated feature film *Alice in Wonderland* (1951) was full of surreal suggestions, most notably the Daliesque deconstruction and reconstruction of the Mad Hatter's watch during the tea party scene. Although the movie was not a great financial success, its experimental aesthetics and, equally as important, its assertion that Wonderland's staged insanity was only temporary, would be repeated throughout Fantasyland. *Alice in Wonderland* ends with Alice waking up, grabbing her cat Dinah, and walking out of her dream. The attractions at Fantasyland, particularly the dark rides like Peter Pan's Flight and Snow White's Adventures, would be timed in the same manner, with riders concluding their magical and sometimes frightening journeys (most of which are only a few minutes in duration) by standing up and walking out into the relative security and order of the rest of the theme park.

Of course, Salvador Dalí and Ludwig II were hardly the only sources of fantasy for Disney's 1950s Imagineers. As Disney directed his artists to search the world for viable theme park motifs and tourist attractions, the architecture of pageants and World's Fairs, from the neon-hued exhibition buildings at the

ix. Model of the projected castle at Falkenstein, 1884. Max Schultze, architect (1845–1926). From *The Castles of Ludwig II of Bavaria*, figure 93. CCA Library.

1933–34 Century of Progress Exposition in Chicago to the Art-Deco drama of the four-hundred-foot Tower of the Sun at the 1939–40 San Francisco Golden Gate International Exposition, was undoubtedly studied in detail. But many of the Imagineers may simply have looked around the vernacular landscape of Southern California for abundant examples of make-believe architecture. Long before the eruption of Postmodern historicism, California's built environment featured plenty of restaurants pretending to be Moorish castles, apartment buildings disguised as Spanish Colonial missions, movie theaters designed as Chinese palaces, and a factory (the Samson Tire and Rubber Company) posed as an Assyrian temple.

In the 1920s, Los Angeles sported lunch stands designed as giant hamburgers, ice cream parlors transformed into igloos (with polar bear attendants), diners shaped as pigs and dogs, and a chi-chi restaurant (the Brown Derby) built as a giant hat. As Michael Sorkin writes, Disneyland is clearly modeled after the city of Los Angeles, whose "genius" lies in its "invention of the possibility of the Loirish Bungalow sitting chockablock with the Tudoroid." Fantasyland's present-day juxtaposition, for example, of the Gothic-Bavarian-surreal-style Sleeping Beauty Castle with the faux-Tudor-style mansion setting of Mr. Toad's Wild Ride more than proves his point. Disneyland's greatest debt to Southern California simulacra may rest, however, in the gigantic pastel-colored cups and saucers fashioned for the Mad Tea Party, the whirling, spinning outdoor ride that was Fantasyland's fastest and most dizzying midway-style joyride when the park first opened in 1955.

Prior to Disneyland, Southern California's most extraordinary examples of fantasy architecture were its so-called outsider artworks, the home-made creations and visionary environments of usually self-taught artists. From Tressa Prisbrey's *Bottle Village* in Simi Valley, a vast assortment of houses hand-built from cement and tens of thousands of glass bottles (to house a collection of over seventeen thousand pencils and an equally large number of dolls), to Baldasare Forestiere's *Underground Gardens* in Fresno, an elaborately tunneled subterranean setting of some fifty earthen rooms, the California landscape has long been host to the fantastic environments of various folk or outsider artists. In the 1950s, the most obvious example of outsider art in Los Angeles was that built in Watts by Italian laborer Sam (or Simon) Rodia. In the mid-1920s, on a triangular lot near train tracks in what was still a fairly rural area, Rodia began to sculpt an elaborate garden with three enormous towers, the tallest over 104 feet in height. Designed in an intricate filigree pattern, the cement-covered steel-rod towers, as well as the ornamental garden sculptures and the scalloped wall surrounding the entire property, were encrusted with all sorts of found objects, from bits of broken bottles and cracked ceramic tiles (Rodia apparently worked at Malibu Pottery between 1926 and 1932), to seashells, shattered plates and cups, and imprints made of tools, corncobs, and his own hands.

Like most outsider artists, Rodia never really explained his motives in building Watts Towers, although the visual similarities between his castle-like minarets and the decorative architectural maquette (called *giglio*) that is carried in parades during the feast day of Saint Paulinus in Nola, a small town in southern Italy near Rodia's birthplace, may provide some clues as to his spiritual and/or nativist intentions. He lived in and worked on Watts Towers for some thirty-odd years and then, in 1954, simply walked away from the site, never to return.

Easily visible to riders on the "little red train" that once ran daily from Long Beach to Los Angeles, Watts Towers received a good deal of press around the same time Disneyland was being imagined. One 1951 *Arts and Architecture* article called Rodia's enigmatic environment "a bizarre yet pleasant world," a description similar to Fantasyland's own blend of imagination and security. Rodia's gardens and Fantasyland both embody architectural visions of other worlds; both are eccentric, off-beat places where visitors participate in perceptually and physically disorienting experiences and may, thereby, consider new and alternative visions of reality. Of course, as art historian John Beardsley points out, there are vast differences between Rodia's recycled visionary environment and Disneyland's $17 million version of commercialized fantasy. Still, as Disney's Imagineers were searching for aesthetic models on which to base their construction of a fanciful environment for America's families, the magical spaces of California's outsider artists may have worked their way into Fantasyland's final architectural conceptualization.

One recent critique of the Disney theme parks finds them to be mainly suffocating, hegemonic places where families are under constant pressure to consume and conform. But Fantasyland, in particular, is hardly so one-dimensional. For millions of American families—even, perhaps, for the make-believe family unit depicted in the 1957 insurance ad that began this essay—Fantasyland's off-beat buildings, outlandish characters, and other-worldly attractions offer opportunities for individual choice and personal transformation. Inside the dark rides of Snow White's Adventures and Peter Pan's Flight, children and adults experience playful and perhaps empowering moments of disruption and defamiliarization. For a few, brief minutes, in controlled physical settings, Fantasyland's audiences are urged to free their minds and exercise their imagination. Accommodating abiding cultural desires for magic and security, for release and restraint, Fantasyland remains a place where Americans truly can "feel the fantasy" suggested in recent Chanel ads (directed by *Blade Runner* filmmaker Ridley Scott)—and at the end of the day, return to the real world.

Catherine Wagner. *Jungle Cruise; Adventureland, Tokyo Disneyland, Tokyo.* Collection CCA.

DISNEYLAND

ITS PLACE IN WORLD CULTURE

Yi-Fu Tuan with Steven D. Hoelscher

Disneyland is a quintessential American dream come true. Both its enormous success and the attack it has drawn from academic critics bear witness to this fact. Other people in other times have also had highly ambitious dreams of a perfect place. Like those of Walt Disney, these were translated into reality with a technical prowess that commands admiration even today. Disney's achievement can be viewed in the context of these other achievements, taking into account certain similarities and differences in the scope and ingenuity of material construction, conceptions of time and space, the provisioning of both moral uplift and entertainment, and the idea that a good place—any good place—has to have a boundary that separates it from and yet allows traffic with the larger world.

Cosmic City—Cosmic Theme Park?

An aerial photograph taken in 1954 of the first stage in the construction of Disneyland shows a vast rectangle carved out of orange and walnut groves (see Fig. 1). The heart-shaped berm that would enclose the theme park has not yet emerged. What we see instead is a piece of cleared space—a blank sheet. To a student of the ancient urban scene, it is a clear reminder of the first stage in the construction of the cosmic city, and, in particular, of the Chinese cosmic city, which likewise begins its life as a blank sheet—a gigantic walled-in space—on which architects can impose their design of palaces and parks, avenues and streets. Also within the rectangle are villages and farms. For all its artificiality, the cosmic city includes nature—controlled nature. One might even exercise poetic license and call a city that is so thoroughly planned a sort of cosmic theme park. Its theme or overarching purpose is to promote contentment, as the overarching purpose of the Disney park is to promote happiness.

"Contentment" is a more passive word than "happiness," and one might see in this a significant difference between the Chinese dream and the American dream. But whether "contentment" or "happiness," that which is feared is disorder, chaos, violence. Officials of the cosmic city try to constrain behavior by confining suspicious people, including street entertainers, itinerant traders, and unruly students within designated compounds; and indeed the guards at the city gates keep an eye on all who come and go. I see here a parallel with the social thinking behind Disneyland. The well-ordered park is Walt Disney's answer to the rowdiness, dirt, and threat of social chaos and bodily excess that afflict amusement arcades and parks in decay—egregiously, Coney Island. Chinese officials, no less than Disney officials, both fear and deprecate the sort of uninhibited carnivalesque atmosphere so beloved of the critics of bourgeois order, notably Mikhail Bakhtin.

Great European Gardens—Technological Forebears?

Much closer to the spirit and purpose of Disneyland are its European forebears—the princely gardens, especially those that were built between 1500 and 1800. The great European garden is an idealized world separated from both nature and the city, and also from the frustrating social imbroglios within the main house, to which the garden is attached. A major source of inspiration for the garden is the biblical Eden. From it comes such images of perfection as a climate of eternal spring, and a wealth of exotic plants and animals that live peacefully together under the benevolent care of their natural masters—the human beings. At one time, Europeans believed that this biblical Eden could actually be found, that it has a geographical location. An improved knowledge of geography erased that possibility. Remaining, however, was the challenge to build such an Eden, such a paradise, on earth. The perfect climate was and remains largely beyond human power to achieve, and it cannot be found outside a few favored places such as southern Italy and California. But human ingenuity can rise to meet most other requirements. Such was the belief of the Renaissance and baroque potentates, and such, in our time, was the belief of Walt Disney.

Certain fundamental similarities between the premodern European garden and the modern Disney theme park can be seen in the architectural and engineered character of the historic gardens. Their builders did not hesitate to distort nature if by doing so they could make it more aesthetic and amusing. Consider that marvelous manufacture of Renaissance hydraulic engineers—the fountain. Water was compelled to dance, to soar unnaturally skyward, for human pleasure. Fountains were a delight to the eye and to the ear, but they could also be used as squirt guns to splash visitors, causing them momentary dismay, but the element of surprise—of unpredictability within a thoroughly controlled environment—added to their overall enjoyment. Disney engineers who conceived the drenching pleasures of Splash Mountain would have appreciated the Renaissance water jets, both for the thrill they offered and for the ingenuity of their construction and placement.

A major challenge to builders of sixteenth-century gardens was how to accommodate animals. To simulate paradise, animals must be present. Moreover, they have to live peacefully with one another and with people, as all living things do in paradise. In the real world, wild animals cannot of course be let loose in a garden. Putting them behind bars is also not an answer, for it clearly destroys the desired paradisiac illusion—unless they are birds, which can be caged and the cages then cleverly hidden among the foliage. To meet the challenge of including animals, builders in the past, as today in Disneyland, resorted to technology. Michel de Montaigne encountered some remarkable examples of mechanical simulation during his visit to Italy in 1581. At one Tuscan villa, he found toy animals that could drink, jump into the water, and swim about. At another, he heard birds singing but what he really heard were the sounds produced by the impact of water falling on trapped air. "Touch a spring," Montaigne noted in amazement, "and you give motion to an artificial owl, which, on presenting itself on top of a rock, causes a sudden cessation of the previous harmony, the little birds being supposed to have become alarmed at his presence."

Disneyland, as a happy Edenic place, must have animals, and indeed visitors may have the impression that they are everywhere. But, with the exception of a few "petting animals" (ponies, goats, and the like) once sequestered in Big Thunder Ranch, a few ducks in the Rivers of America, the odd horse that draws a trolley on Main Street, U.S.A., uninvited birds that swarm into the ecologically lush park, they are not real and they are certainly not wild. Rather what one finds in Disneyland is a strange assortment of animated beings. These include: original creations played by human actors, automated robots designed to look like animals but exhibiting decidedly human traits and talents, and automated robots designed to both look and behave like real animals. Mickey Mouse is a supreme example of original art—a mouse only by the wildest stretch of the imagination, a human being in personality and behavior, but superior to most people in his inimitable blend of courtliness and innocence.

Anthropomorphized characters appear in a variety of exhibits and rides—Brer Rabbit, for example, and the Country Bears, who sing and stomp through a Western-style hoe-down. And then there are large beasts like the elephants and hippos in Jungle Cruise, whose realistic appearance and menacing behavior are intended to impress and thrill young visitors. Disneyland is thus alive with animated creatures. Their presence, thanks to robotics technology and human actors, helps to sustain the illusion of a paradisiac world in which animals and people, animals that are larger than life and look like huggable cherubim, can all live in close proximity, offer one another, if not intimate friendship, then wonder and excitement without risk of bodily harm (Fig. x).

Paradise is perfection. Change is incompatible with what has already been perfectly achieved. But human beings are easily bored. They require not only variety but constant change. This was certainly true of Louis XIV and his courtiers. At the Sun King's favorite retreat, Marly, improvements never ceased. Great stretches of thick woodland were transformed into lakes, where people were rowed about in gondolas, and were then changed back to forests so dense that daylight was banished as soon as the trees were planted. Goldfish ponds, decorated with gilding and paintings, were scarcely finished before they were unmade and rebuilt to a higher standard of perfection. Walt Disney was famously proud of the fact that his creations are always in process, never finished: new rides, parades, and performances are periodically added, tempting visitors to return to the park again and again for more helpings of happiness. Both Marly and Disneyland can appear to be in a constant state of flux: courtiers such as the duc de Saint-Simon complained about the confusion, as in our time visitors to Disneyland might complain about construction work, especially when it

Disneyland: Its Place in World Culture 193

x. Bird's-eye view of Jungle Cruise ride, Adventureland, Disneyland. Disney legend has it that the ride was based on the movie adventures of Bogart and Hepburn in *The African Queen*. Harper Goff. Brown and black ink on paper. 23 x 28. 1954.

occurs on the sites of favorite old attractions now demolished. In fact, at both places meticulous planning has been the order of the day. Improvements at Marly were never whims. They were thoroughly tested before being carried out. First, the king would see a watercolor rendering, which might undergo several revisions before it won final royal approval; then a full-scale model was built, and only when this, too, met with approval would the new design be implemented. One could easily substitute Walt Disney for the Sun King in this sketch: both are restless yet meticulous in their search for ideal workmanship and both have vast powers—technological as well as human—at their command.

What does one do in paradise? How did high European society use its splendid gardens? The aims were many, including sheer fun. Pictures of Tudor gardens show men and women paddling on a stream, rolling on the ground, teasing monkeys, splashing each other with water, and appreciating the thrill of disorientation in elaborate mazes. In eighteenth-century France, the charm of simple life in a timeless country scene was considered an important amenity of the royal pleasure ground (Fig. xi). As European aristocrats two hundred years ago indulged in pastoral nostalgia, so middle-class Americans today indulge in Main Street nostalgia. Given the stage of a prettified farm, a Marie Antoinette could play at being a milkmaid, as in Disneyland visitors entering a quaint store on Main Street can play at being shoppers in a presumably more innocent time. Quiet socializing in a shaded grove and, at the other extreme, watching mythic figures frolicking on an elaborate stage of cloud-

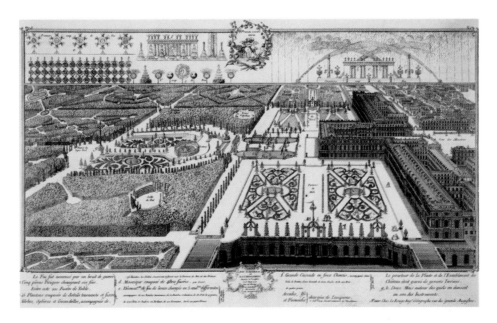

xi. Fireworks and Illuminations at Versailles in Honour of the Marriage of the Count of Provence (later Louis XVIII) to Louise-Mari-Joseph de Savoie. Unknown artist. Etching with burin work, hand-touched with yellow watercolor. 17 1/2 x 29 1/2. c. 1771. CCA DR:1982:105.

bedecked heaven and pastoral earth were both features of the court theater during the sixteenth and seventeenth centuries. Again one can find parallels in Disneyland: munching hamburgers with family and friends in a shady corner of the Hungry Bear Restaurant is one kind of experience; another is watching the hieratic Lion King and his court moving majestically down Disneyland's own axis mundi (Main Street, U.S.A.).

Playing and role playing are part of the "fun" of being in a pleasure garden or in a Disney park. Play accommodates—indeed requires—illusion. Historically, a close bond exists between the illusions of a garden and those of pictorial painting, between garden and theater. A number of Italian Renaissance gardens boasted permanent theaters for entertainment, as did French gardens toward the end of the seventeenth century. The *bosquets* of Versailles were decorated green halls that could seat as many as three thousand spectators. In overall design, too, the great gardens of Europe owed much to both painting and theater. Architects and landscape architects were not uncommonly also landscape painters, and have close links with the stage. These brief excursions into the past prompt the question: what was the professional background of Walt Disney, a supreme creator of "gardens of delight" in our day? Predictably, for someone so in tune with and indeed ahead of his time, Disney's background was not painting and theater, but rather their quintessential American progenies—cartoon, cinema, and television.

Cosmos vs. Theme: Overcoming Time

The differences between the cosmic city, the European garden, and the Disney theme park are at least as revealing as their similarities. One striking difference is in the conception of time. The time of the cosmic city is cyclical—the orderly rounds of day and night and of the seasons, which have their ultimate source in the motion of the stars. A quite different temporal image is associated with the garden. Modeled initially on earthbound Eden rather than on heaven, its timelessness is that of an innocent place before the fall, before death, before society. Nevertheless, the great garden retains a vertical orientation, for one of its precursors is the monastic courtyard, termed "paradise"—and "paradise," unlike Eden, points to both heaven and earth. To complicate the meaning of the garden further, secular aesthetic values such as "vista," "scenery," "landscape," and "prospect" have been added to the religious ones of cosmos and Eden, and with these additions an ideal of expansive space and distance emerges, which in turn evokes a linear conception of time. What lies at the distant horizon, a patch of blue sky or a church steeple, is the future; or, more rarely, it is what a person sees when he looks back—the receding past. Surprisingly, the walled cosmic city of tradition and Disneyland of contemporary America now have an important feature in common: in neither is the eye directed to a distant horizon; in the confined spaces of both the one truly open space is up. If heaven is the hoped-for destiny of religious persons in the cosmic city, the sky (toward which the rocket in Tomorrowland conspicuously points), rather than some terrestrial horizon, now stands for the boundless future of secular men and women.

These historical observations and comparisons bring into focus certain distinctive features of the Disney ideal. Consider time once more. In modern society, the watches that people wear are a symbol of their servitude. Walt Disney, like builders of the cosmic city and the garden, attempts to liberate people from time's burden by creating an essentially atemporal world. But how different are their methods!

Absent from Disneyland are both the cosmic city's celebration of the eternal round of seasons and the garden's encouragement of the transcendence of time through meditative contemplation. These ideals, products of cultures that value a stable and serene way of life, are alien to the American delight in action and dynamic change. But I have put the difference too bluntly and will now have to qualify and elaborate. Consider a key Disney idea—the "theme." What exactly is a theme? A theme, as Disney conceives it, is a milieu or ambiance (the jungle of the Jungle Cruise, the quaint shops and streets of New Orleans Square) so distinctive and entrancing that when immersed in it one forgets time. To be there is to have arrived: no need therefore to worry about being elsewhere. The timelessness of "center," ritually evoked in the cosmic city, is at least hinted at in Disneyland. As for the eternal round of seasons, it cannot hold for Disneyland if only because it is located in Southern California where mean temperatures vary little from month to month. "Perpetual spring" itself conveys a sense of timelessness: it certainly conforms with accepted images of Eden or paradise. Unfortunately, a seasonless climate and unchanging vegetation can induce boredom. So Disney introduces variety and change by replanting flowers, trees, and lawns in the park, giving it an art-aided temporal variety that is greater than nature's own rhythms in the surrounding landscapes.

One technique that Disney has famously exploited to mitigate time's burden is to exclude the extended and unoccupied present that can attract discomfort and mundane worries into its vacuous midst. Visitors to Disneyland step either into the past, as represented by Frontierland and Main Street, or into the future, as represented by Tomorrowland. Burdensome time is not, however, so easily sidetracked. It still weighs on all who must stand in a long line to get into a popular tour. Disney's solution is to segment the line, produce a zigzagging path with mini-exhibits so that people, even as they shuffle toward their goal, feel that they are as good as there. In some rides and exhibits, the idea of a holding area where unstructured time may intrude practically disappears. Star Tours, for instance, features a spacious waiting room that is integral to the experience of travel. The room itself is full of things to see and hear—

glimpses of a workshop, posters of planets that tempt the space tourist, announcements of departure time, even what appears to be an accident, with fumes spewing out of a docked spacecraft, to the alarm of its robotic caretaker.

Kinesthetic Thrill, Spectacle, Landscape

On almost any long stretch of the American interstate highway, signposts encourage travelers to get out of their car and admire the view. For all the well-known American need to move efficiently toward stated goals, the restorative pause is allowed provided it doesn't last too long. Now, Disneyland has many charming nooks and corners for rest and refreshment and many carefully framed scenes on its rides, but they do not open out to panoramic vistas. In one of the few places (New Orleans Square) where one can get a broad view at the ground level, it is curiously disturbing, for in it are juxtaposed two towering prominences—the Alps' Matterhorn and the American West's Big Thunder Mountain—that are clearly incongruous and offend the ideal of a unified theme that Disney studiously upholds elsewhere. Disneyland offers an extraordinary range of visual stimuli. Nevertheless, some historically significant conceptions of landscape are absent, including a broad spread of earth and sky that invites ruminative daydreaming or contemplation.

I have noted earlier that in Europe, gardening and painting were closely related arts: builders of great gardens were either themselves landscape artists or connoisseurs of landscape painting; a landscape painting, even though it may embody or suggest time, induces calm rather than energetic action. Walt Disney was not a landscape painter but a cartoonist; and in the animated cartoon a personality—a dynamic character—occupies the center stage. Scenery, by contrast, is background—almost an afterthought to the artist in the preliminary stages of design.

Consider some of the distinctive sensory-aesthetic experiences (rewards) that visitors to Disneyland can expect. First in order of encounter and of importance, in the sense of leaving a lasting imprint, is the theme itself—the mood of a place. In its regard for the primacy of theme and mood, Disneyland has more in common with the cosmic city and the great European garden (where builders use all the skill at their command to establish an overall atmosphere), than with the ordinary amusement park, whose carnivalesque atmosphere is more or less happenstance. At Disneyland, one does not look at but is immersed in an ambiance. For that reason, visitors may not be consciously aware of it. Its effect, when successful, is to generate a sense of well-being, a fragrance that lingers.

The second special reward—the ride—is kinesthetic. Riders, as they plunge into the dark tunnel, are made to feel that they are not just spectators of an adventure but participants in it. Note that a difference already exists between watching a movie screen and watching a theater's stage. The movie makes the viewer feel like a participant: the camera's eye is the moviegoer's eye, and as the camera shows a car's hood pointing and moving down a road, I in the dark cinema feel as though I am behind the wheel myself, steering the car down the road. Nothing like this order of participation can occur when I watch a performance on a theater's confined stage. It is this movie-house experience that Disney wishes to carry over into the ride, greatly enhanced by the jerky, thrusting motions of a car or boat that is attached to the conveyor belt.

Any roller-coaster ride will provide kinesthetic thrills. What then is so special about this ride in Disneyland? The answer is the spectacle of a craftsmanship and splendor seldom seen elsewhere. This is the third substantial reward. Take Splash Mountain. It has plenty of surprises and excitement, climaxing in the plunge down a high waterfall, but along its half-mile track riders are taken through swamps, caves, and other scenes, and entertained by more than one hundred Audio-Animatronics® characters, including Brer Rabbit, Brer Bear, and Brer Fox, who sing "Zip-A-Dee-Doo-Dah" and other jolly songs.

The reward of spectacle raises the question: what is the difference between it and landscape? One answer might be: spectacles excite whereas landscapes generally do not. A landscape may, however, function as a spectacle if riders, rushing along, see it for only a few seconds and it is gone. That flash of color and form, unavailable for prolonged viewing, is what makes it a spectacle, as sword fights and fireworks, too quick in their individual movements to be considered a stable composition, are spectacles. Many rides last only four or five minutes, and even the longest do not exceed a quarter of an hour. Severe time constraint in itself rules out the kind of leisurely viewing that a landscape painting or a real landscape can command. If this is the case, why don't Disney people reduce the number of scenes so as to permit longer viewing? Isn't the longer pause justified by the scenes' craftsmanship and splendor? I have indeed attributed these qualities to them. But these qualities, egregiously absent in run-of-the-mill amusement parks, have their limitations even in Disneyland. A few seconds of starry-eyed watching is fine, more than this risks dis-illusionment and boredom.

A detour helps to explain the problem. Consider an important difference in how people respond to stage as distinct from movie scenery. A stage set that shows landscape quickly becomes boring unless something happens, whereas this is not necessarily true of a movie landscape. On film, the human drama may be dull but its background—even if it is the Nevada desert—can still command attention because it is the image of a real place: the tumbleweed one sees dancing in the picture's lower left corner and numerous other details are put there by nature, not by a director's or artist's limited imagination and skill. Although Disney's medium is film, his cartoon landscapes are obviously of human design—that is, they do not even pretend to be anything other than a product of fantasy. As such, unless they are supremely well done, they cannot hold the viewer's attention. In *Snow White and the Seven Dwarfs*, the scene that shows the dwarfs' cabin in the forest has a certain charm and is technically accomplished in the evocation of pictorial depth, but it is artistically rather vapid compared with the earlier scene that shows the forest personalized, with an evil will of its own, its branches taking the shape of human arms and fingers, reaching out at fleeing Snow White. In the Disneyland ride, the film's anthropomorphized forest predictably plays a major role, whereas its pretty landscapes scarcely appear. Indeed, the wicked queen and witch completely overshadow the princess heroine, and the ride itself is given a new title, Snow White's Adventures.

Landscapes in an animated cartoon can nevertheless have an important supporting role, even a key role, as Disney soon realized. Take just one element—color. Disney discovered how effectively its use in landscape could accent the personality of his characters and alter the mood of his viewers. Contrasts of darkness and light are a favorite technique for projecting chaos and evil on the one hand and harmony and goodness on the other. A well-known example occurs in the last two sequences of *Fantasia*, in which the somber, sinister tones of "A Night on Bald Mountain," set to the music of Moussorgsky, are contrasted with dawn in a misty forest that turns into the rosy-hued interior of a cathedral, set to Schubert's "Ave Maria." In Disneyland, this method of dramatization—the gently polarized forces of the cosmic city's yin and yang transmuted into the radically opposed forces of darkness and light in the West's Gnostic imagination—is employed over and over again. Theme park rides lend themselves to such dramatization. Many take place in the dark. Riders enter a winding tunnel where they are subjected to a succession of horrors until they finally emerge into the bright California sunshine. Where are the good people—Mickey, Minnie, Donald, Pluto, Goofy, Pooh, and others of their kind? Naturally, they are out in the open, on Main Street, at the central plaza, in pastel-colored Mickey's Toontown, greeting guests, hugging children (Fig. xii). By contrast, the villains—Big Bad Wolf, Cruella De Vil, Captain Hook, Stromboli, and their kind—lurk in the underworld of tunnels and caves where they belong.

The Good and Exciting Place

Human beings have always been tempted to envisage a world better than the one they know. The literature on Eden, paradise, or utopia is vast. Besides fictional writers, humanist scholars, and social scientists (including Karl Marx) have tried to envisage life in the good place. Even the greatest minds have failed, however, in one test—important to William James among others—namely, that such a place should stimulate the imagination, that its effect must not dull too soon. Understandably, Walt Disney does not score total success where so many talented people before him have failed. Yet I would like to argue that he has succeeded to an extraordinary degree—that he has introduced elements into his conception of a good and happy place that others have missed.

Let it be admitted at the start that Disneyland is successful because it never aspired to be a place of permanent residence—a home. Its people are visitors, or, as Disney officials say, guests. How else can it claim, tongue-in-cheek, a population of three hundred million in a compound of only 185 acres? People visit for a day or two and then leave; they hardly have time to be bored. Disneyland is of course more a visionary model than an achieved habitat. But when critics dismiss it as just a mindless entertainment center, they reveal their own lack of perceptiveness. They forget, for one, that Disneyland is also a busy workplace. Its several thousand employees, or "cast members," possess collectively a broad range of skills and talents, from those of the gardener, architect, electrician and hydraulic engineer, to those of the vendor, cook, nurse, guide, musician, and Matterhorn climber. Some work at the front of the stage, others work backstage: roles are flexible and employees know how to respond to the demands of the situation.

Backstage work can no doubt be tedious and hard. Walt Disney, to his credit, paid tribute to it. He believed in hard work for himself and for other Americans. It is part of his image of the good place. A feature that non-American visitors (especially those from servant-rich Asia) may find surprising is the prominence given to workshops and work life in Disneyland. At several major rides and performances, as visitors wind their way to the principal event, they are treated to a display of tools and activities that seem to say, "Before there can be magic, there must be work." On the way to meet Mickey in his studio, one sees the labor behind filmmaking and one is invited to admire household appliances, including a washing machine that tumbles Mickey's dirty overalls and four-digit gloves. And before one enters a spacecraft for Star Tours, one is made to look behind the scenes at the workshop, its clutter of tangled wires, welding tools, generators, conveyors, and arrays of monitoring dials and meters that make space flight possible.

An invaluable heritage from the studio's cartoons is the park's air of fun and wackiness. Only two shows are undeviatingly serious: Great Moments with Mr. Lincoln and the patriotic travelogue (no longer in operation) American Journeys. Others have at least a touch of fun and humor in them. These qualities, which depend on a subconscious awareness of human pretentiousness and fallibility, are a saving grace of Disney's utopia. Their absence from other utopias is one reason why they so quickly pall. In Disneyland, wackiness is predictably rampant in Mickey's Toontown, which is designed especially for young children and their giddy sense of fun (Fig. xii). There one finds, for instance, a service station sign which says, "If we can't fix it we won't," a Fireworks Factory that periodically explodes, an impact crater shaped like Goofy, marking the spot where he missed his swimming pool while high diving, and so on. Elsewhere too, one finds instances of self-deflation and fun: for example, the guide of Jungle Cruise who puns shamelessly and the robotic captain of Star Tours who casually announces to strapped-down passengers that, well, it is his first flight.

Disneyland is intended to be a happy and sunny place. Curiously for such a place, it is packed with horrors, disasters, and death—with witches, ogres, pirates, earthquakes, burning log cabins, and train wrecks, as well as "bones, lots of bones; human bones, cattle bones, dinosaur bones.... There have got to be more bones at Disneyland than at the Smithsonian Institute and UCLA Medical School combined." True, almost all the horrors are underground: a well-fed Pooh walks the streets, not some skeleton or Captain Hook. Almost everything one sees at the surface is bright and cheerful. But the ultimate source of Disneyland's sunny exuberance lies in the belief that Good triumphs over Evil, that the little fellow, through a combination of luck, courage, and cunning, can always overcome in the end the big bad person in his or her numerous guises, all of which signify Power and its abuse. It is this overarching theme of optimism in Disneyland—fairy tale and seductive dream—that cultural critics have found hard to forgive. Yet without it in some (subtler) form, human beings may have to make do with a gray and constantly wary world unrelieved by jollity and hope—a world that slips easily into fatalism, or cynicism and despair.

Contentment, peace, and harmony are of high value in traditional Asian cultures, and in Western culture, too, before the modern period. The cosmos signifies harmony, the garden contentment and peace; utopia is a peaceful—contented and stable—society. Disneyland's special distinction, its divergence from historically ideal places, lies in this. On the one hand, it too embraces these values and finds them in the past—on Main Street, U.S.A., in New Orleans Square, and on Mark Twain's Island, where, after a rain shower, the ground trampled into bare earth by children's feet turns into authentic mud wallows. On the other hand, Disneyland looks exultantly to technology and the future. What delicious irony! For it is this futuristic technological orientation that now dates Disneyland, making it seem a "historic theme" out of the late nineteenth and early twentieth century.

Borders: Who Can Enter?

Is the good place open to everyone? Shouldn't it be? This was not a contentious issue in earlier times. After all, Heaven itself had its gate, guarded by Saint Peter, and only a small proportion of souls could enter. Good places seemed, almost invariably, to have borders around them, some protected by guards. The cosmic city was a walled and guarded compound. The great European gardens were private domains. True, Louis XIV, as the universal Sun King, at times opened Versailles to all Parisians, but he also regretted his generosity, finding the swarming populace too obtrusive. Good places were often difficult to access: that, too, limited the number of people who could enter. "Narrow is the gate, hard the way, that leads to life [the Kingdom of God]," we learn from the Bible (Matt. 7:13). Historically, the paradises, Edens, and utopias of the imagination all tended to be far off, separated from tumultuous humanity by ocean, mountain, or forest.

In a nation that aspires to be free, democratic, and egalitarian, this question of who are welcome in paradise can be highly contentious. Is prosperous Orange County, in which Disneyland is located, to welcome all comers? For that matter, what about that larger promised land—the United States of America itself? Changes in Disneyland reflect changes in the larger society. Originally intended for middle-class families with youngish children, the park now caters increasingly to older groups. Rock concerts have been introduced and are very popular with the high school set. As part of the same trend, thrills that can fleetingly disorient even teenagers are installed, the latest being Indiana Jones™ Adventure. Unaccompanied adults are being catered to, which entails the maintenance of restful nooks and corners as well as the provision of shows that entertain without kinesthetic excess, an outstanding example of which is the old favorite—the sing-alongs of Country Bear Playhouse.

On the other hand, young families are not forgotten, as the ambitious new feature—Mickey's Toontown—testifies. The age range of visitors to Disneyland is now noticeably greater than it was. Likewise, the range of ethnic types. Main Street on a busy day is delightfully cosmopolitan—a colorful palette to challenge that of It's a Small World—and not at all the sea of bobbing white that it was in the first decade of its existence.

The important question is, how far can this diversification go on without destroying Disneyland's ambiance—its thematic unity? It has gone far—much farther than Disney himself thought either likely or desirable—but to go farther still without disintegration it must hold on with conviction its unique quality of wacky optimism backed by virtues of know-how and hard work. That sunniness, that optimism, is essentially childlike, by which I mean (among other qualities) a tendency to accept the good things of life—for the most part—as they are. Historically, perfect places such as Eden and the Kingdom of God were reserved for the pure in heart and the starry-eyed, for children rather than sophistic doctors and priests. Why shouldn't this notion of limited membership also be applied to Disneyland? The young in heart ought to be made welcome in principle. Who then are suspect? Who must be searched for weapons before admittance? If in the past they were doctors and priests, today they are their unsmiling descendants—those literary and cultural mandarins who have made profitable careers for themselves by finding only cinder in Cinderella, the toad in every prince.

xii. Goofy's Gas, Mickey's Toontown, Disneyland.

FORTY YEARS OF OVERSTATEMENT

CRITICISM AND THE DISNEY THEME PARKS

Greil Marcus

> Disneyland is dedicated to the ideals, the dreams and the hard facts which have created America.
>
> *Walt Disney, dedication plaque, Disneyland, 1955*

> "Oh my God," said [seven-year-old] Mitchell, holding my hand as we strolled down one of the simulated Main Streets. "We're trapped in a production of *The Music Man*, directed by Leni Riefenstahl."
>
> *Libby Gelman-Waxner, "If You Ask Me: Mondo Disney," Premiere, February 1996*

> I am a very strong supporter of both States' rights and the local elected government, and believe the U.S. Senate really has no business refereeing—pardon the pun—every Mickey Mouse dispute around the country.
>
> *Senator Ben Nighthorse Campbell of Colorado, Hearing before Subcommittee on Public Lands, National Parks and Forests on Proposed Location of Disney's America Project and Its Potential Impact on the Manassas National Battlefield Park and Other Significant Historic Sights in Northern Virginia, June 21, 1994*

Any critical discourse takes place within a milieu of certain shared referents, common definitions, readily comprehensible metaphors, a lingua franca. The criticism of Disney theme parks as it has taken shape over the past forty years is no different, and the quotations above, from Walt Disney himself to fictional seven-year-old to real-life senator, seem to me to outline the borders of the critical theme park in which Disney criticism conducts its rides and spins its occasionally revelatory, more often creepy wonders and illusions. These are borders of touching naïveté—within which Disney's dedication plaque is always paid promise or looming threat, and never anything so plain as a come-on, a cannily patriotic 1950s version of a carny's shill—and they are borders of steely-eyed suspicion, a rolling chorus down the decades of "You can't fool me," "*You can't fool me*," "YOU CAN'T FOOL ME!"

Before looking into what professional critics have made of Disney land-work, it's worth pausing over this lingua franca—ordinary Disney language as caught in comments collected at random from the everyday media in the course of the last year. Here, one can perhaps get a sense of what people say and mean when they talk Disney, of how much or how little they do talk about. Such talk raises a key question of Disney theme-park criticism: that of whether the critical discourse of books and scholarly journals, pop culture critics such as Tom Carson and political critics such as Michael Harrington, semiologists such as Umberto Eco and Jean Baudrillard, architects such as Charles Moore and Reyner Banham, journalist Richard Schickel or social theorist Susan Willis, actually goes beyond the ordinary conversation.

Catherine Wagner.
New York Streetscape, Backstage Studio Tour;
Disney-MGM Studios Theme Park,
Walt Disney World, Orlando, Florida.
Collection CCA.

Literate America heaved a collective groan last week: huge ads in several national newspapers promoted the upcoming film *Jefferson in Paris* by displaying part of the American Constitution. But Thomas Jefferson had as much to do with drafting the Constitution as he did with writing the recipe for American cheese. Says a spokeswoman for Walt Disney Co., which releases the film March 31: "We all walked in Monday morning and said, 'Oh, f---! It should have been the Declaration of Independence.'" This from the company that wanted to build a theme park celebrating American history.

Newsweek, 1995

Is it just a coincidence that Paul Verhoeven's *Showgirls*, Mike Figgis' *Leaving Las Vegas*, and Martin Scorsese's *Casino*, three would-be down-and-dirty tributes to lost Vegas, all went into production at more or less the moment when, led by the refurbished MGM Grand Hotel, America's fastest-growing metropolis began promoting itself as the new Orlando? Lost Vegas became Vegasland, a wholesome middle-American theme park resort. "Today it looks like Disneyland," whines *Casino*'s old-time casino boss. And vice-versa: the ten-story sphinx guarding the thirty-story disco Egyptian glass pyramid that is the Luxor Las Vegas is a dead ringer for Disney's Hollywood Pictures logo.

J. Hoberman, "American Myths: Stardust Memories,"
Artforum, January 1996

The ABC anchors and reporters were jittery when they learned that Disney had gobbled their network. They were thinking deeply, I'm sure, about journalistic integrity. Interviewing Thomas Murphy and Michael Eisner on *Good Morning America*, an edgy Charlie Gibson blurted: "I never thought I'd work for a guy named Mickey.". . . What will happen when ABC and Disney begin plugging each other's shows and promoting each other's events? Will Brit Hume do his White House stand-up on a toadstool? Will Pocahontas be the hot forensic babe in Jimmy Smits' precinct on *NYPD Blue*? Will Ted Koppel explain to the nation the precise scientific meaning of flubber? Will Cokie Roberts be mistaken for Cruella DeVil? Will Grumpy turn up with a Prozac overdose on *General Hospital*? What will George Will look like animated? . . . For Republicans who cherish nostalgic visions of returning America to the 1950s, this is not a merger, this is a miracle. They are delighted with Mr. Eisner's promise to make the giant news conglomerate reflect "what this country stands for." (Davy Crockett, C.E.O.).

Maureen Dowd, "Mickey Mouse News,"
New York Times, August 3, 1995

Just a bit more:

#13. *Pocahontas* Early settlers sang, danced, cut down trees, and exploited fuzzy animals for profit. Sounds like they founded the first Disneyland.

Jim Mullen, "The Year That Was Hotsheet,"
Entertainment Weekly, December 29, 1995

Is America so hypnotized by deregulation that it no longer cares about antitrust or monopoly control? Or have media companies been moved to some Magic Kingdom where these hard-won protections do not apply?

James Ledbetter, "Merge Overkill,"
Village Voice, January 16, 1996

Great America is so soul-destroying. Really, if you take Disneyland as a tiny, small-scale model of a perfect fascist regime, Great America is a mere third-world tin-pot dictatorship, slipshod and uncomfy. In fact, rather than the country it purports to celebrate, Great America resembles Uruguay, or Bulgaria, in that it's full of long lines, poor and expensive food, and very bad plumbing.

Gina Arnold, "Fools Rush In: Yesterday's Back,"
Express (Berkeley), September 1, 1995

Two different visions compete for the soul of the blues. One defines them as a folk art, a collective expression of black American culture and a record of oppression. The other sees the blues as a modernist art of individual genius melding tradition and innovation with technology and commerce, one whose influence pervades all of pop music today.

Nowhere is the conflict more sharply drawn than in the House of Blues. To some, it is the last best chance to keep the form vital; to others, it reduces one of the most profound forms of American music to a Disney cartoon.

Phil Patton, "Who Owns the Blues?"
New York Times, November 26, 1995

News item—the Walt Disney Co. expects to make only modest changes at its future subsidiary, ABC, henceforth known as Anaheim Broadcasting Co.

To wit:

Disney respects the integrity of *ABC World News Tonight* and won't overhaul it except for a minor personnel change. Peter Jennings has been reassigned and replaced by Pocahontas to reflect the company's strong belief that news anchors should mate for life . . . on the drama front, ABC plans to revive the old TV series *The Millionaire*. Each week, the mysterious John Beresford Tipton will present unsuspecting recipients with a cashier's check for a million dollars—just enough to cover air fare, the hotel bill, gate admission and concession costs for a family of four to visit Disney World in Orlando.

John Carman, "Why? Because We Own You,"
San Francisco Chronicle, August 2, 1995

Now, some of this is funny—I think Carman's *Millionaire* riff is a scream—some of it is flat, some of it is cheap, a bit of it is slick, and a lot of it is glib. But I think all of it is telling. Who hasn't talked like this or thought like this? Disneyland, Walt Disney World—Disneyism as most fully embodied in its theme parks—rises out of these cuttings like a Godzilla of entrepreneurial, mass-psychologized Americanism, and just about all any of the writers cited can do in defense is condescend.

Condescension is not thinking, but it can be politics. Gina Arnold proves that all too well with a throw-away line (a "small-scale model of a perfect fascist regime") in an argument about something else, not because what she says necessarily sums up Disneyland, but because it does sum up virtually everything the academic authors of the weirdly, militaristically named The Project on Disney's *Inside the Mouse*—a book published in 1995 by Duke University Press—have to say about Walt Disney World.

Because condescension isn't thinking, it disarms the critic, who whatever her form or style must, to succeed, engage the reader and lead him to think along with her. It's fascinating that a Disney park so completely defeated the previously invulnerable Libby Gelman-Waxner (the nom de film crit of playwright Paul Rudnick). This is a critic so fearsome she once explained to her "adorable seven-year-old daughter, Jennifer," who had begun to ask about death, "that hell is basically like the smoking section of a restaurant—a place where everyone's clothes smell bad and the utensils and glassware have water spots. I said that most people and all animals except pit bulls go to heaven, and that the Richard Nixon Library & Birthplace in Yorba Linda, California" (described by many Disney critics as Disneyland's chief local competition, and by some as Disneyland's doppelgänger) "is spoken of as the entrance to the underworld in the Dead Sea Scrolls."

What does this have to do with the criticism of the Disney theme parks? Well, plenty. This is the sort of writing the places need—outrage and humor and wonder all mixed up together. Something in the Disney parks, if not Disneyism as such, brings out not necessarily the best or the worst but so often the most in people—it strips them bare, reduces them to babble or prompts curses and slurs. Examples tend to the awful, as with actor Robert Duvall's comment—in his role as gentleman farmer of (savor the name) Upperville, Virginia—on the plan to construct Disney's America near the Manassas battle-field. "It's like building at Auschwitz," Duvall told the acute *Forbes* reporter Lisa Gubernick. "But then [Disney Chairman Michael] Eisner's ancestors only came over in the last hundred years. The Civil War isn't part of his history." These disgusting words might be countered by an argument such as, "Even though my ancestors came to the United States after the American Revolution, I've always considered the Declaration of Independence part of *my* history"—but what they really need is a response on the level that comedian Dennis Miller, on his HBO show, offered as part of his weekly news summary just before the 1994 congressional elections.

"DEMONSTRATORS MARCH ON WASHINGTON TO PROTEST DISNEY THEME PARK IN VIRGINIA"

flashed a headline; "You really have to wonder," Miller said, "about people who fear Mickey Mouse more than Oliver North."

Most Disney critics forget this kind of language—swift and tough—as soon as they begin, if they ever knew it. What they mostly produce instead is polemical, ideological, or merely self-congratulatory, smug: treatises so fixed on decoding Disney's own Rosetta Stone of a dedication plaque they can hardly be bothered to investigate which rides are fun and which aren't, let alone why.

That, one might think, is where any criticism of Disney theme parks ought to begin. Instead it may well begin with novelist and screenwriter Julian Halevy's notorious "Disneyland and Las Vegas," published in the *Nation* in 1958—which is to say, again, that it begins with the Disney plaque.

In 1958, the United States was still poisoned by McCarthyism; in Hollywood the blacklist was still in effect. In the pages of the left-wing *Nation*, any product labeled "American" was to be treated as suspect, but Halevy went in armed. He began by informing his readers that though a U.S. citizen, he was a resident of Mexico; having "just returned" from an anthropological foray into the United States, he was "now once more enjoying the taste of unfrozen orange juice and fresh fish, conversations lasting four or five hours in which all sorts of cabbages and kings are discussed, meetings with friends where no one asks if I watched TV last night to see Mickey Rooney do Oedipus Rex . . ." Today it is very hard to read such stuff: not only to be reminded, as critic Tom Carson would write in 1992 in his wildly ambitious "To Disneyland," that "Anywhere this side of utopia, the opposite of 'commodity culture' isn't nature but privilege," but to realize that against the capitalist democracy of the United States, in 1958 profoundly inegalitarian but in the first stages of an equally profound self-renewal, Halevy was promoting Mexico, with its economy a mix of feudalism and racketeering and its politics those of a tin-pot dictatorship, as morally superior. And yet this too—in language that, over the decades, modernizes but does not really change—is utterly typical of Disney criticism. There's a way in which the whole main stream of the discourse is a search for a way to say "The horror, the horror," without sounding too corny.

"As in the Disney movies," Halevy writes,

the whole world, the universe, and all man's striving for dominion over self and nature, have been reduced to a sickening blend of cheap formulas packaged to sell. Romance, Adventure, Fantasy, Science are ballyhooed and marketed: life is bright colored, clean, cute, titivating, safe, mediocre, inoffensive to the lowest common denominator, and somehow repugnantly inhuman. The mythology glorified in TV and Hollywood's B movies has been given too solid flesh. . . . Give 'em mumbo-jumbo. One feels our whole mass culture heading up the dark river to the source—that heart of darkness where Mr. Disney traffics in pastel-trinketed evil for gold and ivory.

Picking this apart—noticing that Halevy compares "Mr. Disney" to slave traders as smoothly as he covers his bets with the A-movie producers he's presumably pitching his scripts to—is much less interesting than following the path, or river, Halevy opened up. Disney fan Ray Bradbury responded in a mocking letter to the *Nation* and, later, in a piece that tried to turn Halevy's Disney-Las Vegas opposition ("The satisfactions sold in Las Vegas are subtler and more profound," Halevy said: "they touch on the real lives, the real anxieties") on its head. "Vegas's real people are brute robots, machine-tooled bums," Bradbury wrote. "Disneyland's robots are, on the other hand, people, loving, caring and eternally good." Science-fiction novelist Bradbury was not speaking ironically, and in a way it's too bad no one has ever tried to figure out what what he said means—stacks of Postmodernist Disney exegesis could have been preempted. But though Halevy said what many, many people thought—and think— he was too brazen; to retain credibility, critics had to turn the volume down. Thus a few years later the *Nation* published "Disney's Fantasy Empire" by John Bright, another novelist-screenwriter, who attacked Halevy as a snob out of touch with "the new masses." "All escape is not neurotic," Bright wrote. "What's sick about a vacation?" And yet, as he proceeded through several pages of attempting to like Disneyland (while at the same time trying to throw up a roadblock against Disney's then-planned Mineral King resort near Yosemite National Park), Bright wasn't very convincing, and neither was Richard Schickel, attacking Halevy in his groundbreaking 1968 study *The Disney Version*. To Halevy's complaints about a "papier-mâché crocodile" and a "muddy ditch" on Disneyland's Jungle Cruise, Schickel correctly stated that "the alligator is technologically far advanced over papier-mâché" and that the water was "sparkling clean." "Nor can one blame Disney for the impoverishment of our national mental life," Schickel went on—oddly, since to a good degree his book tried to make just such a case.

The Disney Version, the first book to combine biography, business history, and cultural critique in an attempt to make sense of the Disney phenomenon, began with a hard, blunt assertion—"As capitalism, it is a work of genius; as culture, it is mostly a horror"—and then spent the rest of nearly three hundred pages avoiding its burden. There is the prissy assertion, regarding the Disney Studio's appropriation and revision of Stravinsky's "Rite of Spring" in *Fantasia*, that "had Disney actually possessed the soul of an artist . . . he could not have treated Stravinsky as he did," as if all those possessed of the soul of an artist are fine fellows, but this is not horror. That comes only at the very end of the book, when Schickel attempts to present the original Disneyland Abraham Lincoln robot as a Frankenstein's monster, about to despoil the countryside, as it were, from within the breast of each villager. "Are we really supposed to revere this ridiculous contraption," Schickel wrote, "this weird agglomeration of wires and plastic"—which in 1969 Schickel's description made me desperate to see—"transferring to it, in the process, whatever genuine emotions we may have toward Lincoln in particular, toward mankind in general?"

Actually, one is not supposed to revere this contraption, but Schickel is not to be stopped: "If so, we are being asked to abjure the Biblical injunction against graven images and, quite literally, we are worshipping a machine." So Schickel tries to nail his argument:

At this point the Magic Kingdom becomes a dark land, the innocent dream becomes a nightmare, and the amusement park itself becomes a demonstration not of the wondrous possibilities of technological progress, as its founder hoped, but of its possibilities of horror.

For the reader of Schickel's book, this can be very confusing—for not ten pages earlier, Schickel can be found quite accurately disparaging Disneyland's Jungle Cruise as "nothing deeper intellectually or emotionally" than jungle cruises "in a hundred movies and television shows," and then, paddling up Halevy's river, insisting that "to go beyond that Disney and his 'imagineers' would have had to create, in three dimensions, an objective correlative to the mood of terror Conrad invokes, through means that are in the last analysis inexplicable and therefore inimitable, in *Heart of Darkness*." So, instead of the "dark land" the Magic Kingdom becomes with the Lincoln robot, Schickel wants a new subsection of the park, Darkland?

But let us leave the confusion of just what "The horror, the horror" might mean as a ride, and get back to what it means for Schickel. Disney's Lincoln is supposed to demonstrate Disneyland's possibilities for horror, for Disney culture as a horror, but what exactly does this horror consist of? "Disney labored over Mr. Lincoln as he had not labored to bring forth his Mouse," Schickel writes, "and brought forth a monster of wretched taste." Bad taste is not a horror—but one suspects that, here, Schickel has really said exactly what he means, and all he means. A careful reader is left altogether at sea. Disney's "love for the Lincoln Legend knew few bounds," the reader will have found Schickel saying: "he could quote long passages from his speeches." If one knows anything of Lincoln, one will be intrigued—which speeches? Lincoln was no dispenser of bland homilies, tribune avant la lettre of Disneyfication—what of Lincoln's philosophy, his terrors, his pain, his dark visions, his balanced, Shakespearean imagery, might Walt Disney have been responding to? This is the sort of question that does not get asked in Disney criticism, not because the specific answers might be out of reach, as here they probably are, but because the question raises others. If Walt Disney's attachment to Lincoln was deep and profound, that might tell us more about Walt Disney or Lincoln than some of us want to know.

With the ground broken, Disneyland and later Walt Disney World, Tokyo Disneyland, and Disneyland Paris were opened to Postmodernists and semiologists. For such Old World writers as Umberto Eco, in *Travels in Hyperreality*, Jean Baudrillard in *America*, Reyner Banham in *Los Angeles: The Architecture of Four Ecologies*, Disneyland was indeed a playground. Meaning floats free as signifiers dance attendance. Disneyland side by side with a Jack in the Box stand, the Watts Towers, the Brown Derby, Grauman's Chinese Theater, and the like makes sense in Banham's book; his claim that Disneyland is orchestrated "with such consummate skill and such base cunning that one can only compare it to something completely outrageous, like the brothel in Genet's *Le Balcon* . . . an almost faultless organization for delivering, against cash, almost any type at all of environmental experience that human fancy, however inflamed, could ever devise . . ." translates as, "can I go now?"

As always, Eco gets you in the mood to think; he could care less if you agree with him. "The 'completely real' becomes identified with the 'completely fake'" is his premise; as you puzzle that out through such examples as the reconstruction of the Oval Office at the Lyndon B. Johnson Presidential Library in Austin, Texas, Eco leads you into "the most typical phenomenon of this universe," his favorite Disneyland rides, the Pirates of the Caribbean and the Haunted Mansion. He has nothing particularly remarkable to say about these rides, other than to communicate over the course of two pages that they are absolutely incredible and that he can't get them out of his mind—or, in another sense, into it. The critical faculty that works so well on the ambience of Disneyland ("Disneyland can permit itself to present its reconstructions as masterpieces of falsification, for what it sells is, indeed, goods, but genuine merchandise, not reproductions. What is falsified is our will to buy") falls apart in the face of fun. As for Baudrillard, master of the slipknot school of criticism, he might not have stepped on a single ride at all. His major argument begins and ends at that old Disney sign: "Disneyland is there to conceal that it is the real country." Here we are confronted with snobbery as deep as Robert Duvall's, and based in similar old-soil values. As opposed to an organic nation like France, America is made up, no less a contraption, with all of its mechanical checks and balances, than Disney's Lincoln. What the overwhelming symbology of Disneyland conceals is that America is all symbol; it does not exist. In other words: "Can I go now?"

From here it is a short step to a whole redoubt of American criticism—the basic question of which is, "How do I get out of here?," a question raised with varying degrees of anxiety. By far the best work in this vein is political scientist Michael Harrington's 1979 "To the Disney Station: Corporate Socialism in the Magic Kingdom." Uninterested in Disney culture, he is riveted by Disney capitalism, and by the theme parks as a nation ("Disney World is not a company town; it is a company state"). Disney World "embod[ies] one of the most powerful desires of the late Seventies," Harrington wrote: "that it is possible to reach apolitical, anti-intellectual, corporate, and technocratic solutions to the problems of society." Though before too long his argument begins to tip toward Godzilla-fantasies of omnipresence and omnipotence, Harrington's voice is clear and muscular throughout. The same cannot be said of Mike Wallace's "Mickey Mouse History: Portraying the Past at Disney World" (*Radical History Review*, 1985), or Alexander Wilson's "The Betrayal of the Future: Walt Disney's EPCOT Center" (*Socialist Review*, 1985) or Michael Sorkin's "See You in Disneyland" (from Sorkin's 1992 anthology *Variations on a Theme Park*). All have their moments of interest and all devolve quickly into a kind of critical voice that can perhaps best be called spite.

This is not a good posture from which to practice criticism—an angry defensiveness, a fear that somehow one's faculties or tools of analysis are not up to the job disguised as contempt for the job itself—and nothing makes this more clear than The Project on Disney's *Inside the Mouse: Work and Play at Disney World*. Here, courtesy of three academics and one photographer-essayist who pretend to be working collectively (the various essays in this collection are unsigned, though the first use of the first person results in a footnote distinguishing Susan Willis from Karen Klugman, Klugman from Jane Kuenz, Kuenz from Shelton Waldrep), is the Anhedonic School of Disney criticism without doubt or restraint. "I always approach culture as a consumer," Willis says; she wonders if "there is any pleasure in mass culture"; she alerts her readers that "As a critic of consumer culture, I don't find shopping pleasurable"; that Walt Disney World is "the quintessential enactment of the hysterical bourgeois subject"; and that the costumes of the sales clerks at Walt Disney World "make them indistinguishable from the merchandise" they sell. To which one might reasonably reply, your notion of culture is vastly impoverished; your notion of pleasure must be inconceivably refined; you're probably in the wrong business; speaking of hysterical . . . speak for yourself, sister.

The critics at work here are suspicious, afraid, envious, chilled. Often one begins an essay sharing their trepidation over the fundamental colossalness, the *all-presentness*, of Walt Disney World, but one cannot keep up with the nearly instant and then unvarying retreat to ideology, buzzwords (like the FBI in the 1950s, the Anhedonics see "subversion" everywhere; the difference is they're all for it), distaste—to, finally, retreat from their putative subject itself. Rooted mindlessly in the notion of "resistance through rituals"—in which, in a sort of everyday-life inversion of *Invasion of the Body Snatchers*, people happen upon habits and hunches that allow them to maintain a semblance of subjectivity in a world defined by the overwhelming objectification of mass society—*Inside the Mouse* is meant as a field guide for the avoidance of complicity with the culture that is in fact one's own. "Instead of feeling like an anonymous peasant with particular interests that are not recognized in the vast kingdom," Karen Klugman writes, "you can think of yourself as the court jester." And you can then think of everyone else as a peasant—or, as with Willis and the Walt Disney World sales clerks, as merchandise.

Here we have reached bottom: dedicated, smart people who have somehow managed to convince themselves that all the great social and political reforms in the United States over the past forty years have produced a society at least as unfree as the society in which Disneyland first appeared, and as if, somehow, one can read the hidden protocols of this unfreedom through the spectacle of Walt Disney World. "Shopping is a ride not unlike the other amusements," Willis says—and perhaps it is, if you never really ride the rides.

While at least spiritually staying off the rides is a fundamental premise of Disney theme park criticism, if not the fundamental premise, there are at least two critics who understand that, as Karl Marx might have put it, criticism of Disney theme-park rides is the prerequisite of all Disney theme-park criticism. In the 1984 *The City Observed: Los Angeles—A Guide to Its Architecture and Landscapes*, architect Charles Moore jumps right on. Instantly, Disneyland begins to make sense: as a funfair where good ideas meet fantastic execution, where ideas stillborn nevertheless function adequately, where small-mindedness restricts but does not extinguish delight, where surprise lurks in apparent banality and banality in what at first glance looks like vision. An enthralling account of Pirates of the Caribbean ends up right where a lot of people have found themselves when they got off, which is to say utterly, fabulously confused, half-humiliated, half-filled with wonder: "It's astonishing how this pin-brained apotheosis of sloth and stupidity can be so fascinating." With the Haunted Mansion, Moore has no such reservations; you're not even sure his one cavil isn't a joke, or a backhanded prophecy of an age when the word "handicapped" would be replaced by "physically challenged":

The Haunted Mansion is a badly flawed ride, if only for the smug and superciliious treatment it bestows on ghosts, just because they are dead. Even so, it is surely one of the most skillful, sophisticated and engrossing spatial sequences on the planet. It is useful to see the ride as a progression from outside the event, where the observer and the observed are at some distance, to the inside, where the observer, mind and body, has entered into the observed, so that it finally envelops him and even at the end makes an attempt to enter him.

Here we are all the way into a dream—a constructed dream unfolding on its own terms. Taking an attraction on its own terms—not on the mystifying terms of the Disneyland plaque or the self-protecting terms of fashionable shibboleths—is Moore's great strength. Reading him, you might simultaneously feel pleasure in plain speech working hard and bafflement that such language applied to Disney theme parks is so rare. Moore can tell you why Mr. Toad's Wild Ride can stay with a child for years. He can rail against It's a Small World, and its accompanying theme song, without making them stand for the American soul or the Temptations of Mammon ("The trouble with this experience, aside from the fact that it so exaggerates the goody-goody aspects of Disneyism as to make them intolerable, is that the damn song stays in your head for months. Therefore, gentle reader, consider this heartfelt proposal that you not go near the place"). He can let someone who first visited Tomorrowland in the 1950s understand why it was disappointing even then ("A good case can be made on evidence collected from all over that the future came and went in about 1957"). Moore is so sharp, so thoughtful and engaging, that you want him to go farther, to expose himself as he exposes this ride or that—but here one must turn to Tom Carson.

Carson, a critic whose work has most often appeared in the *Village Voice*, began writing about music and television and moved on to writing about politics—politics as culture, sometimes as a theme park. Writing in 1992 in the *LA Weekly*, the Los Angeles version of the *Village Voice*, Carson entered Disneyland, as he had many times before, with a smile on his face and a flutter in his belly. "*Nothing looks fake,*" he marvels. "Fabricated, yes—fake, no. Disneyland isn't the mimicry of a thing. It's a thing."

This is where Disney theme-park criticism opens up: with the acknowledgment that Disney's idea and its execution, whether judged liberating or imprisoning, fun or a bore, was something new. It cannot be taken for granted; it was not always here. Where, though, is Disneyland's here? Carson goes all over the map to find it. "'A happy East Germany,'" he says to himself, trying out the notion. "Imagine East Germany happy. Imagine East Germany." East Germany was gone as he wrote; Disneyland was still there. Another try:

Disneyland is unilateral, literally a control freak's paradise. It can't be experienced in any way, or yield any meanings, other than those Walt meant it to. If Walt had really wanted our imaginations to soar, He would have given us wings, not mouse ears.

Yet I know it's precisely this imminent abnegation of all independent will that thrills me each time I cross the parking lot to those heraldic ticket booths. The feeling's akin to the blissful relinquishing of responsibility I experience on airplanes, where I'm still happier than any place on Earth. I may die. But I won't be asked to *live up to* anything.

Moving through the park, testing its rides and attractions against much of what's been written about them, contrasting the smooth operation of the park with a long interview with a park worker—who not infrequently played Goofy while on LSD—Carson recreates the Disneyland environment in such a way that it is at once demystified, full of questions without answers, and mystified beyond all reason, to the point where it seems the place can turn a visitor's unfocused unease into a ride everyone is on. Carson himself ends in a grand collapse of history into popular culture, as if all at once a wailing chorus of Los Angeles voices—those of Nathanael West, William

Faulkner, the Beach Boys, the Eagles, Ed Sanders, Charles Manson, Aimee Semple McPherson, Theodor Adorno, F. Scott Fitzgerald, Ronald Reagan, and on, and on—is speaking through him. He tours the park with Tom Joad, who it turns out survived the migrant camps and began working for Disneyland in 1955, and hasn't voted for a Democrat "since I first ate in a sit-down restaurant. And that's a *long* time ago."

We had passed into Fantasyland. In the lengthening shadows—it was nearly sunset—the great carousel spun. Sleeping Beauty's Castle's violet turrets stood out against a violet sky. I saw tears in Tom Joad's eyes.

"This was everything we ever dreamed of, back then," he said. "We thought all Californy would be like this."

This won't work for everyone. The "Californy" is off, a pulling away from the story, a distancing, the self-protection that infects so much Disney criticism. But the passage gets at something deep about Disneyland. Tom Joad is beside the point—the man in *The Grapes of Wrath* expected no castles in California—but also a way in. There's a way in which all Californians believe all California should feel like Disney's vision, and a way in which it does. There is a way in which California called Disneyland into being, and in which Disneyland only reflects back the light of its own place.

So far, this is as far as the criticism of Disney theme parks goes, and self-evidently it is not very far. The real literature remains to be written; the parks have a forty-year head start.

xiii. Walt Disney working on his live steam train, c. 1950.

INTERVIEW WITH FRANK GEHRY

BY KARAL ANN MARLING AND PHYLLIS LAMBERT
JANUARY 6, 1996

Catherine Wagner. "The Darkroom," Hollywood Boulevard; Disney-MGM Studios Theme Park, Walt Disney World, Orlando, Florida. Collection CCA.

KARAL ANN MARLING: I wanted to talk to you a little bit about some of your own experiences with theming, and what you think the whole thing is about, particularly in your own work at Festival Disney.

FRANK GEHRY: I was not given the Festival Disney project to theme, and from the beginning I was worried about that. Bob Fitzpatrick, who was the head of Euro Disney [now Disneyland Paris] when we started, was very clear that he was not asking me to do a themed project. However, when I saw the building finished, in the context of other themed projects, it became clear to me that my building was a Frank Gehry theme. It was a theme de facto, whether I liked it or not.

KAM: Could you talk to me a little bit about what a Frank Gehry theme is?

FG: Because I had my own language, and because this project, I suppose, grew out of my body of work, it was sort of recognizable; it had its own sensibility. So it was complete and compact.

KAM: Which is, of course, the real virtue of something like Main Street, U.S.A.

FG: Yes, it had those qualities, even though it was modern and different. Because it was encapsulated by all these other hermetic kinds of ideas, it also became one of them. That was a surprise to me. Actually, before I started it, Michael Eisner wanted Claes Oldenburg to collaborate with me on the project. Claes and his wife said they couldn't let themselves get that close to Mickey Mouse because they would be co-opted by the relationship. They got fussy about it; they did not want to do it. Then, Fitzpatrick went to visit them. For a millisecond, they agreed to participate. They entertained the possibility for maybe three or four days. Then they called me and said no, they shouldn't do it and I shouldn't do it because—they said— "you'll see, you'll be part of something you're not really interested in being part of." Given the way the project came to me, I disagreed. I thought it wasn't going to happen. Bob Stern is going to theme something and Michael Graves is going to theme something. But that's not the way our project is going to be. So I was more optimistic.

KAM: Whenever you take a commission, I suppose there is a program involved: build an art gallery, build a shoe store, and in a sense, you are theming. Aren't you building a fantasy of what that thing is?

FG: Yes, except if you are given a hotel and told to make it New York, a commission Michael Graves was given. I was in the room when the theming symposium happened in New York. Each one of the guys was given a theme, and they talked about New York and about the essence of New York. I remember people writing furiously as they listed these essences. Then Michael had to go back and design a building that was evocative and respected those essences. He made these pseudo towers that looked like high-rise towers with punched openings and different colors, and he made a New York bar.

KAM: And a subway in the basement.

FG: Yes. Actually, his interiors—I think you'll agree with this—really did it. The interiors of that New York hotel. You go into one of those restaurants and you feel like you're really in New York.

KAM: Yes, the Rainbow Room piece is wonderful.

FG: It's a superb effort. He wasn't as successful on the outside, and he says that too. Whereas Bob Stern was very successful on the outside. The outside is New England.

KAM: Sort of Newport, New England.

FG: He got it! The French architect Antoine Grumbach did the best one for me because it maintained a toughness and an abstraction. It was supposed to be the Adirondacks or the

210 Designing Disney's Theme Parks

xiv. Perspective view, Festival Disney, Disneyland Paris. Frank Gehry, architect, 1992.

wilderness at any rate. But in that context, if you walk around the string of pearls—the hotels with themes—and then you get to Festival Disney, what is it? So Festival Disney has a look. You can say: what look is that? And that's why I say it had my look—that in relationship to all of that, I became a theme.

KAM: It certainly does turn your attention to ideas of contemporary America because here you are, you do walk around this circle, you do come out of the railroad station complex, and you do walk through it. It functions in a way as a kind of second main street.

FG: Did you know of Venturi's proposal? That was one of the most spectacular things I have ever seen. It was Bob Venturi at his pinnacle, just the best. I couldn't believe it. I was on the floor howling with laughter when he presented it. It was in New York, at Bob Stern's office, and all the architects were there. We were fussing about a master plan and how we were all going to work together.

Venturi came in with his best Princeton professorial demeanor. He had the cardigan sweater. Of course he doesn't smoke a pipe. He stood up and presented the fall line. An *allée* of 150-foot-high flat cutouts of Mickey Mouse and Minnie Mouse, every 50 feet on center, from the entry to the Castle. You would come in off the main road and be confronted with this *allée*. He had pictures of it in relation to the distance between Place de la Concorde and the Arc de Triomphe. It was the same distance. You would be confronted with Mickey and Minnie frontally, holding hands across this *allée* every 50 feet, 150-feet high. It was breathtaking and spectacular.

He presented it like an architecture professor from Princeton, very dry, comparing it to the Champs-Élysées, filled with historical references. I was on the floor; I couldn't contain myself. I had to walk out of the room several times. Michael Eisner just loved it. I guess in Disney's context it would have been the wrong thing to do, but it was so strong, so beautiful, and so to the point of what the whole thing is about. They would have, in one fell swoop, replanted the Champs-Élysées and taken control of it for Disney. It was just hilarious.

Disney president Frank Wells got up and said, "You can't do this, Robert." So he threw cold water on it. It pointed out to me something very important—that it would have been the same issue with Claes, that Venturi plays close to their edge, but he does it in a way that is art, that is meaningful, that is relevant to where we are in the world and what we are doing. He tells the truth. There is an essence and a truth in Venturi's portrayal of this whole thing. That's why he could not do work for them. From then on, he never got to do the hotel.

He played too close to their edge and they can't accept that. It would be disastrous, I suppose, for them to do so.

PHYLLIS LAMBERT: It was appropriate that Robert Stern imitate a New England environment because that is what Robert has been into for so long. He is like all those eclectic architects of the nineteenth century. I find it terribly interesting that it is that sort of architect—a stylist essentially—who can successfully work for Disney in that context.

FG: It's interesting that Venturi cannot.

PL: Yes, because Venturi is something else, is he not?

FG: But it's that something else that is really why he cannot do it.

PL: Do you think it is something like the same problem Oldenburg had, being too close to it to begin with?

FG: Right. Those two get very close to the mouse. But Oldenburg and Venturi are commentators; they are also commentators.

KAM: It's that irony that I think is one of the big problems. It's interesting to me that some things Oldenburg is interested in, like L.A. roadside architecture, architecture as statue, are things that Disney has never done. It's always within a context very close to reality that Disney chooses to theme something.

FG: Would Disneyland work if it got into that? I don't know. Would masses of people go to Disneyland? I think the French would have liked it. I think if they had pulled those cards in France, they would have been more successful. Because the French love that.

KAM: I'm not so sure that's what Americans go to Disney World to look for. I suppose one of the principles Disney operates on in terms of theming is a pleasure and comfort level they've been trying to create among patrons that's a little bit different from what Venturi had in mind.

FG: Right. But Peter Eisenman talked about Disney's dark side; he presented an underworld hotel. I was sort of squeaky clean, Mr. Good Boy. I went in and took them at face value. They said that when people leave the Magic Kingdom at four o'clock in the afternoon and head for the hotels or the train, they wanted something that would light up and attract them so they could get their last half-a-buck out of them.

This is exactly the way they portrayed it to me. What they wanted to do was pretty straightforward and honest. They wanted it to be specially lit and to deal with the French skies, which are mostly gray in the winter. They wanted to do something that would light up this place, starting at four p.m., and make it come to life.

That's when I did the colonnade with the stainless steel

and the light. The only piece I took from theming was when we started the project, when somebody talked about the railroad and whether Festival Disney could have something to do with the history of the area and relate to the railroad. The railroad sounded interesting to me because so much passion is evoked in going to stations: seeing your loved ones off, greeting people. That, for me, was the essence of Walt Disney: he loved trains and had a miniature choo-choo that he used to go around the garden on. He tinkered with trains and loved all that nostalgia. I've spent a lot of time at the Walt Disney house because of the work with Mrs. Disney on Disney Hall. I've seen the little train, the train shed where he tinkered, their house, the kind of art they lived with, and a lot of flowers. And that's how it all started. To collide with the train station excited me because there was a reality to it. I decided to make the colonnade of Festival Disney perpendicular to the station, to the tracks. It's almost as though my row of columns was the residue of some old power station that related to the railroad. That's how I hooked into it.

Unfortunately, when the actual design of the railroad station happened, there was never money to complete that square. I used to think, "Why are they doing this? They're putting so much money in this thing." Then I found out that it wasn't the money, it was the crowd control. One of their senior people, Dick Nunis, was very controlling of that area. He wanted Tiananmen Square. If there was ever a riot or anything, he could bring in the troops and control the area. He didn't want to break it down too much. The scale of Tiananmen Square in front of Festival Disney, the railroad station, and the entrance to the park didn't make any sense. It was too big, it became a no-man's-land. I don't know what they're doing with it now. I went there to the opening for one evening and left, and I've never been back.

KAM: It's pretty much a no-man's-land to this day.

FG: Yes. That was something we all agonized about. I remember talking to Michael many times, saying get the clock from Grand Central, because the clock still exists in New York. The Transit Bureau still has that clock in the basement. Nobody is using it. You could probably get it.

KAM: There *is* a little railroad train that runs outside one of the buildings, which is themed now on its interior and a little bit on its exterior to be a sort of deco train station.

FG: The interiors of the stores, the signage, and all those things were done by others. I was offered the chance to work on them. When they were given to others, I was given the opportunity to comment on what they did. I don't know why, but I got holier than thou. I said, "I can't do Mickey Mouse; I'll make the building, and you guys put your stuff in it. I don't know how to do that."

In retrospect, I think I was wrong. I could have done it. Once I was pregnant, I should have done it. I should have because it would have been fun. I don't how far it would have gotten. I might have run into the same problem Venturi did in the end and not have been able to do it. The Mickey Mouse image has the power to co-opt anything, almost anything.

KAM: Has your brush with theming left any influences?

FG: I don't know. They know I'm not a themer, so I never get asked to do those projects. I was asked to do an office building, which I did—a back-of-house office building, which we just completed. At one point I said, "Why don't we put a Mickey statue up on the prow that looks like a big ship and just make a little Mickey statue?" I was willing to do it, and they said no, no, no, stop, that's not you. They're very respectful. I did the hockey rink, which is not themed. They like it.

So I am in a different category in their minds too. They never bother me about stuff. They offered me the animation building, the one that Stern did. But I was already working on two Disney projects and it would have represented more than 50 percent of my office with Disney work. That's not healthy for either party, so I turned it down. I had been there before with the Rouse Company; it didn't work.

KAM: But how about that moment of revelation, when you did a non-themed project at Festival Disney and discovered that, in fact, you had themed it? Has that been a revelation of any use to you?

FG: Yes, it was. Had I understood it, had I been smart enough to figure that out, had I known that in advance, I would not have done it. Claes, I think, was trying to tell me that, and I didn't get it. I thought I was going to do my stuff and it didn't matter.

In the world we are involved in, I don't know that it's a catastrophe or that it means anything. You can get precious about it. I loved the people. I wanted to work with Eisner. He's very intelligent; he loves architecture. He's personally caught up in architecture.

KAM: Actually, I'm interested in the same things you are. I am absolutely captivated by the Walt Disney who doesn't know anything about architecture, zipping around his backyard on his little train and saying to himself, "I could make a pleasure garden," and coming at architecture in that way.

xv. Festival Disney (detail), Disneyland Paris. Frank Gehry, architect, 1992.

SOURCES

Catherine Wagner.
Special Effects Tank, Backstage Studio Tour;
Disney-MGM Studios Theme Park,
Walt Disney World, Orlando, Florida.
Collection CCA.

Expository Expositions: Preparing for the Theme Parks
by Neil Harris

On the Philadelphia Centennial, Charles W. Robinson, "Exposition Management," *Harper's Weekly* 34 (February 1, 1890): 90.

Denton J. Snider, *World's Fair Studies* (Chicago: Sigma Publishing, 1895), p. 124.

On the 1893 fair as the dawn of a new era, F. Hopkinson Smith, "The Picturesque Side," *Scribner's* 14 (November 1893): 611.

John Goodman, "Altar Against Altar," *Art History* 15 (December 1992): 437.

Russell Kirk, "From The Academy," *National Review* 19 (August 22, 1967): 911.

Amusement and Recreation in Milwaukee (Milwaukee: Milwaukee City Club, 1914), p. 5.

Olmsted quoted in Roy Rosenzweig and Elizabeth Blackmar, *The Park and the People: A History of Central Park* (Ithaca: Cornell University Press, 1992), p. 332.

"The Park and the Botanical Garden," *Harper's Weekly* 41 (July 17, 1897): 702.

John J. Ingalls, "Lessons of the Fair," *Cosmopolitan* 16 (December 1893): 143.

Frank Morton Todd, *The Story of the Exposition*, I (New York, London: Putnam's, 1921), p. 170.

On Midwestern entrepreneurs at Coney Island, Gary Kyriazi, *The Great American Amusement Parks: A Pictorial History* (Secaucus, N.J.: Citadel, 1976).

Richard Harding Davis, "The Last Days Of The Fair," *Harper's Weekly* 37 (October 21, 1893): 1002.

Edwin E. Slosson, "The Amusement Business," *Independent* 57 (July 21, 1909): 134.

Frederic Thompson, "Amusing The Million," *Everybody's Magazine* 19 (September 1908): 386.

"St. Louis and the Fair," *New York Times*, October 14, 1904, p. 6.

Day Allen Willey, "The Trolley-Park," *Cosmopolitan* 33 (July 1902): 267–68.

"Exhibitions and Expositions," *Nation* 125 (October 26, 1927): 441.

"Chicago Fair," *Newsweek* 4 (November 18, 1934): 32.

"Is It Progress?" *Christian Century* 50 (June 28, 1933): 839.

Lincoln Kirstein, "A Century of Progress," *Nation* 138 (June 20, 1934): 697.

On Sally Rand, Bruce Bliven, "A Century of Treadmill," *New Republic* 77 (November 15, 1933): 11.

Bruce Bliven, "Los Angeles," *New Republic* 51 (July 13, 1927): 197.

Edmund Wilson, "The City of Our Lady the Queen of the Angels," *New Republic* 69 (December 2, 1931): 67–68.

Sarah Comstock, "The Great American Mirror," *Harper's* 156 (May 1928): 718.

On Los Angeles, Lillian Symes, "The Beautiful and Dumb," *Harper's* 163 (June 1931): 24.

Julian Hawthorne, "Novelties at Buffalo Fair," *Cosmopolitan* 31 (September 1901): 491–92.

Imagineering the Disney Theme Parks
by Karal Ann Marling

My understanding of the architecture of the Disney theme parks is based upon the collections of Walt Disney Imagineering, Glendale, California. In addition to the original Walt Disney Studio library, and video versions of the Disney films, TV shows, and press conferences, WDI also maintains a massive working reference library of the drawings, plans, and other visual tools from which the parks (and every detail thereof) were built. These renderings constitute the primary documentation for this essay.

The second key source has been interviews and conversations with the men and women who built the parks. During the summer of 1995, I conducted formal interviews with Marty Sklar, John Hench, Wing Chao, Marvin Davis, Bill Cottrell, Card Walker, Bill Evans, Ward Kimball, Sam McKim, Rolly Crump, Tony Baxter, Barry Braverman, Eddie Sotto, Bob Weis, Tim Delaney, Tom Morris, Eric Jacobson, Jan Sircus, Susan Bonds, and Joe Lanzisero, and many of their associates.

In addition, I have consulted written material at WDI and in the Walt Disney Archives, Burbank, California, and photographic records at both WDI and the Walt Disney Company Photo Collection in Burbank.

For a cultural-historical approach to the parks, see Karal Ann Marling, "Disneyland, 1955: Just Take the Santa Ana Freeway to the American Dream," *American Art* 5 (winter/spring 1991): 168–207; "Kenbai vs. All-American Kawaii at Tokyo Disneyland," *American Art* 6 (spring 1992): 102–11; and chapter 3, "Disneyland: The Place That Was Also a TV Show," in *As Seen on TV: The Visual Culture of Everyday Life in the 1950s* (Cambridge: Harvard University Press, 1994).

My research team for this project consisted of Andrew Lainsbury, Barbara Coleman, and Adam Harris. Our basic bibliography of published sources began with Kathy Merlock Jackson, *Walt Disney: A Bio-Bibliography* (Westport, Conn.: Greenwood Press, 1993).

Imagineers Bruce Gordon and David Mumford published *Disneyland: The Nickel Tour* (1995) during our period of residence at WDI: their interest and encouragement were most helpful. Bruce, David, Kevin Rafferty, and Randy Webster were then working on *Walt Disney Imagineering: A Behind the Dreams Look at Making the Magic Real* (New York: Hyperion, 1996); our debates, discussions, and disagreements are all reflected in this text.

Arline Chambers arranged interviews and transportation. Randy Webster served as our guide to the pictorial documentation, models, photos, and other artifacts. He was, at all points, a full collaborator on the research that supports this essay.

The Ideal City
Bosley Crowther, "The Dream Merchant," *New York Times*, December 16, 1966.

Parks and Railroads
Walt on amusement parks, quoted in Richard Schickel, *The Disney Version: the Life, Times, Art and Commerce of Walt Disney*, rev. ed. (New York: Simon and Schuster, 1985), p. 310.

Walt to Roger Broggie, quoted in Roger Broggie interview, July 16, 1968, Walt Disney Archives, Burbank, Calif.

Walt on the berm, Pete Martin and Diane Disney, interviews, c. 1956, Walt Disney Archives.

On Walter Knott, see editorial statement, *Ghost Town News* 5, no. 30 (April 1946): 2. Published by "Knott's Berry Place," this magazine was purchased by subscription by the original Walt Disney Studio library, now the Imagineering Research Collection, Glendale, Calif.

The Chicago Railroad Fair
Ward Kimball, quoted in Leonard Mosley, *Disney's World* (New York: Stein and Day, 1985), p. 230. The fullest account of the trip is "An Interview with Ward Kimball," *Storyboard, The Journal of Animation* 2, no. 5 (October/November 1991): 16–19, 34.

Disneylandia
Walt on his stove, quoted in a report prepared by David R. Smith, archivist, to accompany an inventory of the miniature collection in Disney's studio office, February 1, 1978, Walt Disney Archives.

Roger Broggie, quoted in Bruce Gordon and David Mumford, *Disneyland: The Nickel Tour* (Santa Clarita, Calif.: Camphor Tree Publishers, 1995), p. 13.

The Burbank Park
Walt to Harper Goff, quoted in Randy Bright, *Disneyland: Inside Story* (New York: Harry N. Abrams, 1987), p. 39.

Memo of 1948, quoted in Bob Thomas, *Walt Disney: An American Original* (New York: Simon and Schuster, 1976), pp. 218–19.

Undated six-page prospectus (Burbank) appended to "The Disneyland Story" (April 20, 1954), IRC Library, Walt Disney Imagineering, Glendale, Calif.

Burbank politician, quoted in Bright, *Disneyland*, p. 41.

Enter the L.A. Architects
Becket on clients, quoted in Robert Cahn, "The Man Who Changes Skylines," *Saturday Evening Post* 231 (November 27, 1958): 33.

Walt on Wright, quoted in Bob Thomas, *Walt Disney: An American Original* (New York: Hyperion, 1994), p. 193.

Walt on rejected Main Street building, quoted in Bob Thomas, "Uncle Walt's Greatest Stand: How There Was Almost No Disneyland," *Los Angeles,* (December 1976), 209.

Bruce Becket, interview, July 13, 1995.

The Art Directors
Disney on Main Street, quoted in Bob Thomas interview with John Hench, fall 1989, Walt Disney Archives.

Marvin Davis, interview, July 26, 1995.

Goff on Main Street, in Disneyland, Inc., "Report on Amusement Parks," June 1954, Walt Disney Archives.

Research and Development
Harrison Price on SRI study, address to National Fantasy Fan Club convention, Anaheim, Calif., July 22, 1995.

Description of Disneyland in WED Enterprises, "Disneyland," 1953, p. 3, prefaced by undated memo from Bill Cottrell, in IRC Library, Walt Disney Imagineering.

Harrison A. Price, William M. Stewart, and Redford C. Rollins, "An Analysis of Location Factors for Disneyland," August 28, 1953, Walt Disney Archives.

Marvin Davis on new rides, interview, May 28, 1968, Walt Disney Archives.

Other People's Amusement Parks
"Disneyland, Inc., Report on Amusement Parks," 1954, Walt Disney Archives. George Whitney, Jr. and Bruce Bushman were the other members of the research team.

Bill Cottrell, interview, July 12, 1995.

Castles in the Air
Walt to Herb Ryman, quoted in Thomas, *Walt Disney*, 1994, pp. 245–46.

Ryman's mother, quoted in Bright, *Disneyland*, p. 55.

Marvin Davis on Ryman, interview, 1968, Walt Disney Archives.

Disneyland: The Place That Was Also a TV Show
Walt on TV, quoted in Schickel, *The Disney Version*, p. 313.

Walt to Pete Martin, interviews, c. 1956, Walt Disney Archives.

Walt on hub, quoted in Bright, *Disneyland*, p. 61.

Walt on "museum foot," quoted in Thomas, *Walt Disney*, 1994, p. 251.

Selling Disneyland
David Mumford on building Main Street, interview, June 29, 1995.

Imagineers on building techniques, Joe Lanzisero and Susan Bonds, interviews, June 27 and 29, 1995.

The Architecture of Reassurance
Walt's distrust of blueprints, cited in J. Tevere MacFadyen, "The Future: A Walt Disney Production," *Next,* July/August 1980, p. 30.

Measurements of Main Street, in Allan B. Jacobs, *Great Streets* (Cambridge: MIT Press, 1993), pp. 170–71.

Inventory of stores, in Leon J. Janzen, "Walt Disney's Live Steam Legacy (Part 1)," *The "E" Ticket* (winter 1990–91): 25.

Walt on street as toy, quoted in Schickel, *The Disney Version*, pp. 323–24.

Hench on chaos, quoted in Bright, *Disneyland*, p. 48.

Hench on scenes, quoted in Thomas Hine, "At EPCOT Center, the Message is Mixed," *Philadelphia Inquirer*, October 22, 1982.

Walt on being corny, quoted in Diane Disney Miller with Pete Martin, "My Dad, Walt Disney," *Saturday Evening Post* 230 (January 5, 1957): 82.

Walt to his architects, quoted in Thomas, "Uncle Walt's Greatest Stand," p. 209.

Main Street Memories
Richard Neutra, quoted in David Gebhardt and Harriette von Breton, *L.A. in the Thirties: 1931–1941* (n.p.: Peregrine Smith, 1975), p. 109.

Main Street Urbanism
Eddie Sotto on Paris, interview, June 28, 1995.

Cowboys, Artificial Rivers, and Plastic Hippos
Early ideas for Jungle Cruise, in David Mumford, "Jungle Cruise Comments," *The "E" Ticket* (summer 1989): unpaginated.

Bill Evans, interview, June 30, 1995.

Julian Halevy, "Disneyland and Las Vegas," *Nation* 186 (June 7, 1958): 511. See also John Ciardi, quoted in Michael R. Real, *Mass-Medi*ated Culture (Englewood Cliffs, N.J.: Prentice-Hall, 1977), p. 80.

On architectural style of Indiana Jones™ Adventure, Susan Bonds, interview, June 29, 1995.

Walt's Ten-cennial TV show, WDI Video Reel 4943.

On Chinatown district, Gordon and Mumford, *The Nickel Tour*, pp. 233–34.

John Hench on Tiki Room, interview, June 22, 1995.

Fantasyland
Claude Coats on animation and theme parks, interview, April 20, 1978, Walt Disney Archives.

Ward Kimball on Frontierland station, interview, July 14, 1995.

Buildings and 'Toons
Joe Lanzisero, interview, June 27, 1995.

Marty Sklar, interview, June 23, 1995.

It's a Small World After All
Rolly Crump, interview, June 27, 1995.

Cities of Tomorrow
On 1995 Tomorrowland, Eric Jacobson, interview, July 6, 1995 (including team members Rick Rothschild, Ron Chesley, and Paul Osterhout). See also Kevin Rafferty, Dan Molitor, and Kerry Smith, "It's a Great Big Beautiful Tomorrow(land)," *The Disney Magazine* 30, no. 1 (winter 1994): 20–23.

On Discoveryland, Tim Delaney, interview, July 6, 1995.

Report of 1967, quoted in Gordon and Mumford, *The Nickel Tour*, p. 238.

On Monsanto Home, Jack E. Janzen, "The Monsanto Home of the Future," *The "E" Ticket* (winter 1991–92): 12–19.

Tomorrowlands
Victor Gruen, *The Heart of Our Cities: The Urban Crisis, Diagnosis and Cure* (New York: Simon and Schuster, 1964), pp. 19–49.

Walt to John Hench, quoted in Richard R. Beard, *Walt Disney's EPCOT: Creating the New World of Tomorrow* (New York: Harry N. Abrams, 1982), p. 11.

Project X
"Walt's Florida Press Conference," September 15, 1965, WDI Video Reel 18122.

Walt on EPCOT acronym, Marvin Davis, interview, July 26, 1995.

EPCOT film (industry version), December 1966, WDI Video Reel 17062.

Notes of a meeting with Walt Disney about the film, in Marty Sklar, "Walt Disney World Background and Philosophy," WED memo, September 21, 1967, and attached storyboards for EPCOT film.

On context of utopian thinking, John M. Findlay, *Magic Lands: Western Cityscapes and American Culture after 1940* (Berkeley: University of California Press, 1992): 105–11.

EPCOT after Walt
Davis on EPCOT as wienie, quoted in "Disney Planned a City," *Sales Meeting*, July 1969, pp. 85–86.

On monorail in lobby, Marty Sklar, interview, June 23, 1995.

On Becket hotels at Magic Kingdom, press releases, U.S. Steel, April 30, 1969.

Future World
On rented pencils, David Mumford, interview, June 29, 1995.

On Kodak building at EPCOT, Tony Baxter, interview, July 6, 1995.

On design of General Motors building, Marty Sklar, conversation, July 25, 1995.

Barry Braverman, interview, July 7, 1995.

Inside the Berm—and Outside
Ariane Mnouchkine on Disneyland Paris, quoted in Jenny Rees, "The Mouse That Ate France," *National Review*, May 11, 1992, p. 57.

Ray Bradbury, quoted in Arthur Miller, "Citizen Disney," *Los Angeles*, November 1964, p. 34. See also Ray Bradbury, *Yestermorrow* (Santa Barbara: Capra Press, 1991), pp. 146–48.

James Rouse, quoted in Bright, *Disneyland*, p. 29.

Card Walker, interview, July 17, 1995.

Bob Weis, interview, July 14, 1995.

Tim Delaney, interview, July 6, 1995.

Jan Sircus, Bobby Brooks, Tom Figgins, and Stuart Bailey, interviews, July 17, 1995.

Making Imagination Safe in the 1950s: Disneyland's Fantasy Art and Architecture by Erika Doss

Insurance by North America advertisement, *Life* 43, no. 21 (November 18, 1957): 96.

Russell B. Nye, "Eight Ways of Looking at an Amusement Park," *Journal of Popular Culture* 15, no. 1 (summer 1981): 70; Walt Disney quoted in *Disneyland, The First Thirty-Five Years* (Anaheim, Calif.: Walt Disney Company, 1989), p. 11.

On Wright see Vincent Scully Jr., *Frank Lloyd Wright* (New York: Braziller, 1975), pp. 30–31; on May see Harold Kirker, *Old Forms on a New Land: California Architecture in Perspective* (Niwot, Colo.: Robert Rinehart Publishers, 1991), pp. 92–96.

Warren Susman, "Did Success Spoil the United States? Dual Representations in Postwar America," in Lary May, ed., *Recasting America: Culture and Politics in the Age of Cold War* (Chicago: University of Chicago Press, 1989), pp. 30–33.

On "Kiddieland," Randy Bright, *Disneyland: Inside Story* (New York: Abrams, 1987), p. 42.

In his paper "Redefining the Pleasure Garden: The Cinemaesthetics of EuroDisneyland," presented at the American Studies Association Annual Conference, November 11, 1995, in Pittsburgh, Andrew Lainsbury reported that Disney staffers consider being stationed at the It's a Small World ride a hardship assignment because of, among other things, the "endlessly droning tune." Their reaction is not atypical: recently, while riding on It's a Small World in Walt Disney World with my three-year daughter (who would ride on nothing else in Fantasyland without screaming), various adult reactions to the seemingly interminable ride included adding obscene lyrics to the song and standing up in the boat and pretending to machine-gun the dolls.

Richard Schickel, *The Disney Version: The Life, Times, Art, and Commerce of Walt Disney*, rev. and updated (New York: Touchstone, 1968, 1985), p. 322; Disney quoted in Bright, *Disneyland*, p. 81. See Karal Ann Marling, "Disneyland 1955: Just Take the Santa Ana Freeway to the American Dream," *American Art* 5 (winter/spring 1991): 197, for a discussion of Fantasyland's participatory mode.

Miles Orvell, "Understanding Disneyland: American Mass Culture and the European Gaze," in Orvell, *After the Machine: Visual Arts and the Erasing of Cultural Boundaries* (Jackson: University of Mississippi Press, 1995), p. 156. Jack Zipes, *Breaking the Magic Spell: Radical Theories of Folk and Fairy Tales* (Austin: University of Texas Press, 1979), p. 18. See also Zipes, *Fairy Tales and the Art of Subversion: The Classical Genre for Children and the Process of Civilization* (New York: Wildman, 1983).

Jean Laplanche and Jean-Bertrand Pontalis, *The Language of Psychoanalysis*, trans. David Nicholson-Smith (New York: W. W. Norton, 1973); see also Victor Burgin, James Donald, and Cora Kaplan, eds., *Formations of Fantasy* (New York: Methuen, 1987).

Umberto Eco, *Travels in Hyperreality*, trans. William Weaver (New York: Harcourt Brace Jovanovich, 1986), pp. 3–58; The Project on Disney, *Inside the Mouse: Work and Play at Disney World* (Durham: Duke University Press, 1995), p. 166 and *passim*; Anne Norton, *Republic of Signs: Liberal Theory and American Popular Culture* (Chicago: University of Chicago Press, 1993), p. 21.

On Main Street vs. strip malls, Marling, "Disneyland 1955," p. 195.

Walt Disney quoted in Bright, *Disneyland*, p. 100.

Hench quoted in "EPCOT Center: It's a Very Carefully Planned Place," *Philadelphia Enquirer*, October 21, 1982, as noted in Stephen M. Fjellman, *Vinyl Leaves, Walt Disney World and America* (Boulder, Colo.: Westview Press, 1992), p. 203; Disney quoted in Bright, *Disneyland*, p. 63. See also Bright, p. 61, Fjellman, p. 204, and Marling, "Disneyland 1955," p. 197, for discussion of Disney's wienie theory.

On the Castle and Disney films, Frank Thomas and Ollie Johnston, *Disney Animation, The Illusion of Life* (New York: Abbeville Press, 1981), p. 371. See also Schickel, *The Disney Version*, p. 299. For discussion of Disney's live-action films and television projects see Schickel, pp. 298–314 and Douglas Gomery, "Disney's Business History: A Reinterpretation," in *Disney Discourse: Producing the Magic Kingdom*, ed. Eric Smoodin (New York: Routledge, 1994), pp. 75–78.

"Disneyland, Uncle Walt packs his new park with the stuff children's dreams are made on," *Life*, August 15, 1955, p. 41; Zipes, *Breaking the Spell*, p. 9. On Tokyo's Castle see Karal Ann Marling, "Letter from Japan: *Kembei* vs. All-American *Kawaii* at Tokyo Disneyland," *American Art* 6 (spring 1992): 108.

On Bavarian prototype, Bright, *Disneyland*, p. 87.

On Falkenstein, Heinrich Kreisel, *The Castles of Ludwig II of Bavaria*, trans. Margaret D. Senft-Howie (Darmstadt: Franz Schneekluth Verlag, 1954), pp. 75–79.

As Kathy Merlock Jackson notes in *Walt Disney: A Bio-Bibliography* (Westport, Conn.: Greenwood Press, 1993), "Following World War II, both the Disney Studio and its distribution company RKO had millions of dollars worth of frozen funds that could be spent only in England." Disney's solution was to produce films overseas (see pp. 46–47). Ray Bradbury notes Disney's attention to European art and architecture in "The Hipbone of Abraham L.," in *Yestermorrow: Obvious Answers to Impossible Futures* (Santa Barbara: Capra Press, 1991), pp. 143–44, and Bright, *Disneyland*, p. 49, notes Disney's fondness for Tivoli Gardens.

In *Disneyland*, p. 52, Bright reports that Disney commissioned the Stanford Research Institute to analyze attractions throughout America and abroad in preparation for a Disneyland feasibility study.

Steven Watts, "Walt Disney: Art and Politics in the American Century," *Journal of American History* 82, no. 1 (June 1995): 85; David Low, "Leonardo da Disney," *New Republic* 106 (January 5, 1942): 16–18; Eisenstein quoted in Jay Leyda, ed., *Eisenstein on Disney*, trans. Alan Upchurch (Calcutta, 1986), as noted in Watts, p. 90, note 9; Genauer, "Walt Disney's Music Pictures Range from Beautiful to Banal," *New York World Telegram*, November 16, 1940, as noted in Watts, p. 90, note 8.

Watts, "Walt Disney," p. 88.

On Graham, see Thomas and Johnston, *Disney Animation*, pp. 71–72, 538–39; on the Jean Charlot lectures see the Disney Archives, Burbank. See also Charlot's article, "But Is It Art? A Disney Disquisition," in *The American Scholar* (summer 1939): 261–71. Disney quoted in Leonard Maltin, "*The Disney Films* (Crown: New York, 1984), p. 74.

Hench quoted in A. Eisen, "Two Disney Artists," in *Crimmer's: The Harvard Journal of Pictorial Fiction* (winter 1975): 35; Bradbury quoted in "The Hipbone of Abraham L.," p. 144; Disney quoted in Thomas and Johnston, *Disney Animation*, p. 71 (see also p. 332), and in Robert De Roos, "The Magic Worlds of Walt Disney," *National Geographic* 124 (August 1963): 174.

On "Destino" see Leonard Shannon, "When Disney Met Dali," *Modern Maturity*, December/January 1978–79, p. 50–52; for one view of Disney's South American ventures see Julianne Burton-Carvajal, "'Surprise Package': Looking Southward with Disney," in Smoodin, *Disney Discourse*, pp. 131–47.

Breton quoted in William Gaunt, *The Surrealists* (New York: G. P. Putnam's Sons, 1972), p. 7; Barr quoted in Miller, *American Realists and Magic Realists*, p. 5. Dalì appeared on the December 14, 1936 cover of *Time* and Disney first appeared on the December 27, 1937 cover of *Time*, in a feature titled "Mouse and Man."

On the 1939 Levy exhibition see "Salvador Dalì: New Yorkers Stand in Line to See his Six-in-One Surrealist Painting," *Life*, April 17, 1939, pp. 44–45; on Dalì's Ballet see "Life goes to Dalì's new Ballet," *Life*, November 27, 1939, p. 91.

"World's Fair: It Turns Out to be a Wonderful Place," *Life*, July 3, 1939, pp. 66–67. Disney's specific interest in surreal styles may also be linked to deepening political disillusionment he experienced during the 1941 labor strike at the Disney Studio and throughout World War II. Watts observes that Disney, like other prewar Populists, developed a "hardened political viewpoint" after the war, becoming an ardent anti-Communist; see "Walt Disney," pp. 104–105. On Dalì's American popularity, see Erika Doss, *Benton, Pollock, and the Politics of Modernism: From Regionalism to Abstract Expressionism* (Chicago: University of Chicago Press, 1991), pp. 291–303. On Disney's financial state during the building of Disneyland see Bright, *Disneyland*, p. 53.

Smith quoted in Shannon, "When Disney met Dali," pp. 51–52.

Michael Sorkin, "See You in Disneyland," p. 217, in Sorkin, ed., *Variations on a Theme Park: The New American City and the End of Public Space* (New York: Noonday Press, 1992). Sorkin also discusses Disneyland's ancestry in nineteenth and twentieth century World's Fairs, pp. 208–13. For a general analysis of these fairs see, for example, Robert W. Rydell, *World of Fairs: The Century-of-Progress Expositions* (Chicago: University of Chicago Press, 1993), and Patricia F. Carpenter and Paul Totah, *The San Francisco Fair, Treasure Island, 1939–1940* (San Francisco: Scottwall Associates, 1989). For illustrations of Los Angeles vernacular architecture see the catalogue *Architecture in California, 1868–1968* (Santa Barbara: University of California Press, 1968), and David Gebhard's essay "One Hundred Years of Architecture in California", pp. 6–29. For more on this type of architecture see Karal Ann Marling, *The Colossus of Roads: Myth and Symbol along the American Highway* (Minneapolis: University of Minnesota Press, 1984).

On outsider art see John Beardsley, *Gardens of Revelation: Environments by Visionary Artists* (New York: Abbeville Press, 1995), and Eugene Metcalf and Michael Hall, eds., *The Artist Outsider: Creativity and the Boundaries of Culture* (Washington, D.C.: Smithsonian Institution Press, 1994).

For further information on Rodia see Jules Langsner, "Sam of Watts," *Arts and Architecture* 68 (July 1951): 23–25; Calvin Trillin, "A Reporter at Large: I Know I Want to Do Something," *The New Yorker* 41 (May 29, 1965): 72–120; Leon Whiteson, *The Watts Towers of Los Angeles* (Oakville, Ont.: Mosaic Press, 1989); and I. Sheldon Posen and Daniel Franklin Ward, "Watts Towers and the *Giglio* Tradition," Library of Congress *Folklife Annual*, 1985, pp. 143–57.

Langsner, "Sam of Watts," p. 25; see also "Popular Art: Sam of Watts," *Architectural Review* 111 (March 1952): 201–3. Beardsley, *Gardens of Revelation*, pp. 12–13. See Jackson, Walt Disney, p. 309, Appendix E, for a breakdown of the costs for each Disney theme park.

On Disney parks as hegemonic environments, see The Project on Disney, *Inside the Mouse*, p. 69.

Disneyland: Its Place in World Culture
by Yi-Fu Tuan

On the Chinese cosmic city, A. F. Wright, "Symbolism and Function: Reflections on Changan and Other Great Cities," *Journal of Asian Studies* 24 (1965): 667–79.

On the purpose of Disneyland, Bob Thomas, *Walt Disney: An American Original* (New York: Hyperion, 1994), pp. 13, 273.

On guards at the gates of the cosmic city, Etienne Balazs, *Chinese Civilization and Bureaucracy* (New Haven: Yale University Press, 1964), pp. 69, 71.

On Disney's response to disorder, John M. Findlay, "Disneyland: The Happiest Place on Earth," in *Magic Lands: Western Cityscapes and American Culture after 1940* (Berkeley and Los Angeles: University of California Press, 1992), pp. 55, 66, 73.

On critique of bourgeois order, Mikhail Bakhtin, *Rabelais and His World* (Cambridge: MIT Press, 1968).

On the actual location of Eden, Henry Baudet, *Paradise On Earth: Some Thoughts on European Images of Non-European Man* (New Haven: Yale University Press, 1965), pp. 15–20.

On Renaissance fountains, Henry Rouse and Simon Ince, *History of Hydraulics* (New York: Dover, 1963), pp. 59–138; David R. Coffin, *The Villa d'Este at Tivoli* (Princeton: Princeton University Press, 1960), p. 28.

On the display of animals, John Prest, *The Garden of Eden: The Botanic Garden and the Re-Creation of Paradise* (New Haven: Yale University Press, 1981), pp. 25–26; William Howard Adams, *The French Garden 1500–1800* (New York: Braziller, 1979), p. 18.

On the mechanical owl, Michel de Montaigne, *The Complete Works of Michael de Montaigne*, "Montaigne's Journey into Italy," William Hazlett, trans. (New York: Worthington, 1889), p. 612.

On Marly, Lucy Norton, *Saint-Simon at Versailles* (London: Hamish Hamilton, 1958), p. 265.

On approval of designs at Marly, Olivier Bernier, *Louis XIV: A Royal Life* (New York: Doubleday, 1987), p. 222.

On Tudor gardens, Nan Fairbrother, *Men and Gardens* (New York: Knopf, 1956), p. 94.

On Marie Antoinette as a milkmaid, Pierre de Nolhac, *The Trianon of Marie-Antoinette* (New York: Brentano's, n.d.), pp. 203–204.

On court theater of the sixteenth and seventeenth centuries, Stephen Orgel, *The Illusion of Power: Political Theater in the English Renaissance* (Berkeley: University of California Press, 1975), pp. 51–52.

On architects as landscape painters, Derek Clifford, *A History of Garden Design* (London: Faber and Faber, 1962), p. 140.

On the ride experience, Margaret J. King, "Disneyland and Walt Disney World: Traditional Values in Futuristic Form," *Journal of Popular Culture* 15 (spring 1981): 120.

On Splash Mountain and disaster scenes, Bob Sehlinger, *The Unofficial Guide to Disneyland* (New York: Prentice Hall Travel, 1994), pp. 75, 113.

On the cinematic background, Jean-Paul Sartre, *Sartre on Theater*, ed. M. Contat and M. Rybalka (New York: Pantheon, 1976), p. 60.

On scenes in *Fantasia*, John Culhane, *Walt Disney's Fantasia* (New York: Abradale Press, 1987), pp. 181–205.

On utopia, William James, "What Makes A Life Significant?" in *Essays on Faith and Morals* (New York: New American Library, 1974), pp. 288–89.

On Disney at work, Steven Watts, "Walt Disney: Art and Politics in the American Century," *Journal of American History* 82, no. 1 (1995): 96–102.

On the triumph of good over evil, Ollie Johnston and Frank Thomas, *The Disney Villain* (New York: Hyperion, 1993).

Forty Years of Overstatement: Criticism and the Disney Theme Parks
by Greil Marcus

Libby Gelman-Waxner on hell, "Afterlife, After Lunch," in *If You Ask Me* (New York: St. Martin's, 1994), p. 122.

Duvall quoted in Lisa Gubernick, "The Third Battle of Bull Run," *Forbes*, October 17, 1994, p. 67.

Julian Halevy, "Disneyland and Las Vegas," *Nation*, June 7, 1958, p. 510.

Tom Carson, "To Disneyland," *LA Weekly*, March 27–April 2, 1992, p. 22.

Halevy on heart of darkness, "Disneyland and Las Vegas," p. 511.

Ray Bradbury, "The Machine-Tooled Happyland," *Holiday*, October 1965, p. 100.

John Bright, "Disney's Fantasy Empire" *Nation*, March 6, 1967, p. 300.

Richard Schickel, *The Disney Version* (New York: Avon/Discus, [1968] 1969), p. 279.

Schickel on the Disney phenomenon, *The Disney Version*, p. 10; on Stravinsky, p. 207; on machine worship, p. 286; on Disneyland as dark land, p. 287; on mood of terror, p. 287; on Mr. Lincoln, p. 285; on Disney's love for the Lincoln legend, p. 285.

Reyner Banham, *Los Angeles: The Architecture of Four Ecologies* (London: Penguin, 1971), p. 127.

Umberto Eco, *Travels in Hyperreality* (New York: Harcourt Brace Jovanovich, [1983], 1990), p. 7.

Eco on ambience of Disneyland, *Travels in Hyperreality*, p. 43.

Jean Baudrillard, *America*, trans. Chris Turner (New York: Verso Press, 1988).

Michael Harrington on Disney capitalism, "To the Disney Station: Corporate Socialism in the Magic Kingdom," *Harper's*, January 1979, p. 39.

Harrington on Disney World as embodiment of desires, "To the Disney Station," p. 36.

Mike Wallace, "Mickey Mouse History: Portraying the Past at Disney World," *Radical History Review*, March 1985; Alexander Wilson, "The Betrayal of the Future: Walt Disney's EPCOT Center," originally published in *Socialist Review*, November–December 1985, collected in Eric Smoodin, ed., *Disney Discourse: Producing the Magic Kingdom* (New York and London: Routledge, 1994; Michael Sorkin, "See You in Disneyland," collected in Sorkin, ed., *Variations on a Theme Park* (New York: Hill & Wang/Noonday, 1992).

The Project on Disney, *Inside the Mouse: Work and Play at Disney World* (Durham, N.C.: Duke University Press, 1995), pp. 2, 40, 42 (Willis).

Klugman on vast kingdom, *Inside the Mouse*, p. 164.

Willis on shopping, *Inside the Mouse*, p. 40.

Charles Moore (with Peter Becker and Regula Campbell), *The City Observed: Los Angeles—A Guide to Its Architecture and Landscapes* (New York: Random House, 1984), p. 44.

Moore on Haunted Mansion, *The City Observed*, p. 45; on It's a Small World, p. 50; on Tomorrowland, p. 51.

Carson on mimicry, p. 17; on East Germany, p. 18; on abnegation of will, p. 18; as Tom Joad, p. 24; on Fantasyland, p. 25.

CHRONOLOGY

compiled by Andrew Landsbury

December 5, 1901
Walt Disney born in Chicago, Illinois; his father, Elias, had worked on the great Chicago World's Columbian Exposition of 1893.

April 1906
The Disney family moves to Crane Farm, a forty-eight-acre spread outside Marceline, Missouri. Walt Disney never forgets Kansas Street in Marceline, which becomes one important prototype for Disneyland's Main Street, U.S.A.

1918
Walt Disney drops out of high school and joins the ambulance corps as a driver in France during World War I; he falls in love with Paris.

1923
Walt Disney's Kansas City animation business goes bust. He moves to Los Angeles and, with his brother Roy, founds the Walt Disney film company.

Spring 1926
The Disney movie studio moves to quarters at 2719 Hyperion Avenue.

November 15, 1932
In preparation for a feature-length cartoon, Walt Disney sets up an art school to train animators. Here Disney and his artists perfect the use of the storyboard to plan animated sequences. Eventually, this combination of picture and story would influence Walt Disney's approach to architecture.

1934
The Farmer's Market opens in Los Angeles and becomes one of Walt Disney's favorite haunts.

1936
Crossroads of the World opens on Sunset Boulevard, featuring a variety of make-believe architectural styles and a pedestrian environment.
Walt Disney is named to the French Legion of Honor for "creating a new art form in which good is spread throughout the world."

December 21, 1937
Snow White and the Seven Dwarfs, the first feature-length animated film, premieres at the Carthay Circle Theater in Los Angeles (later replicated in the Disney-MGM Studios Theme Park). Workers at the studio present Walt Disney with a backyard playhouse for his two daughters, a child-size copy of the dwarfs' cottage from the film.

1938
Disney animator Ward Kimball buys a real 1881 steam locomotive and founds the Grizzly Flats Railroad in his yard in San Gabriel, California.

February 18, 1939
The Golden Gate International Exposition opens in San Francisco. Mrs. James Ward Thorne exhibits her miniature rooms at the San Francisco fair and at the New York World's Fair (see below).

April 30, 1939
New York's World's Fair opens, celebrating "The World of Tomorrow." Disney prepares a special Mickey Mouse film for the Nabisco pavilion. The fair is held at Flushing Meadow, Queens, site of the later 1964 Fair at which Walt Disney would unveil his new Audio-Animatronics® figures.

1940
Walt Disney's friend Walter Knott buys the first structures for his Ghost Town in Buena Park, California.

February 7, 1940
Release of *Pinocchio*. The famous "Pleasure Island" sequence showing an amusement park with roller coasters and other familiar rides as a place of depravity and disorder expresses the beliefs of a father who takes his daughters to such places on weekends and longs for an environment the whole family could enjoy together.

April 1940
Walt Disney visits Henry Ford's historical Greenfield Village in Michigan.

May 6, 1940
The Disney studio completes a move into new quarters in Burbank, designed with the help of Kem Weber. With twenty-five buildings on fifty-one acres, the complex was begun in 1939.

November 13, 1940
Release of *Fantasia*. Using classical music and themes drawn from high art, *Fantasia* is a highbrow failure. Walt Disney gradually directs his energies away from the movie business into dreams of a pleasure garden.

May 29, 1941
Disney is struck by the Screen Cartoonists Guild.

June 20, 1941
The feature film *The Reluctant Dragon*, showing how cartoons are made, also provides a tour of the new studio.

August 17, 1941
Disney leaves on a goodwill tour of Latin America, accompanied by Mary Blair and other animators and designers later involved in his plans to create a three-dimensional form of animation in his theme parks.

October 23, 1941
Release of *Dumbo*. Disney's cheapest animated feature to date, it includes a delightful train, "Casey, Jr.," later replicated at Disneyland.

1946
Animator Ollie Johnston builds a small-scale live steam railroad in his backyard.
Walt Disney visits New Orleans. He is captivated by the city and brings home a mechanical toy—a bird that sings when a key is wound.

1947
Ward Kimball helps the Disney set designers create an authentic Victorian railroad station for the film *So Dear to My Heart*. In 1948, Walt Disney gives him the set for use as a real station on the Grizzly Flats line. In 1953, Disney tries to get it back for Disneyland.

Christmas 1947
Walt Disney sets up an electric train layout in his office, ostensibly a gift for a nephew.

1948
Architect Welton Becket, a friend and neighbor of Walt Disney, designs Bullock's new department store in Pasadena.
So Dear to My Heart completed. Having the small-town look of Marceline, Missouri, it is Disney's favorite of all his films (and it would be shown on his TV program in 1954). He works in secret with art director Ken Anderson making a miniature version of one of the sets from the movie.

Summer 1948
Walt Disney and Ward Kimball visit the Chicago Railroad Fair together. On the way home, they stop at Greenfield Village. Kimball thinks this trip was a determining factor in Walt Disney's decision to build Disneyland.

August 1948
First internal memo describing a place that is recognizably Disneyland in the making.

December 21, 1948
Release of *Seal Island* documentary film. The series of nature and travel films begun with *Seal Island* will provide the inspiration for Adventureland at Disneyland.

1949
Walt Disney visits Paris and shops for miniature furniture and accessories.

Christmas Eve 1949
Walt Disney's Lilly Belle steam engine is tested at the studio. The engine is part of the rolling stock of the Carolwood Pacific Railroad, Disney's layout in the garden of his new house in Holmby Hills. To pacify the neighbors and reduce noise, he hides the train behind an earthen berm, similar to the thirty-five-foot embankment later constructed around Disneyland.

1950
Walt Disney tours Tivoli Gardens in Copenhagen with radio personality Art Linkletter.

September 1950
The sculptor Christadoro is hired by Walt Disney to carve figures for his handmade sets or miniature rooms. Disney works in secret to find the means to make these figures move.

December 25, 1950
Walt Disney's first television show airs on Christmas Day: *One Hour in Wonderland*.

1951
Walt Disney meets art director Harper Goff at the Bassett-Lowke train store in London. He hires Goff, who prepares a rendering for a park on sixteen acres adjoining the Burbank studio.
Release of *The African Queen*; the movie will inspire Goff's later designs for the Jungle Cruise ride at Disneyland.

1952
Walt Disney shows his handmade model of Granny's Cabin from *So Dear to My Heart* at the Festival of California Living in the Pan-Pacific Auditorium, Los Angeles.
Walter Knott opens his Ghost Town and Calico Railroad, with old mining engines.

March 1952
The Burbank Leader carries a report on Walt Disney's presentation to the city council. Burbank doesn't want a conventional amusement park—and the plot of land across the street from the studio proves too small for all of Walt Disney's new ideas.

December 1952
Walt Disney founds WED (Walter Elias Disney) Enterprises to carry out the planning for and building of Disneyland.

January 1953 (?)
Harper Goff draws plans for Main Street, U.S.A. based on his own boyhood hometown of Fort Collins, Colorado.

May 1953.
Walt Disney rejects a master plan for Disneyland commissioned from Luckman and Pereira. He hires Marvin Davis to draw up a master plan instead.

July 1953
Marvin Davis draws another version of Main Street. Walt Disney hires the Stanford Research Institute (SRI) to find a suitable park site and study the feasibility of the investment.

August 28, 1953
SRI draft study selects Anaheim, California, as the best place for Disneyland.

September 1953
Artist Herb Ryman spends a weekend with Walt Disney and creates the first complete vision of how the park will look. Roy Disney takes Ryman's renderings to New York to persuade the TV networks to finance his brother's park. The agreement struck with ABC calls for a weekly Disney show in return for financial backing.

June 1954
Bill Martin, Bill Cottrell, and several other Disney intimates tour museums, parks, and other tourist attractions around America looking for ideas. Many such research trips precede the opening of Disneyland.

October 27, 1954
The first show in the "Disneyland" series airs on the ABC network. Walt Disney appears with a dazzling new rendering by Peter Ellenshaw of the projected park and talks about the place. The weekly topics of the show are keyed to the segments of the park plan.

1954–55
Welton Becket builds the Capitol Records building.

1955
The Museum of Modern Art's influential photo show, *The Family of Man*, takes place in New York City.

May 25, 1955
Davy Crockett goes into theatrical release. Originally made as a serial for the "Disneyland" TV show, this Western influenced the design of Frontierland.

July 17, 1955
Disneyland opens in Anaheim on live TV, with twenty-four cameras and Art Linkletter, Ronald Reagan, and Bob Cummings as hosts.
Later that summer, the "plussing" begins, with several new attractions, including the Dumbo Flying Elephants.

October 3, 1955
The Mickey Mouse Club debuts on afterschool television.

December 1955.
Mike Fink Keelboats, actually used in the filming of the *Davy Crockett* series, brought to Disneyland for use as a ride.

1955–56
Victor Gruen completes Southdale, the first fully enclosed shopping mall, in Edina, Minnesota, a suburb of Minneapolis.

1956
New attractions at Disneyland include Storybook Land and a skyway ride connecting Fantasyland and Tomorrowland.

November 17, 1956
The first of eight installments of "My Dad, Walt Disney," by Diane Disney Miller (as told to Pete Martin) appears in the *Saturday Evening Post*.

1956–58
Plans drawn (unexecuted) for an International Street parallel to Main Street.

February 1957
A delegation of Imagineers visits New Orleans. An MIT-designed Monsanto House of the Future rises in Tomorrowland, showing Walt Disney's interest in using his park to influence real-world architecture.

January 29, 1959
Release of *Sleeping Beauty*; the Disneyland castle had already been named after the film.

June 1959
Major alterations to the park, with the addition of the Matterhorn, the Submarine Voyage, and the monorail. Tomorrowland and parts of Fantasyland had been left incomplete at the time of the opening because of time pressures and a lack of funds. The 1959 campaign aims to remedy these problems. Vice President Richard Nixon and his family attend the dedication ceremony on June 14.

1960
Excited by the new technology in use at Disneyland, Walt Disney approaches Las Vegas with the idea of running a monorail down the strip; he is turned down.

May–June 1960
Nature's Wonderland, a fabricated Disneyland landscape of the Old West, is explored by means of a mine train ride and a pack mule ride.

1961
Walt Disney spearheads the merger of the Los Angeles Conservatory of Music and the Chouinard Art Institute to form the California Institute of the Arts (Cal Arts), a professional college-level school from which many Disney employees are drawn.

June 1961
The monorail is extended across the parking lot to the Disneyland Hotel. The hotel had been designed by Luckman and Pereira.

November 1961
Walt Disney wants everything in the park to be clean and bright, even the Haunted Mansion. So the planned ghost house is redesigned to conform to his wishes.

Summer 1962
New, more realistic creatures are added to the old Jungle Cruise ride in Adventureland. They are placed in "gag" or comic situations designed by Marc Davis.

November 1962
Concrete and steel tree installed in Adventureland. The Swiss Family Tree House is based on the sets of the 1960 Disney feature film *Swiss Family Robinson*.

1963
New Orleans Square, the first new "land" to be added to Disneyland, opens.

June 1963
The Enchanted Tiki Room in Adventureland is the proving ground for Walt's ongoing experiments with robotics.

November 1963
Walt Disney and a chosen group of confidants scout a tract of central Florida swampland called the Reedy Creek Basin.

1964
Victor Gruen publishes *The Heart of Our Cities*.

April 22, 1964
The New York World's Fair opens with four Disney attractions for Ford, General Electric, Pepsi-Cola, and the State of Illinois. Robert Moses, the fair's planner and promoter, urges Walt Disney to take over the fairgrounds as a "Disneyland East" when the show closes.

Summer 1964
Anonymous buyers snap up land around Orlando, Florida. Walt Disney has spent an estimated $5 million to acquire 27,400 acres through middlemen and dummy corporations.

1965
Welton Becket's firm supplies drawings for a New Tomorrowland and for a building to house the GE Carousel of Progress at Disneyland. The GE exhibit in New York included Medallion City, a model American subdivision.
Walt Disney completes purchase of forty-three square miles of Florida property. He wants to build a model city there—a utopia eventually called EPCOT (Experimental Prototype Community of Tomorrow). The city is previewed in a model exhibited inside the Carousel of Progress attraction, which has been moved from New York to Disneyland.

January 3, 1965
The "Disneyland" show observes its tenth anniversary and Walt Disney introduces a host of coming attractions including enhancements to New Orleans Square and It's a Small World (formerly the Pepsi pavilion).

February 3, 1965
WED Enterprises, personally owned by Walt from 1952 to 1965, is incorporated as a subsidiary of Walt Disney Productions.

July 1965
The robotic Abe Lincoln from the New York Fair moves to Disneyland with a new script in time for Independence Day.

October 1965
The Orlando Sentinel identifies Walt Disney as the mystery buyer of Florida land. In a secret office at WED, Disney's team is working on Project X for Florida—Walt Disney's new city.

November 15, 1965
Governor Hayden Burns confirms that a new Disneyland will be built outside Orlando and calls this "the most significant day in the history of Florida."

1966
Walt Disney continues to supervise plans for Project X, calling on American corporations to locate their research facilities and light-industry plants on the property.

Summer 1966
Two additional World's Fair attractions—It's a Small World and a primeval world diorama from the Ford pavilion—complete the transition to Disneyland.

December 15, 1966
Walt Disney dies at the age of 65.

1967
Tomorrowland is redesigned again by Imagineer John Hench as a "cartilaginous" city centered on a Spaceport transit hub. Some of the ideas for Project X are reflected in Spaceport.

February 2, 1967
Roy Disney outlines his late brother's plans to build the world's first futuristic metropolis, or EPCOT. Eventually, the working city will disappear from the plan. EPCOT becomes a kind of permanent World's Fair instead.

February 1967
Pirates of the Caribbean opens in New Orleans Square, Disneyland. This is the most advanced of the robotic environments Walt Disney had envisioned in the 1930s.

Summer 1967
Ground-breaking for the new Disney theme park in Florida and the Disney-built hotels around it. There were to have been five themed hotels: Asian, Venetian, Persian, Contemporary, and the Polynesian Village. Of these, only the Contemporary and the Polynesian were built.

August 1969
The Haunted Mansion finally opens in New Orleans Square at Disneyland. It is the bright, clean, happy house that Walt Disney wanted.

June 22, 1970
The Walt Disney Archives are established on the studio lot in Burbank.

June 17, 1971
The one hundred millionth guest enters Disneyland.

October 1, 1971
New park opens in Florida. The complex is christened Walt Disney World. On opening day, there is a single theme park on the grounds, a "Disneyland East" called the Magic Kingdom.

December 20, 1971
Roy Disney dies.

October 1972
Florida's Magic Kingdom has attracted 10.7 million visitors in its first year. It welcomes more foreign guests per year than most nations.

December 1972
Lake Buena Vista, a leisure-oriented second-home community designed by Disney opens its first townhouses (furnished and maintained by Disney) to corporate guests.

January 15, 1975
The Magic Kingdom adds a new ride designed especially for this park: Space Mountain, a themed, fully enclosed roller coaster, or Disney's first real thrill ride.

March 22, 1975
Walt Disney World Village opens on the periphery of the Florida park—a functioning shopping center surrounded by resort hotels.

September 1979
Big Thunder Mountain Railroad, Disneyland's own unique thrill ride, opens to the public. In May, Disneyland had acquired a version of Florida's Space Mountain.

October 1, 1979
Ground is broken for EPCOT Center at Walt Disney World.

July 17, 1980
Disneyland is twenty-five years old.

December 3, 1980
Ground is broken on reclaimed land in Tokyo Bay for Tokyo Disneyland.

1981
Planned community of Seaside, Florida, is designed by "new urbanists" whose ideas on space and reassurance in the built environment share common ground with Walt Disney's.

October 1, 1981
Walt Disney World celebrates its "Ten-cennial."

1981–82
Another new New Tomorrowland for Disneyland is planned and executed.

October 1, 1982
EPCOT Center opens as a theme park at Walt Disney World. Resembling a permanent World's Fair, EPCOT consists of two parts. Future World contains corporate pavilions; World Showcase recreates the architecture of famous tourist sites.

April 15, 1983
Tokyo Disneyland opens.

Spring 1983
A revised Disneyland Fantasyland includes old rides equipped with new, three-dimensional facades.

September 23, 1984
Michael Eisner is chosen to lead Walt Disney Productions.

1986
A new entrance for the Pirates of the Caribbean at Disneyland includes a staircase that spirals up to a private apartment, built for the Disney family but never occupied. It becomes a Disney Gallery, where artwork created in the course of building the Disney parks is sold and exhibited.

October 1986
The fifteenth anniversary of Walt Disney World. By January 1, 1987, the total number of people who had visited the park would be larger than the population of the United States.

1987
The first Disney Store opens in the Glendale (California) Galleria. Five hundred more stores will be opened around the world in the years to come.
A collaboration with filmmaker George Lucas results in a Star Tours attraction for Disneyland.

1988
Imagineer-conceived Grand Floridian Hotel at Walt Disney World opens a major building campaign at the resort. If Walt's real city was not yet built, a metaphorical one had been created, composed of thousands of guests in overnight residence in a vacation city. Orlando International Airport surpasses New York's Kennedy International as the fastest-growing airport in the nation.

June 22, 1988
Who Framed Roger Rabbit jointly produced by the Disney Company and Steven Spielberg's Amblin Entertainment, opens. It reactivates interest in Disney's early work and inspires plans for Mickey's Toontown at Disneyland.

1989
Eisner selects Postmodern architect Michael Graves to design the first hotel at Walt Disney World—the Swan—not created with the input of the Imagineers. The grand opening of the Swan demonstrates Eisner's fascination with avant-garde architecture as a component of the Disney corporate image.
Eisner is pelted with eggs in Paris, where he announces plans to build a theme park in France.
Walt Disney Productions opens an animation studio in Montreuil-sous-Bois, a Paris suburb.

May 1, 1989
Disney-MGM Studios Theme Park opens at Walt Disney World. This is the third theme park on the property. The others are the Magic Kingdom and EPCOT.

October 1989
Pleasure Island, an adult nightclub complex named to commemorate Walt Disney's view of the depravity of amusement parks in *Pinocchio*, opens at Walt Disney World, adjacent to the Village.

1990
Officials announce the beginning of the "Disney Decade": a fourth theme park in Florida, twenty-nine new attractions in existing parks there, seven resort hotels, and five hundred condominums for guests.

1991
Postmodernist Team Disney office building, designed by Arata Isozaki, is built on the Florida property. In California, the Imagineers begin to work on a Toontown addition to Disneyland.

April 12, 1992
EuroDisney Resort opens in Marne-la-Vallée, France, outside Paris. The Festival Disney entertainment complex outside the main gate is designed by Frank O. Gehry.

August 1992
A Disney store opens on the fashionable Champs-Elysées in Paris. Commentators quote an irate French critic who had earlier called EuroDisney "a cultural Chernobyl."

January 26, 1993
Mickey's Toontown opens at Disneyland.

Fall 1993
The Walt Disney Gallery debuts in Main Place, Santa Ana, California; the store appeals to upscale shoppers with a sophisticated mix of Disney art and themed mall architecture.

November 11, 1993
The Walt Disney Company announces its intention to build a new theme park dealing with American history in Haymarket, Virginia, just outside Washington, D.C. It is called Disney's America.

Summer 1994
Disney makes its presence felt in New York City, agreeing to renovate a theater and working on plans to rebuild and sanitize Times Square.

June 1994
Tower of Terror, with a thematic reference to TV's *The Twilight Zone*, is added to the Disney-MGM Studios Theme Park.

August 30, 1994
Ground-breaking ceremony for a Disney Wedding Pavilion at Walt Disney World.

October 1994
The company yields to local criticism and announces it will seek another site for its projected Americana theme park (originally scheduled to open in 1998).

December 1994
The new Disney Animation Building in Burbank is designed by Robert A. M. Stern. *The Los Angeles Times* calls it an "instant landmark."
The new Alien Encounter attraction at Walt Disney World opens briefly but is closed again for modifications when Michael Eisner decides it is not scary enough.

February 1995
The latest new and improved Tomorrowland celebrating *past* visions of the future opens at Walt Disney World and seems to provide an ideal solution to the problem presented by an ever-changing future.

March 3, 1995
Indiana Jones's Temple of the Forbidden Eye rises over Adventureland in Anaheim; a product of the most advanced robotic and ride-control technology built to date, the attraction is a result of another collaboration with George Lucas.

April 1995
Blizzard Beach, the third Walt Disney World water park, opens. The other water parks are the forty-acre Typhoon Lagoon (1989) and River Country (1976).

Summer 1995
Two-hundred-acre international sports complex begun at Walt Disney World.
Disneyland Paris (formerly EuroDisney) adds De la Terre à la Lune, a unique interpretation of the Space Mountain idea.

1996
Inauguration of the Disney Institute, a center for adult recreational learning at Walt Disney World.
Had Disneyland Paris not experienced financial difficulties, a new version of the Disney-MGM Studios park would have opened on the French site.
After years of planning, future residents buy homes in Celebration, a real town built on the Florida property. Although there are no factories, skyscrapers, or electric cars, Celebration does have schools and other features of true urbanism. It is the company's answer to Walt Disney's utopian dreams.

Spring 1998
A fourth theme park is slated to open at Walt Disney World: Disney's Animal Kingdom.

Page 6
Catherine Wagner.
Beanstalk outside Sir Mickey's Store; Fantasyland, Disneyland Paris, Marne-la-Vallée, France.
Gelatin silver print.
22 1/16 x 17 13/16 (image). 1995

Page 8
Catherine Wagner.
Autopia; Tomorrowland, Disneyland, Anaheim, California.
Chromogenic color print.
17 5/16 x 22 (image). 1995.

Page 12
Catherine Wagner.
Mickey Mouse's House; Mickey's Toontown, Disneyland, Anaheim, California.
Chromogenic color print.
17 5/16 x 22 (image). 1995.

Page 18
Catherine Wagner.
World Bazaar; Tokyo Disneyland, Tokyo.
Gelatin silver print.
17 15/16 x 22 (image). 1995.

Page 28
Catherine Wagner.
Storybook Land; Fantasyland, Disneyland, Anaheim, California.
Chromogenic color print.
22 x 17 5/16 (image). 1995.

Page 53
Catherine Wagner.
World Bazaar; Tokyo Disneyland, Tokyo.
Gelatin silver print.
17 7/16 x 22 (image). 1995.

Page 106
Catherine Wagner.
"Molly Brown" Sidewheeler; Frontierland, Disneyland Paris, Marne-la-Vallée, France.
Gelatin silver print.
17 3/4 x 22 (image). 1995.

Page 133
Catherine Wagner.
Minnie Mouse's Kitchen; Mickey's Toontown, Disneyland, Anaheim, California.
Chromogenic color print.
17 3/8 x 22 (image). 1995.

Page 153
Catherine Wagner.
Avenue of the Planets; New Tomorrowland, Magic Kingdom, Walt Disney World, Orlando, Florida.
Gelatin silver print.
22 x 17 5/8 (image). 1995.

Page 167
Catherine Wagner. *Swan Hotel, Tower of Terror, and Spaceship Earth* (from left to right); *EPCOT, Disney-MGM Studios Theme Park, Walt Disney World, Orlando, Florida.*
Gelatin silver print.
17 5/8 x 21 13/16 (image). 1995.

Page 178
Catherine Wagner.
It's a Small World; Fantasyland, Disneyland, Anaheim, California.
Gelatin silver print.
21 13/16 x 17 5/8 (image). 1995.

Page 190
Catherine Wagner.
Jungle Cruise; Adventureland, Tokyo Disneyland, Tokyo.
Chromogenic color print.
17 5/16 x 22 (image). 1995.

Page 200
Catherine Wagner.
New York Streetscape, Backstage Studio Tour; Disney-MGM Studios Theme Park, Walt Disney World, Orlando, Florida.
Gelatin silver print.
17 7/8 x 22 (image). 1995.

Page 208
Catherine Wagner.
"The Darkroom," Hollywood Boulevard; Disney-MGM Studios Theme Park, Walt Disney World, Orlando, Florida.
Chromogenic color print.
17 5/16 x 22 (image). 1995.

Page 214
Catherine Wagner.
Special Effects Tank, Backstage Studio Tour; Disney-MGM Studios Theme Park, Walt Disney World, Orlando, Florida.
Gelatin silver print.
17 7/8 x 22 (image). 1995.

In 1995, the Centre Canadien d'Architecture/Canadian Centre for Architecture commissioned photographer Catherine Wagner to photograph the four Disney parks. The photographs in this book are drawn from the collection of 32 works from that commission that are now in the CCA collection.

Photoengraving by Evolutif, Montrouge
Printed and Bound by Pollina s.a., 85400 Luçon - France - n° 74450
Printed on BVS Plus Demi-matt 150 g/m² chlorine free paper